Hiking Trails
in the Midwest

Hiking Trails in the Midwest

Jerry Sullivan and Glenda Daniel

Contemporary Books, Inc.
Chicago

Library of Congress Cataloging in Publication Data

Sullivan, Jerry, 1938-
    Hiking Trails in the Midwest.

    Bibliography: p.
    1. Hiking—Middle West—Guide Books.   2. Back-
packing—Middle West—Guide-books.   3. Middle West—
Description and travel—Guide-books.   4. Trails—
Middle West—Guide-books.   I. Daniel, Glenda, joint
author.   II. Title.
GV199.42.M53S94   1980   917.7043   79-8752
ISBN 0-8092-7007-2

Copyright © 1980, 1974 by Jerry Sullivan and Glenda Daniel
All rights reserved
Published by Contemporary Books, Inc.
180 North Michigan Avenue, Chicago, Illinois 60601
Manufactured in the United States of America
Library of Congress Catalog Card Number: 79-8752
International Standard Book Number: 0-8092-7007-2

Published simultaneously in Canada by
Beaverbooks
953 Dillingham Road
Pickering, Ontario L1W 1Z7
Canada

CONTENTS

Hiking Trails
in the Midwest

Like all real treasures of the mind, perception
can be split into infinitely small fractions
without losing its quality. The weeds in a
city lot convey the same lesson as the
redwoods; the farmer may see in his cow-pasture
what may not be vouchsafed to the scientist
adventuring in the South Seas.

Aldo Leopold
A Sand County Almanac

1

AN INTRODUCTION TO MIDWEST BACKPACKING

When we wrote the first edition of this guide six years ago, back-packing was something people went to the Appalachians or the Rockies to do. There were a few trails in this part of the country, and some areas—the Porkies, Isle Royale—that drew large numbers of back-packers. But the people who administered public lands in the Midwest were generally not making a tremendous effort to provide for back-packers, and it was quite reasonable of them not to, since there seemed to be only a limited demand for this kind of recreation.

We have watched things change over the past six years, but it wasn't until we began to dig for information for this revised edition that we realized just how extensive the changes have been. We started out thinking that this edition would be about one-third longer than the original book. It is actually at least twice as long.

New trails have been created in every part of the region, and information about all trails, new and old, is much easier to come by. Vastly improved maps and brochures are now available, and trail coordinators have been appointed in several states. Trails have become a priority item in the national forests, even in the north where canoeing used to get all the recreational attention.

Many trails in the Midwest offer a measure of solitude that is hard to come by in the Sierras or the Smokies. Probably only Isle Royale and the Porcupine Mountains come close to being overcrowded, and many beautiful places are scarcely used. In fact, it is reasonable to say that we should use our trails more than we do in order to ensure that trail maintenance and construction will be kept in the budgets of state and federal agencies.

Backpacking in the Midwest is in most respects like backpacking anywhere. It demands that we cut loose from the usual supports in order to be temporarily self-sufficient. We have to carry everything we need; we have to deal with problems without outside help.

We need certain items of equipment to live well in the woods, and the next chapter provides some guidance on buying the gear you need.

However, a good backpacking experience takes more than equipment. We also need to know something about the environment in which we live. The chapters on each separate state include information on geology and flora and fauna. In this introduction we will discuss some of the things you need to prepare for in order to enjoy backpacking in all of the midwestern states.

CLIMATE

The Midwest is an area of continental climate. This means that we have hot summers and cold winters. You can run into July days in the 90s even in northern Minnesota; and in southern Missouri, January nights can drop to zero or below. Obviously there are significant differences from north to south. Summers are longer and hotter in the south; winters, colder and longer in the north.

Typical summer weather in Missouri is so hot that most backpackers confine their outings to the months between October and May. They do encounter cold and snow, but temperatures around freezing are typical winter weather, and rain is much more common than snow. Indiana, southern Illinois, and southern Ohio are also reasonable places to hike in winter, spring, and fall.

Winter backpacking is a serious undertaking in the upper peninsula of Michigan and in northern Wisconsin and Minnesota. Of course, the snow depth usually requires snowshoes or cross-country skis, and that kind of equipment is for travel that is outside the scope of this book.

With both heat and cold to contend with, midwestern hikers have to know something about heat exhaustion and hypothermia. Heat exhaustion really should not be a problem. Nobody is chasing you, so if you begin to feel hot, just sit down and relax until you feel cool. However, if you begin to feel giddy and weak, or if you turn pale or start vomiting, the solution is gradual cooling. Apply cool, wet cloths to your skin, and have someone fan you gently. Don't drink water in large amounts. The idea is to restore fluid balance gradually.

Heat exhaustion is brought on by an elevation of body temperature. Hypothermia is a potentially lethal condition created by a lowering of body temperature. The symptoms are rather violent, and they form a definite progression corresponding to body temperature. As body temperature drops from normal to 96 or 97 degrees, the victim begins to shiver so violently that a simple act like tying shoes requires intense concentration. At about 92 degrees the shivering becomes spasmodic. Coordination continues to deteriorate, and many people become aware that they are not thinking clearly. At a body temperature of 85 degrees, muscles begin to stiffen and people often become irrational. At 80 degrees, hypothermia victims sink into a stupor. If cooling continues much beyond this point, they die.

In the early stages of this process, the body can regain normal temperature if the victim gets out of the cold. Just crawling into a sleeping bag may be enough. However, as temperature lowers, outside heat is required. Under field conditions, you should always err on the side of safety by assuming that outside heat is necessary.

External heat sources can include hot food and drinks, or a pocket heater held against the body. Body heat from another person is effective. Crawl into a sleeping bag with the victim. Build a fire. If you have a tent, put the victim inside it and build a fire so that its heat reflects on the tent.

Before you initiate any of these measures, remove the conditions that caused the problem. Take off wet clothes and seek whatever shelter is available from wind or rain. If the victim has no dry clothes, have everyone in the party donate a garment.

Hypothermia can set in very quickly. If you are an hour's walk from your car when symptoms begin to appear, don't try to hurry home. Stop and get warm.

Remember that hypothermia is not something that happens only during below-zero temperatures. Rainy, windy days with temperatures in the upper 30s or lower 40s are prime hypothermia weather. If you are wet, the process will happen much more quickly, a fact that points up the importance of adequate rain gear.

ABOUT FIRES

These days a lot of backpackers look on people who build campfires as only slightly less destructive than the Dutch elm disease. Aside from the danger of forest fire, the arguments against campfires are that fires use up downed wood that ought to be rotting back into the soil and that fires leave a scar on the ground that may be quite enduring.

As to the first argument, the minerals in the wood are actually released by burning, and the mineral rich ash sinks into the ground to provide food for plants more or less immediately. The second part of the argument is more compelling. It is depressing to come upon a good campsite dotted with black, charred spots. However, in the humid climate of the Midwest, they will not last too long. In an area that gets a lot of use, just the tramping of feet will prevent new plant growth from covering these unsightly scars.

For cooking, we recommend that you use a small portable stove rather than rely on a campfire. A stove is more convenient, it will function even in a rainstorm, and it doesn't scar the landscape. This recommendation applies with particular force to areas that receive heavy use, such as the Boundary Waters or Isle Royale.

NOXIOUS ANIMALS

The large animal that backpackers are most likely to have trouble with is the black bear. Bears were extirpated in the Ozarks, but recently they have been reintroduced to some of the wilder areas in northern Arkansas. Sighting one in Missouri is very unlikely, but they have been reported in the Devil's Backbone Wilderness Area, so their presence is at least theoretically possible.

Bears are much more common in the north, in the wilder parts of Ontario, Minnesota, Wisconsin, northern Lower Michigan, and Upper Michigan.

The black bear is usually a shy creature that shrinks from human contact. However, it is also an animal with a prodigious appetite. Whenever you hike in bear country you should take certain precautions with your food, viz:

Do not eat in or near your tent. Set up your kitchen 50 feet from your tent and do all your cooking and eating there.

At night, hang your food out of reach. A big bear can reach 8 to 10 feet by standing on its hind legs. A bear can also climb much better than you can; so just draping the food over a big tree limb is not going to do the job. The ideal is to hang it 10 feet high and at least 6 feet away from the trunk or any branch sturdy enough to support a bear.

It is also a good idea to make some noise as you walk through the woods. This will give the bear a chance to get out of your way before you are right on top of him.

If these precautions fail and you find yourself face to face with a bruin, remember these tips:

Do not run. Bears can run much faster than people, and millions of years of evolution have told them that when something runs, they should chase it.

Talk. Sometimes the sound of an ordinary human voice will scare a bear witless.

If plain talk won't do it, resort to more fearsome noises. Bang pots together, shout, and clap your hands.

If the bear continues to approach, retreat slowly, but keep facing the bear. Some people have retreated as much as a mile in this fashion.

If the bear seems determined to go after you, shuck off your pack. He is probably more interested in the food it contains than in your body, and while he destroys everything you have, you can escape.

If he is not interested in your pack, drop to the ground on your stomach and put your arms around your head to protect your face and throat. Lie still. Resistance would be futile and self-defeating.

All these rules should supplement the obvious tips, such as not feeding bears and not trying to approach them too closely. If you see a sow with cubs, move directly away from them at a dignified but steady pace.

Hikers in the Boundary Waters of Minnesota, on Isle Royale, or in

Algonquin Provincial Park may encounter a moose. These are large formidable animals, and a cow with a calf or a male in rut can be dangerous. If you see one, just back off slowly. Do not try to contest the right-of-way. A moose can go anywhere it wants to.

In the southern half of the Midwest, you may encounter poisonous snakes. Such encounters are unlikely, since snakes will strive to avoid them, but they do happen. If you come across a snake, do not freeze the way cowboys used to do in western movies. If a snake is coiling to strike, it is because he perceives you as a threat. Remove the threat by backing slowly away and avoiding sudden movements.

Three species of rattlesnake are native to the Midwest. The pygmy rattler, a small snake as the name suggests, is found only in extreme southern Missouri. The timber rattler can be found in Missouri, eastern and southern Iowa, southeastern Minnesota, southwestern Wisconsin, and extreme northwestern Illinois. It may also be encountered in southern Illinois, Indiana, and Ohio, and in the Illinois River Valley. The Massasauga rattler, another small and very shy snake, ranges as far north as the Straits of Mackinac in Michigan and Georgian Bay (including the Bruce Peninsula) in Ontario. It is also found in southern Wisconsin, southern and eastern Iowa, northern Missouri, and all of Illinois, Indiana, and Ohio, except the extreme southern portions of these states.

Copperheads can be found in Missouri, in the Mississippi Valley as far north as southern Iowa, and in southern Illinois, Indiana, and Ohio. Cottonmouths live in southern Missouri and southern Illinois.

Snakes generally avoid well-trodden footpaths, and they are more active at night than during the day. If you are walking around at night in snake country, using a flashlight is a sensible precaution.

Be careful on rocky hillsides where rattlesnakes and copperheads are more likely to lurk. Cottonmouths are water snakes, so you are more likely to find them in creek bottoms.

Carry a snakebite kit when you hike in snake country and study its use before you hit the trail. The first aid procedures recommended in the kits will suffice on the trail, but they do not substitute for medical attention. Get to a doctor as soon as possible.

These are the animals that can kill you, but there are others that can drive you crazy. The mosquito can stand as a symbol of the North Woods. These pestiferous creatures begin to rise in their clouds in late May. The peak season is June and July. By late August, they are generally not numerous enough to constitute much of an annoyance.

Mosquitoes are most numerous near still water such as lakes, marshes, and swamps. They do not like direct sunlight and are most active in the morning, and in late afternoon and early evening. A good breeze will keep them down, but breezes are often scarce in the deep woods.

Fighting mosquitoes is simple: wear long pants, a long-sleeved shirt, and a hat. Cover exposed skin with a good repellent, such as Cutters or Deep Woods Off. At the worst times, you may want to use a headnet, which is available in most sporting goods stores in the North Woods. It fits over a hat and completely protects your face and head.

The North Woods are also home to a variety of biting flies. Black flies, deer flies, and the tiny (almost invisible but very voracious) flies called no-see-ums are common in summer—even in sunlight during the heat of the day. Protect yourself with the same sort of measures used to fend off mosquitoes.

The bane of hikers in the southern Midwest is the chigger, a pesky beast that burrows into your hide to lay its eggs. Chigger bites can itch for weeks. Repellent applied around your ankles and waist can help prevent them. Sulphur powder is supposed to work too, though it will probably repel your friends as well. Once you have a chigger bite, you can try applying clear nail polish, nail polish remover, rubbing alcohol, and various antiseptic ointments. We have tried them all—generally all at once—so we can report that some or all of them work, but we are not sure which ones.

Early summer is tick season. These arachnids poke their snouts deep under the skin and suck blood until they are several times their normal size. It is usually easy to keep ticks from getting that far because they normally crawl around for some time looking for the ideal spot. You can then feel them and pluck them off. Mutual inspection before retiring is also effective.

PLANT MENACES

Poison ivy grows throughout the Midwest. It can grow as a vine or as an upright shrub. You can recognize it by its alternate leaves, which are divided into three leaflets. Leaf shape is quite variable, but the stalk of the center leaflet is almost always longer than the stalks of the two lateral leaflets.

Poison sumac grows in wet boggy conditions as far north as southern Wisconsin and Lower Michigan. It is a shrub with alternate compound leaves divided into many leaflets. It is distinguished from the harmless sumacs by its leaflets that lack teeth on the edges.

Both of these plants produce skin irritation that can range from mild to very violent, depending on the amount of exposure and the degree of allergy that an individual possesses. Washing with strong soap as soon as possible after the exposure helps, and calamine lotion will suppress the symptoms to some extent. Really serious cases need medical attention.

AVOIDING GETTING LOST

All of the trail descriptions in this book include information on topographic maps. The U.S. Geological Survey issues these maps. They cost $1.25 a sheet and are available from the U.S.G.S., 1200 Eads Street, Arlington, Virginia 22202, for all midwestern states except Iowa and Missouri. Maps of these states should be ordered from the U.S.G.S., Box 25286, Federal Center, Denver, Colorado 80225. When ordering, be sure to include the name of the state in your order.

Topographic sheets (topo sheets) come in two sizes. Maps covering 15 minutes of latitude and longitude are drawn to a scale of 1 inch to the mile. Maps covering 7.5 minutes of latitude and longitude are drawn to a scale of 1 inch to 2,000 feet. In both sizes, the maps show the shape of the landscape and all major natural and manmade features.

In most cases, the trails in this book are well marked and easy to follow, and you can undertake them without a topo sheet to help you. However, topo sheets are a wise addition to your gear in wilderness areas, such as the Boundary Waters, and essential in roadless areas without well-marked trails.

In some cases, we have reproduced topo sheets in this book. In others, we have used maps that are detailed enough to allow you to transfer information to a topo sheet. Anyone who goes into the woods ought to know how to use a compass. A number of good books are now available on map and compass reading, and orienteering—the sport based on these skills. If you don't know how to navigate in the woods, we suggest you obtain one of these books and learn.

A FEW RULES

Backpackers should learn to imitate the animals. It takes a skilled tracker to follow the trail of a deer or bear, and we all ought to try to be just as elusive. The old cliche is, "Take only pictures, leave only footprints." These are sound rules. We might add that you shouldn't leave any more footprints than necessary.

Here are some specifics to help you travel through the woods without leaving heavy traces of your passing:

1. Take out everything you bring in. All trash, scraps of paper and aluminum foil, plastic bags, everything. Burying garbage is useless. It will stay underground only as long as it takes a raccoon to find it.

2. Carry a trowel and toilet paper. When you need to defecate, use the trowel to dig a shallow hole. Use it, put the paper in it, and cover it back up. Always urinate or defecate at least 100 feet from any surface water, such as lakes or streams.

3. Don't camp on lake or stream banks. There is nothing wrong with sitting on the shore and watching the sun go down over the water, but do your sleeping and cooking away from lakes and streams.

2

GEAR

Six years ago, when we were compiling the first edition of this guidebook, we thought the great variety of equipment offered to backpackers made it difficult for beginners to make good choices. We now realize that we hadn't seen nothin' yet. New materials and new designs seem to show up weekly, and even if you are in the business of keeping track of such things, it is easy to miss some revolutionary development.

Some of the new equipment represents real improvement over earlier designs, but a certain amount of gimmickry is inevitable. There is also a lot of specialization. Tents are available for summer, for the desert, for winter camping, and for winter mountaineering.

This chapter provides you with specific advice for buying a basic backpacking outfit, including boots, tent or bivi-bag, pack, sleeping bag, and camp stove. We will talk about the kinds of equipment that are now available, but we cannot anticipate every new product that will be introduced; so we will stick mainly to fundamental advice for beginning backpackers.

The most important thing to think about is how you plan to use your equipment. It is possible to buy a tent that will stand up to 80-mile-an-hour winds and remain upright under 8 feet of snow. But such a tent will cost well over $300, and if all you need is something to keep the rain and mosquitoes off, a $300 tent is a waste of money.

Second, avoid specialization. It is better to have equipment that performs reasonably well in a variety of circumstances than expensive gear that does superbly under some conditions but will offer a lot of needless capacity at other times.

Finally, don't just take our word for it. Throughout this book we have listed the names of organizations that sponsor backpacking outings. There are others that we don't know about. Many schools, for example, have outing clubs, and in some cases local YMCAs offer such outings. Group trips like these are good opportunities to start out in backpacking with guidance, including opinions on equipment, from experienced people. Some organizations of this kind will also give you a chance to rent or borrow equipment so you can try the sport before you spend money. Trail shops in most cities also rent equipment.

BOOTS

Lightweight boots are adequate for most midwestern hiking trips. Vibram soles are not even absolutely necessary, except maybe in the rockier areas of the Ozarks and Minnesota's Boundary Waters Canoe Area. The stiff, heavy climbing and mountaineering boots you see advertised in catalogs and outdoor magazines are meant for use in the Rockies and the Cascades. In Wisconsin's Blue Hills or the Penokee Range, they would merely be extra weight to carry. General wisdom is that one pound on your feet is equivalent to five pounds on your back. Nevertheless, comfort, a good fit, and durable construction are essential. Nothing can ruin an otherwise beautiful trip more effectively than an ill-fitting boot or one that falls apart at the first stream crossing. Here are a few points to keep in mind.

If the boot you decide to buy is imported, make sure it was made with an American last. A last is the foot-shaped mold in which the shoe form is cast. French people apparently tend to have narrower toes than Americans; Italians have narrower heels. Or at least the shoe fashions in those countries seem to indicate those characteristics.

Ask the salesperson whether your boots are chrome-tanned or oil-tanned. It will affect the type of dressing you should use. Remember that even the best of boots need frequent rewaterproofing around the seams. They should also be washed with saddle soap, dried slowly away from a fire, and rubbed with the dressing appropriate for the shoe after each major outing.

There are several ways to attach boot soles to uppers. Those with inside stitching (sometimes known as Littleway construction) or standard two-row outside stitching with welts can be resoled. Injection-molded boots cannot be resoled unless they have a midsole.

Cemented boots have the upper leather folded under a light inner sole and a one-piece rubber lug-sole glued on. There is no stitching, no midsole, and very little support or protection; the boots cannot be resoled.

Quality of leather is a feature to consider. Full-grain leather, made from the outside layer of a cow's hide, resists moisture best and is the most flexible. It is also the most expensive.

Any good boot should also have heel, arch, and toe reinforcing, plus shanks in the sole made of steel, laminated wood, or a stiff plastic to support the arch and protect the instep. Foam rubber padding adds comfort around the ankle, but too much padding can be hot on summer days.

Sewn-in tongues are critical in keeping water, sand, and other debris away from your socks and feet. No self-respecting boot would be without one. Lacing systems have become complicated. They may consist of old-fashioned grommets, hooks and swivel eyelets, hooks and grommeted eyelets, hooks and speed lacing, or any combination of the above. Each system has its advantages. Colin Fletcher, author of *The Complete Walker*, made the most sensible comment we've heard on the subject. He pointed out that if a grommet wears through or works loose, the hole is still usable, whereas a broken hook and swivel eyelet may leave you in bad shape if you are hiking miles from a shoe store.

And finally, here are a few suggestions for telling whether a shoe fits before you've left the store:

1. Wearing the socks you will use on the trail, push your foot as far forward in the boot as it will go with laces untied. Make sure you can place your forefinger inside the shoe behind the heel.

2. When the boot is laced, you should be able to lift your heel no more than $\frac{1}{8}$ inch in normal walking.

3. Your toes should be free to wiggle, but neither the ball of the foot nor the heel should slip when the salesperson anchors the boot to the floor and you try to twist your foot.

4. Boots should be snug in width but generous in length. They won't stretch the way ordinary shoes do.

5. By hammering the floor with the toe, you can make sure that even when you're carrying a full pack and have swollen feet, your toes will never hit the end of the boot.

PACKS

Interior frame packs, designed first for mountaineering, have begun in recent years to rival the standard exterior-frame rectangular packs for general backpacking use. The interior frames have some advantages. Mainly, because they fit closer to your body, they feel more comfortable. And when you lean over to dip a cup of water from a stream, you aren't likely to feel that you're about to topple forward headfirst into the water. Their main disadvantage is that they won't hold as much as an exterior frame pack. The structure and dimensions just don't allow it. Also, you can't lean an interior frame pack against a tree when you stop to rest on the trail.

Exterior pack frames are basically rectangular arrangements of lightweight aluminum poles with two padded shoulder straps at the top and a padded waist belt. Fabric bands are stretched tightly around the exterior frame to keep it and the pack away from the body.

Some packs have just one big compartment, but these are really specialized pieces of equipment for expedition use. Most packs are divided into two main compartments. The bottom one typically is closed with a zipper; the top, with a flap. An assortment of smaller compartments are attached to the outside of the pack bag.

You will learn by experience how to pack a pack to fit your needs. The main thing to remember is that articles you are likely to need during the day should be readily accessible. Your poncho or rain suit, a change of socks, lunch, and your water bottle are among the things you might want to unpack on the trail without too much fuss. Tomorrow's supper and your change of underwear can be tucked away safely at the bottom of the deepest pocket.

Packs and frames come in several sizes. Catalogs generally state the size and give a range of heights that the size is supposed to fit. If your height puts you on the border between one size and another, you should probably look for a chance to try the pack on rather than buying by mail. The waist belt should be at the waist, above your hips but well below your rib cage. The function of the belt is to pull the frame against your body, transferring the weight of the pack from your shoulders to your hips and legs. It won't do the job if it is too short or too long.

Some packs claim to be waterproof. Some do not. To be on the safe side, buy a waterproof cover that will cover the pack bag and anything fastened to the frame outside the bag. Packs made of the new Gore-Tex fabric that is supposed to breathe yet remain waterproof are available but quite expensive.

TENTS

Rain can fall at any time in the Midwest, and biting bugs of various kinds are frequently encountered during the warmer months, so you do need shelter of some kind on any backpacking trip. Shelter for backpackers comes in two forms: tents and bivi-bags.

Bivi-bags have become quite popular since the invention of Gore-Tex. Gore-Tex is a fabric that is permeable to water vapor but impermeable to liquid water. This means that a tent or bivi-bag made of Gore-Tex will keep the rain out and will let the sweat and moisture in your breath escape.

In its most basic form, a bivi-bag is simply a sack big enough to hold one sleeping bag. The bottom is typically a coated fabric; the top, Gore-Tex. You put an arrangement of poles at the head end to keep the cloth out of your face. Put in a mosquito netting panel for ventilation with a Gore-Tex flap that can be lowered over the netting when it rains, and you have a bivi-bag—basic shelter for one person that weighs about two pounds.

Tent designers have produced a sort of creative explosion in the past few years. You can now buy tents that will withstand almost anything, but remember that you pay for every performance feature you get. Don't buy more than you need.

For midwestern backpacking, you are looking for something that will do two things:

1. *Keep the bugs out.* So be sure you have netting on all openings, preferably with zippers to close it. A sewn-in floor helps keep the insects out and aids in keeping you dry as well.

2. *Keep the rain out.* Coated fabric is needed for sure waterproofing. The cheapest backpacking tents are made of a single layer of such fabric. These tents have a disadvantage, however. They keep moisture in as well as out. In cool weather, the vapor you exhale at night can condense on the ceiling and drip back onto you.

More expensive tents solve the condensation problem with an inner tent of uncoated, nonwaterproof fabric and an outer rain fly of coated cloth. Moisture from inside goes through the inner fabric and condenses harmlessly on the inside of the rain fly. Of course, this system adds weight.

New tents made of Gore-Tex are now available that are supposed to provide the best of both worlds. A single layer means lighter weight, and Gore-Tex's permeability to water vapor ends the condensation problem. Such tents are quite expensive, however.

A-frame tents are usually the least expensive, but the sides of most models tend to sag after a while. Pop up or other freestanding tents are appealing because they are easy to assemble and because you can pick up the whole tent and move it if you discover you've set the thing on top of a huge root. Whatever you buy, try to imagine whether you could set it up with a minimum of fuss in the dark in the middle of a rainstorm. And be sure to set the tent up at least once in the backyard or in the nearest park before you take it on a trip.

Many of the new tents are designed for stability in very high winds, a feature of great value to mountaineers. However, high winds are not a problem in the Midwest because we do most of our camping in the woods where the trees dampen the force of the breeze. Winds can become a problem if they are strong enough to blow trees over, but no tent will protect you in such a situation. Also remember that A-frame tents, the cheapest design available, are still favorites with mountaineers because of their stability.

SLEEPING BAGS

Goose down used to be the only real choice for backpackers, but developments in synthetic fillings have changed that. Synthetics such as Polarguard, Hollofil, and FibreFill II are cheaper than down and retain most of their insulating qualities when they are wet. Down still holds an edge in the amount of insulation provided per ounce of weight and in its ability to compress to a small size and bounce back when it is pulled out of a stuff sack. Synthetic-filled bags are bulkier to carry and heavier as well.

Most backpackers favor mummy bags for offering the most warmth for the weight, but if you are willing to carry the extra ounces, roomier bags are more comfortable. For backpacking couples, most sleeping bag models can be zipped together.

Our advice to avoid buying more than you need applies with particular force to sleeping bags. If you want to spend the money, you can get a bag that will keep you warm down to –30°F, but if you never go backpacking after October 1, that kind of bag would be a waste of money. Dealers can supply performance ratings for their bags to help you make a choice.

There are some sleazy operators in the sleeping bag business who will sell you a "goose down" bag that will start crowing every time the sun comes up or a synthetic fiber bag filled with leftover polyester tire cord. Here it is best to stick with established brands and to buy from stores that specialize in backpacking equipment.

SLEEPING MATS

When you are sleeping outside, the ground beneath you can rob you of as much heat as the air above. Since your weight pushes down and flattens the insulation in your sleeping bag, you will need to put a mat under your sleeping bag. The cheapest mats are closed-cell foam pads, available in hip-length or full-length models. Air mattresses are a lot of trouble and tend to be heavy. There is a sort of combination foam pad and air mattress that actually inflates itself. All you have to do is unroll it. It seems to work well, but it costs a good deal more than a simple closed-cell foam pad.

STOVES

Shopping for backpacking stoves is enough to make you go back to building campfires. How can you make a choice among white gas, kerosene, butane, propane, and denatured alcohol? Among Optimus and Phoebus, Coleman, Camping Gaz, and MSR?

We can begin by dividing stoves into two categories: those that require you to handle fuel and those that do not. All stoves that burn white gas, kerosene, or alcohol require you to fill up a fuel bottle before you leave, and all but one require you to transfer fuel from the bottle to the stove's fuel tank. Stoves that burn butane or propane use disposable cartridges that are simply screwed onto the stove when full and detached when empty.

White gas and kerosene stoves also require priming and/or pumping to get them started, but you start a cartridge stove by turning a knob and striking a match.

However, butane stoves have a lower heat output, and cartridge stoves work poorly—if at all—when temperatures are below freezing.

You may also have difficulty in getting replacement cartridges. We once searched all over the upper peninsula of Michigan looking for a butane cartridge—without success. And butane costs more than white gas or kerosene.

FOOD

Freeze-dried and dehydrated foods are available in almost infinite variety these days. They are lightweight and easy to prepare, although they are still exorbitantly priced and, for the most part, taste as bad as ever. They are necessary on long trips, but for weekend outings and even three- or four-day trips, dried food from the grocery store works just as well, tastes better and is cheaper, although it may take a little longer (using more fuel) to cook.

Our own grocery store staples include macaroni and cheese, Japanese-style noodle soups with vegetables, meat-flavored Minute rice, powdered milk, the margarine that comes in a squeeze bottle, instant coffee, tea bags, hot chocolate powder, and instant puddings. Because we live in a large city, we are also able to buy dried vegetables at a reasonable price from Oriental food stores, and we have a recipe of our own for a kind of Chinese beef jerky (see below).

We have also discovered that celery, carrots, and onions keep well for several days when wrapped in foil or plastic Ziploc bags. Their texture alone is morale building at the end of a tiring day.

Everybody has his or her own favorite gorp recipe, most of them containing some kind of fruit, nuts, and candy. We like peanuts, chocolate chips, and raisins for spring and fall hiking. In hot midwestern summers, the chocolate chips tend to melt. Sunflower and pumpkin seeds are popular with a lot of people. And they sound so healthy, too.

Here is our beef jerky recipe, which we found on page 247 of a cookbook called *The Thousand Recipe Chinese Cookbook* by Gloria Bley Miller (Grosset & Dunlap).

Beef Jerky

1½ pounds lean beef
½ cup soy sauce
¼ cup sherry
1 cup stock
3 or 4 tablespoons oil

1. Trim beef of all fat and remove tendons; cube or cut into large chunks.

2. Place in a saucepan with soy sauce, sherry, and stock. Cook, uncovered, over high heat, turning meat frequently until liquid evaporates.

3. Let cool; then refrigerate until chilled (about one to two hours). Shred, mince, or grind beef.

4. Heat oil. Add beef and coat quickly with oil. Cook over low heat, stirring frequently, until meat dries out completely (30 to 40 minutes). Let cool, and store in a covered jar.

CLOTHES

The only hard and fast rule for clothes is that one should dress in layers. Several thin layers of clothing trap air and thus provide more insulation than one thick layer. The layers can also be peeled off one by one as the day progresses and the temperature rises.

Be sure to carry at least one extra pair of dry jeans and socks. Take a sweater or light jacket for evening wear, even in summer. Long sleeves are essential even in warm weather in the North Woods as protection against mosquitoes and black flies. A hat, preferably with a brim, is also good protection against bugs in the North Woods. In the Missouri Ozarks and in southern Indiana, Ohio, and Illinois, you probably won't need to wear a hat except for rain protection. A two-piece rain suit is less cumbersome and more effective than a poncho. A waterproof hat allows more freedom of movement than a hood, but either will work.

Long underwear may be appreciated on spring and fall trips when the evenings are often cold. Mosquito headnets, which fit over brimmed hats, are useful in June in the North Woods (northern Minnesota, northern Wisconsin, the upper peninsula and northern Lower Michigan, and **Ontario**).

MISCELLANEOUS GEAR

Here is a sample list. We seldom take all these items on any individual trip, but they are things to consider: nesting cooking pots; potholder; one bowl, cup, and spoon per person; a washcloth or sponge and dishcloth or two washcloths, one to use for drying the dishes; biodegradable soap; scouring pad (not the kinds containing detergent); pocket knife; length of rope for clothesline and spare tent rope; ripstop nylon repair tape; toothpaste and toothbrush; flashlight; extra batteries; candles and candle lantern; first aid equipment (Band-Aids, moleskin, analgesic cream, mosquito repellent, a sterile needle or more specialized contraption to break blisters, aspirin); extra plastic bags; deck of cards or paperback book for rainy days; notebook and field guides; camera and film; binoculars; and day pack.

These items, of course, should augment the major equipment pieces: tent, pack, sleeping bag and mat, stove and fuel, food, and clothes.

3

MINNESOTA

MINNESOTA—AN INTRODUCTION

Minnesota is a big place with a lot of variety. The northeast is a land of ancient rocks scoured by the glaciers into some of the most rugged terrain in the Midwest. The highest point in the state—Eagle Mountain, 2,301 feet above sea level—is here.

Northwestern Minnesota is extremely flat country. A huge lake—

larger than any of the present-day Great Lakes—occupied much of this part of the state after the glaciers receded. Marshes are common, and there are large areas of peat. At the western edge of the state, in the valley of the Red River of the North, the former prairies are now wheat fields.

Northcentral Minnesota is an area of huge shallow lakes with irregular deposits of glacial till between them. The source of the Mississippi is here.

To the southwest, farms now cover land that was once prairie. The southeastern corner of the state is a part of the Driftless Area, a substantial section of Minnesota, Wisconsin, Illinois, and Iowa that was never covered by ice. The landscape is very old and has been carved extensively by streams into flat ridges divided by narrow, steep canyons.

The best hiking is in the north, particularly in the Superior National Forest and its Boundary Waters Canoe Area. More than one million acres of lake and woodland, it is one of the largest wilderness areas in the U.S. outside of Alaska. Most of the lakes in the upper Midwest occupy depressions in the debris left behind by the glaciers. In northeastern Minnesota the lakes occupy rock basins scoured by the ice as it moved across the land. Bedrock here is not buried under glacial deposits, and extensive rugged outcrops are common. The soil is usually very shallow, and hikers need sturdy boots to protect their feet from rocks at the surface.

The northcentral part of the state is not the greatest hiking country in the world. It is hard to lay out a trail that avoids the extensive wetlands, and the ground is mostly rather flat. However, there are now some interesting trails in the Chippewa National Forest.

In the southeast, where hardwood forests once covered the ridges and canyons, you can also find some enjoyable walking. The state has taken over exhausted farmland and begun the process of bringing back the forests.

James Buchanan knows more about hiking in Minnesota than anyone, and he has made his knowledge available in the *Minnesota Walk Book*. Three volumes of this extensive guide are already available, and doubtless more will be added in the future. Volume I ($4.50) covers northeastern Minnesota and Isle Royale. The island is politically part of Michigan, but ecologically it could be considered a part of northeastern Minnesota. Volume II ($3.95) covers northcentral Minnesota, and Volume III ($4.50) describes the southeastern corner of the state.

These guides cover everything from 1-mile nature paths to long backpacking trails.

The state forest system in Minnesota includes several million acres that are open to hikers and backpackers. In general there has been little recreational development on this land, but if you can handle a map and compass, there are miles of logging roads to explore. In Volume II of his *Minnesota Walk Book*, James Buchanan describes several walks he took on back roads in state forests where traffic is quite light and a measure of solitude is available. Camping is allowed anywhere on state forest lands except where specific rules against it are posted.

Information on the state forests is available from:

Department of Natural Resources
Forestry Division
Centennial Building
St. Paul, Minnesota 55155

TRAILS IN THE SUPERIOR NATIONAL FOREST

The Superior National Forest is primarily canoe country, and traditionally the Forest Service's major recreational efforts have been directed toward providing for the needs of canoeists. There have always been some trails in the forest, but they were often rather poorly maintained. In our first edition, we reported that major trails—like the Sioux–Hustler loop—were brushy and difficult to follow in some places. Sections of other trails were completely impossible to follow.

The past two years have seen a considerable change in that situation. Some very exciting new trails have been created, and many existing paths have been brushed out. There is more work planned for 1980 and beyond, so if you are planning a visit to the Superior, you might write forest headquarters to find out what has been added since this was written.

All but one of the trails described here are at least partly within the Boundary Waters Canoe Area (BWCA), the huge lakeland wilderness that attracts so many of the forest's visitors. The Forest Service has adopted a number of special rules for travel in the BWCA, which hikers as well as canoeists have to follow.

Between May I and November 15, you need a permit to enter the BWCA. These permits are free and they are available from the Forest Supervisor, P. O. Box 338, Duluth, Minnesota 55801, or from ranger stations in Cook, Isabella, Tofte, and Grand Marais, and at the Voyageur Visitor Center in Ely. The permits specify the areas to be visited, the length of the stay, and the number of people in the party.

Between mid-May and Labor Day, the Forest Service has set up a Visitor Distribution Program designed to spread people out in the Boundary Waters to take some of the pressure off the most popular areas. The program is essentially a quota system that limits the number of permits available. Currently, the program applies only to the Snowbank Lake and Angleworm Lake trails. Permits to hike these trails during the portion of the year when the distribution program is in effect can be obtained only from the Voyageur Visitor Center, Box 149, Ely, Minnesota 55731; (218) 365-6126.

It is a good idea to stop at the nearest ranger station before you start a hike. Rangers there can tell you the current condition of the trail and whether there are any special problems you might encounter. Generally you can pick up your permit at that time. However, if you are hiking the Snowbank or Angleworm trails, especially in August and more especially if you are starting your trip on a weekend, you will want to reserve a permit in advance. You can do this by phone or by mail anytime after January 2. However, mail requests must be received at least two weeks prior to the day you plan to start your hike.

Requests to reserve a permit must include the entry point, the starting date (including an alternate if possible), and the name and address of two people in the group.

The rules governing the Visitor Distribution Program are subject to change, and changes are particularly likely in regard to hiking trails. If these trails receive heavy use, more restrictions may be put into effect.

We would suggest that you write to the Forest Supervisor for information as far in advance as possible. That way you can have the information about current rules on hand before you start planning the details of your trip.

Other rules for the BWCA include:

1. Nonburnable, disposable food and beverage containers are not allowed.

2. Groups are limited to ten people.

3. On trails without camping facilities, campsites may be selected at fire-safe locations well off the trail. Permission must be secured from the permit issuing station to build an open fire outside of a developed campsite fire grate. Fire permits must be obtained when you begin your trip, since dry conditions may require that all fires be forbidden temporarily.

4. Use only dead wood for fires.

5. Dig latrines at least 100 feet from the trail and cover before leaving.

6. Do not wash dishes in or near a lake or stream.

7. Drown and stir fires before leaving your campsite. Be sure the fire is completely out.

8. As a precaution, check with the nearest ranger station on the trail condition before starting out.

Since the BWCA is a wilderness, there are rules that prevent much construction to make things easier for hikers. Streams generally are not bridged, and on most of the trails you can expect to get your feet wet. Where trails follow old logging roads, existing culverts are removed.

Trails in the Superior are generally not marked, unless the marking can be done naturally. Stone cairns are used occasionally, and sometimes real blazes—squares of bark cut from trees—may be employed. Such things as paint blazes are employed only in spots that could confuse hikers. Even unmarked, the trails should be easy to follow if you pay attention to where you walk. However, we do recommend that you buy the U.S.G.S. quads that cover the area you are going to hike through, and definitely carry a compass.

THE NORTHERN FORESTS

You'll find a lot of variety in the woods up here. On the better soils, there are spruce-fir forests of the sort that extends from here to the timberline in northern Canada. In this part of the world, the balsam fir and black and white spruce are often overtopped by a super canopy of huge old white pines that sometimes grow to over 200 feet.

White pine and red pine also grow on sandy soils, particularly where circumstances protect them from fire. You will find huge old trees of these species growing along lakeshores. These stands are often open and almost park-like with very little undergrowth.

Jack pine is an important species, too. It is a pioneer that colonizes rock outcrops with only the thinnest covering of soil. Jack pines also are adapted to situations in which fires are frequent, and they often form almost pure stands. You will also find them with black spruce, a combination that would be unlikely farther south.

Where logging and fires have disturbed the woods in northern Minnesota, quaking aspen is abundant, usually growing with red maple and paper birch.

On the plentiful wet ground, you'll find tamarack, black spruce, and white cedar. Many lake basins in this part of the world are gradually filling in with peat formed primarily from sphagnum moss. When the sphagnum has created dry enough conditions, the wet ground trees mentioned above will colonize the peat. This combination creates a northern bog, a strange environment occupied by many specialized plants.

One other plant community can be very important to hikers. Speckled alder—also called tag alder—forms dense thickets of shrubs on low stream banks and other wet areas in which water is moving. Alders grow as a clump of short trunks, and a colony can create a tangle that is nearly impossible to get through—especially with a pack on.

KEKEKABIC—SNOWBANK LAKE—OLD PINES TRAILS

The Kekekabic Trail was built during the 1930s to service the Kekekabic Fire Tower. It begins at the eastern end of the Fernberg Road, which runs east out of Ely, and ends at the Gunflint Trail, Cook County Highway 12, about 45 miles west of Grand Marais. There is parking at both ends of the trail.

Hiking the Kekekabic is a good way to get deep into the BWCA, but it is not the most exciting backpacking experience around. The trail was built for purely utilitarian reasons with no attention paid to scenery, so if you hike it you can expect a lot of tromping through deep woods and few views of lakes and streams.

Consequently, the Forest Service has made some changes in the Kekekabic. At the western end, they have built two loop trails—Snowbank Lake and Old Pines—that can be combined with part of the Kekekabic for interesting hikes that return you to your starting point. At the eastern end, the section from the Gunflint Trail to Agamok Lake is being maintained, but all of the old Kekekabic between Moiyaka and Medas lakes on the west and Agamok Lake on the east is going to be let alone. You can hike it if you wish, but it won't be easy, and as time passes it will become more difficult.

We will describe the western end of the Kekekabic as part of the Snowbank Lake and Old Pines loops.

SNOWBANK LAKE TRAIL
Location: A loop that begins at a parking area near the end of the Fernberg Road, east of Ely, and returns to the Fernberg Road via the Kekekabic.
Length: 22.6 miles for the whole loop, including the 5 miles of the Kekekabic.
U.S.G.S. Quads: Forest Center, Minnesota; Ensign Lake, Minnesota; both 15 minutes.
Description: This is an interesting trail laid out for recreation. It features a number of vistas from high ground overlooking Snowbank Lake. The

Snowbank Lake Trail (circles denote vistas)

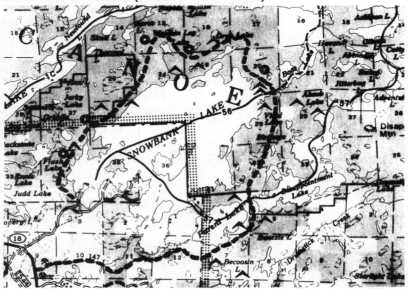

first two miles are on an old logging road that runs between the Fernberg Road and Snowbank Lake. As you approach the lake the trail branches off to the north. Note the good views marked on the map and the wilderness campsites along the shore of Snowbank. Between Wooden Leg Lake and Grub Lake, the steep hills rise 200 feet above the water, and they are just as high where the trail passes between Boot Lake and Snowbank.

There is some wet ground near Birdseye Lake and across the narrow neck of ground between Parent and Disappointment lakes before you hook up with the Kekekabic to return to Fernberg Road.

OLD PINES TRAIL
Location: This is another loop off the Kekekabic. At this writing it is only partially completed. We will describe it according to the proposed route. If you want to hike it, check with the Forest Service to find out if it has been completed and if the actual trail follows the planned route.
Length: From the beginning at the Snowbank Lake Trail just south of Boot Lake, there are two loops. One, 14.7 miles long, goes east to Alworth Lake and around Moiyaka and Medas lakes and returns to the Snowbank Trail south of Parent Lake. The shorter loop, 7 miles, goes around Disappointment Lake. On both loops, the southern leg is actually on the Kekekabic.

Old Pines Trail

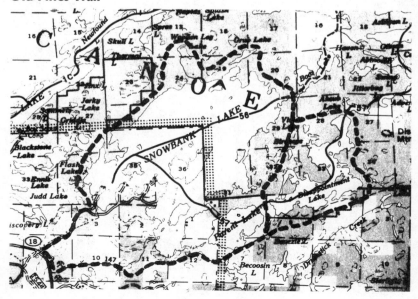

Kekekabic Trail—Eastern End (below and opposite)

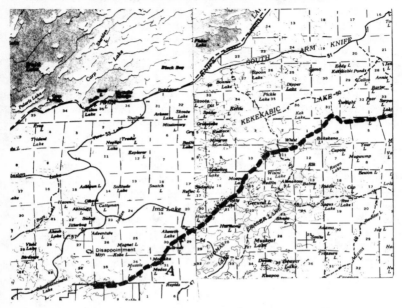

U.S.G.S. Quads: Ensign Lake, Minnesota; Forest Center, Minnesota; both 15 minutes.

Description: Heading east from the Snowbank Trail, this path climbs over a portion of Disappointment Mountain, a massive old hill 300 feet high, nearly a mile long, with many steep slopes. Coming down off the mountain, it skirts Alworth, Moiyaka, and Medas lakes, joining the Kekekabic between the latter two. The Old Pines are a stand of virgin white and red pine on the Kekekabic between Medas and Drumstick lakes.

By combining the Snowbank and Old Pines trails with portions of the Kekekabic, one can make loop hikes of 33, 25, or 24 miles. The longest of these is only 5 miles shorter than the total length of the old Kekekabic and offers the convenience of returning you to your starting point without requiring that you hike the same trail twice.

KEKEKABIC TRAIL—EASTERN END

Location: Begins at a parking area on the Gunflint Trail, Cook County Highway 12, about 45 miles west of Grand Marais.

Length: The whole trail from here to Fernberg Road is 38 miles long. The maintained portion from here to Agamok Lake is 11 miles.

U.S.G.S. Quads (east to west): Long Island Lake, Minnesota; Gillis Lake,

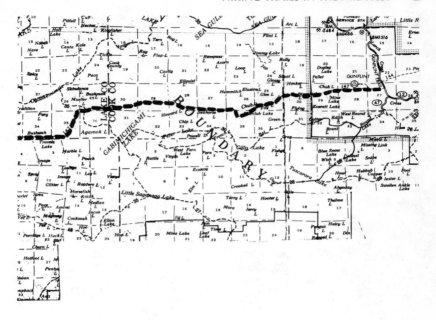

Minnesota; Ogishkemuncie Lake, Minnesota; all 7.5 minutes. These cover the maintained portion. From Agamok Lake west, the quads are Kekekabic Lake, Minnesota, 7.5 minutes; Ensign Lake, Minnesota, 15 minutes; and Forest Center, Minnesota, 15 minutes.

Description: The trail climbs quickly from 1,627 feet at the road to the top of a hill where a short side trail leads to the Gunflint Fire Tower, 2,064 feet. Continuing west, you'll follow an escarpment overlooking Mine Lake where remnants of an old iron mine are still visible. Be cautious here, since the old pits may be hard to see, especially if there is snow on the ground.

There is a good deal of low wet ground along the Gillis Lake section of the trail. You will pass wilderness campsites at Bingshick and Howard lakes.

Some of the hills near Ogishkemuncie Lake are 350 feet high, and there are creeks, ponds, open bogs, and marshes in the low spots between them. The Forest Service built a log bridge in 1968 to take hikers across the gorge between Ogishkemuncie Lake and Agamok Lake. This is where the maintained section ends. Between here and Medas Lake, the trail stays in the woods and crosses a lot of low ground. There are few water sources along the way.

BASS LAKE TRAIL
Location: Starts at County Road 116, the Echo Trail, 6 miles north of Ely.
Length: 5.6 miles.
U.S.G.S. Quad: Ely, Minnesota, 15 minutes.
Description: This newly created trail would make an excellent day hike.
Start in the morning, pack a lunch, and take your time. The trail circles
Bass Lake, and it is laid out to take advantage of some high ground and
good views along the way. You'll pass through some huge old virgin
pines. A portion of the trail crosses an area that was a lake bottom until
the 1920s when the water level dropped 45 feet. The trail is well
marked and easy to follow. There is no drinking water available except
from the lake, so carry a canteen.

Bass Lake Trail

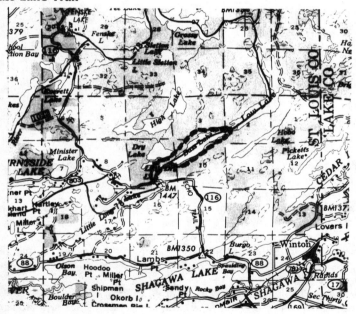

EAGLE MOUNTAIN TRAIL
Location: South end at the intersections of Forest Roads 153 and 158
just north of the forest service's Upper Cascade River Campground.
The trail goes north and west to end at the northern end of Forest
Road 326.
Length: 9 miles.
U.S.G.S. Quads (south to north): Mark Lake, Minnesota; Eagle Moun-
tain, Minnesota; Brule Lake, Minnesota; all 7.5 minutes. Note: only the
extreme southern portion of the trail is on the Mark Lake quad.

Eagle Mountain Trail

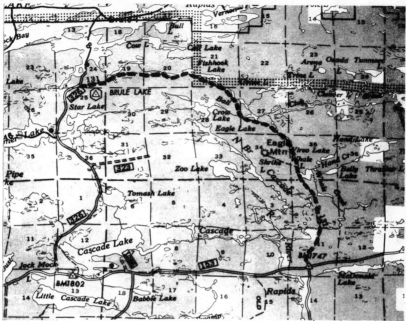

Description: Most hikers use only the first three miles of this trail, walking from F. R. 153 to the top of Eagle Mountain, which at 2,301 feet is the highest point in the state. Spectacular views are available from the summit, especially of the wilderness country to the northwest. There are two campsites on the shore of Whale Lake. From there, you climb about 400 feet in half a mile to the top of the mountain.

The six miles of trail from Eagle Mountain to F. R. 326 are less heavily used and less well maintained than the southern three miles. Coming down off the mountain, you cross Ball Club Creek just north of Crow Lake and then continue west, climbing to the Brule Lake Lookout at 2,120 feet. The road is just beyond the tower.

SIOUX-HUSTLER TRAIL

Location: A loop trail beginning from the Meander Lake Picnic Area off the Echo Trail, County Road 116, about 18 miles northwest of Ely. The other end of the loop is at the Echo Trail about 7 miles west.

Length: 27 miles.

U.S.G.S. Quads (east to west): Shell Lake, Minnesota; Takucmich Lake, Minnesota; both 7.5 minutes.

Description: This loop recently has been brushed out, but hiking it is still a fairly challenging experience. You will enter some remote areas,

Sioux-Hustler Trail

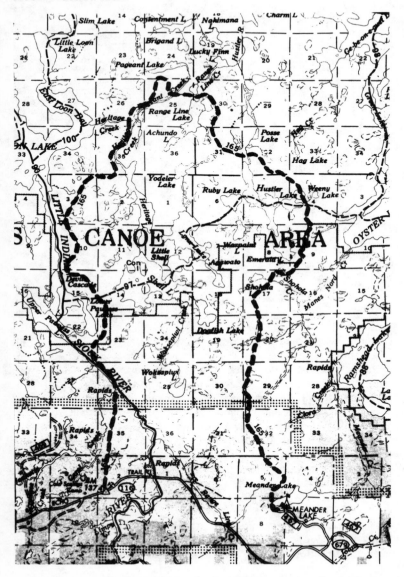

and you can expect to get your feet wet many times. There is some low ground, and there are many stream crossings, none of them bridged.

The Forest Service considers this a trail that only experienced back-packers should try.

From Meander Lake, the trail heads north and then west as far as Pageant Lake. Then it turns south, reaching the Little Indian Sioux River near Devil's Cascade. About a mile below Lower Pauness Lake, it crosses the river and then heads more or less straight south back to the Echo Trail.

There is some up-and-down terrain along the entire route but no substantial hills until you near the river, where the hills are nearly 300 feet above the stream. From there the trail drops down to cross the portage trail between Lower Pauness Lake and Shell Lake. Then it climbs back up onto a steep escarpment overlooking the former lake.

You'll find wilderness campsites at Emerald Lake, about 7 miles from Meander Lake; at Pageant Lake, about 8 miles farther on; and at Devil's Cascade, about 7 miles past Pageant Lake.

ANGLEWORM LAKE TRAIL
Location: Begins at the Echo Trail, County Road 116, 5 miles north of Fenske Lake Campground.
Length: 14 miles.

Angleworm Lake Trail

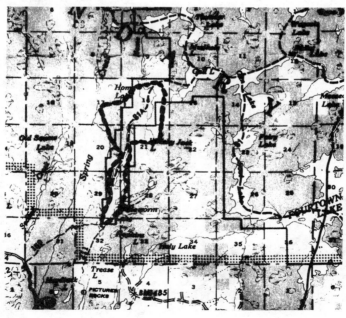

U.S.G.S. Quads: Angleworm Lake, Minnesota; Fourtown Lake, Minnesota; both 7.5 minutes.

Description: The landscape here is a series of ridges running southwest to northeast. Between the ridges are narrow valleys holding streams and/or lakes. Angleworm Lake is a very narrow body of water that occupies one of these valleys.

The trailhead is on one of the ridges. The trail heads northeast on fairly flat ground before dropping down from the ridge to cross Spring Creek on a wooden bridge. Then it climbs over another ridge before dropping down again to Angleworm Lake. You will skirt some swamp on the ridge, and there is more wet ground at the south end of Angleworm.

The valley holding Angleworm Lake is particularly narrow, deep, and steep; you will find some good scenic overlooks on the trail route around the lake. Among the best of these is the hill on the west side of the lake that was once the site of the Angleworm Fire Tower.

LAC LA CROIX TRAIL

Location: Heads north from a parking area on the Echo Trail, County Road 116, about 12 miles northwest of Fenske Lake Campground.

Length: 8 miles.

U.S.G.S. Quads: LaPond Lake, Minnesota; Lake Agnes, Minnesota; Iron Lake, Minnesota; all 7.5 minutes.

Lac La Croix Trail

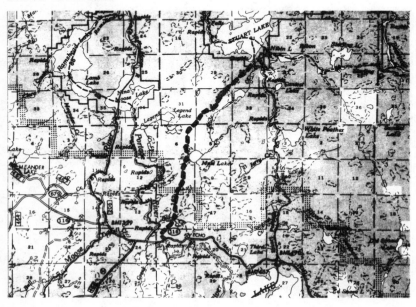

Description: At this time the Lac La Croix Trail does not go to Lac La Croix. It currently runs only as far as Stuart Lake. North of there, it has completely grown over. However, there are plans to brush it out, so check with the Forest Service about the current status if you are interested in hiking beyond Stuart Lake.

This is one of the few trails in the BWCA that is shown on the U.S.G.S. quads, so if you buy the quad sheets, you will have very precise information on the route. The trail follows a string of hills that are like islands in a general sea of swampy lowland.

The first quarter mile of the trail is on a two-track road; after that, you are on a pathway. The first 4 miles are through second-growth forest, but after that you will be hiking in virgin woods.

The crossing of the Stuart River, near the falls at the south end of Stuart Lake, is an easy one. The trail can be followed around the east side of Stuart Lake at least as far as the portage trail between Stuart and Nibin Lakes.

BORDER ROUTE TRAIL

Location: Generally follows the U.S.–Canadian border from Loon Lake on the west to Little John Lake on the east. Access to the west end is off the Gunflint Trail, County Road 12. Forest Road 318 goes north from the Gunflint, about 36 miles west of Grand Marais, skirting the eastern end of Loon Lake. There is a parking area under some power lines. Access to the east end is via County Road 16, the Arrowhead Trail, 17 miles northwest of Hovland.

Access to points along the trail is provided by the South Lake Trail, a 4-mile path from the Gunflint Trail near Poplar Lake to South Lake on the border. This is an interesting trail through old-growth timber, but the trailhead may be difficult to find and there is little parking on the Gunflint.

Other access is provided by taking County Road 66 north from the Gunflint to Clearwater Lake. A 3-mile trail leads from there, via Daniels Lake, to the Border Route.

Length: 32 miles, currently, but work is now going on to extend the trail eastward to join up with the Grand Portage Trail described below, and westward at least as far as Gunflint Lake.

U.S.G.S. Quads (west to east): Gunflint Lake, Minnesota; South Lake, Minnesota; Hungry Jack Lake, Minnesota; Crocodile Lake, Minnesota; Pine Lake West, Minnesota; Pine Lake East, Minnesota; all 7.5 minutes.

Description: This spectacular trail is the creation of the group of Minnesotans called the Minnesota Rovers Outing Club. Based in the Twin Cities, the club brings together backpackers, canoeists, cross-country skiers, rock climbers, cavers, and just about anyone else interested in self-propelled outdoor recreation.

The club offers a variety of outings—usually several each weekend—that are open to members. If you live in the Twin Cities area, the

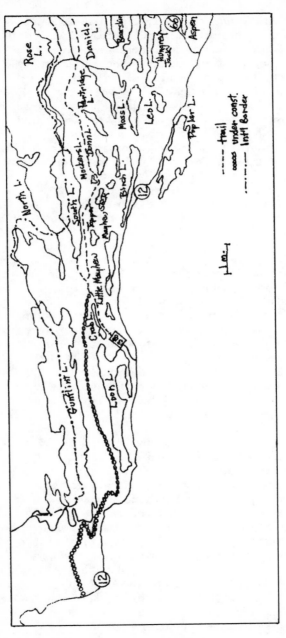

Border Route Trail—west section

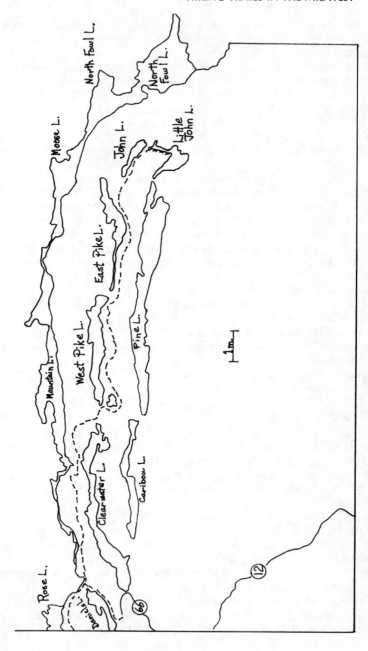

Border Route Trail—east section

Rovers offer an excellent way to meet people with outdoor interests, and if you are a beginner, they provide an excellent means of getting into the outdoors.

Membership is $7 a year, and all dues go to buy equipment that is loaned free—or at a nominal rental—to members going on outings. The club's address is Minnesota Rovers Outing Club, P. O. Box 14133, Dinkytown Station, Minneapolis, Minnesota 55414.

The man responsible for organizing work on the Border Route Trail is Edward Solstad, 3701 Pillsbury Avenue South, Minneapolis, Minnesota 55409. He can supply information on the state of construction, and by spring, 1980, he will have maps of the trail for sale for $1 a set.

You can also find out about the current state of the trail from the Gunflint Ranger Station, Grand Marais, Minnesota 55604; (218) 387-2451.

The landscape along the Border Route is some of the most rugged in the whole Boundary Waters area. If you look at the map, you can see that the lakes here are generally quite long and narrow and oriented east–west. Between the lakes are high, steep ridges that rise more than 500 feet above the water. Cliffs 100 feet high are fairly common, and one precipice, above Stairway Falls where Duncan Lake drains into Rose Lake, is over 300 feet high.

The trail goes northeast from Loon Lake, following the high ridge that overlooks the border lakes for several miles before it turns south between Clearwater and West Pike lakes and then continues east on a ridge to Little John Lake. There are excellent scenic overlooks all along the trail route.

Wilderness campsites are located on South, Rose, Daniels, and Clearwater lakes.

POW WOW LAKE TRAIL
Location: Trailhead is at Forest Center Landing near Lake Isabella. From Isabella on Minnesota Highway 1, go east on Forest Road 172, then left on Forest Road 368, left on Forest Road 173, right on Forest Road 373, right on Forest Road 377 to Forest Center.
Length: Currently about 30 miles, but work is still going on to extend the trails.
U.S.G.S. Quads: Forest Center, Minnesota, 15 minutes; Parent Lake, Minnesota, 7.5 minutes.
Description: This is actually a sort of network of trails that follow the remains of old logging roads. The roads had completely grown over with a considerable tangle of brush before the Forest Service went in to clear them.

The map shows the current state of things, but check in with the Isabella Ranger Station before you start hiking, since much that is new may have been added.

The country here has all been logged, but there is considerable

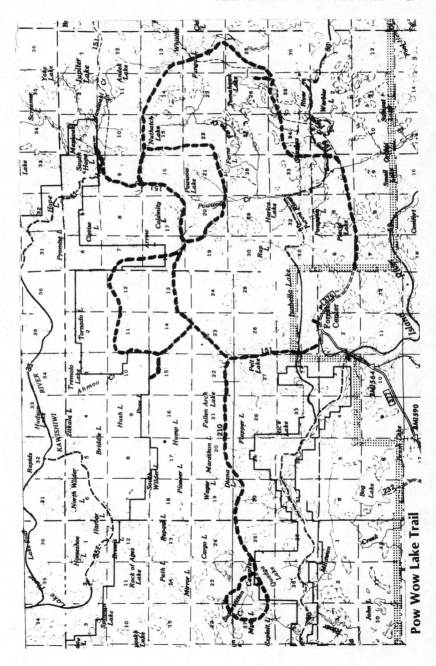

Pow Wow Lake Trail

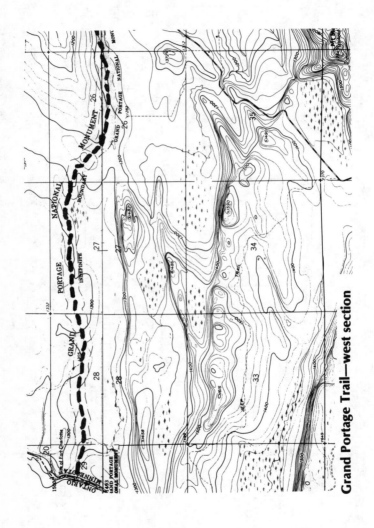

Grand Portage Trail—west section

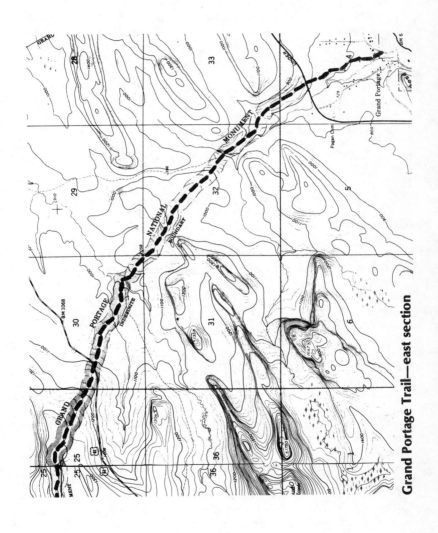

Grand Portage Trail—east section

variety in vegetation along the trails. You will see mixed woods of aspen and balsam fir as well as swamps and marshes. Part of the trail passes a 1,000-acre area that was burned in 1976 and is now furiously growing in. The landscape ranges from rolling to flat.

You will need the usual BWCA permit between May 1 and November 15, but since this area is not on a canoe route, it is free of other restrictions. You can camp where you like, and you need not be concerned with quotas.

GRAND PORTAGE NATIONAL MONUMENT
GRAND PORTAGE TRAIL

Location: Begins at the reconstructed stockade in Grand Portage National Monument in the village of Grand Portage. Ends on the Minnesota–Ontario border on the Pigeon River at the site of Fort Charlotte.
Length: 9 miles.
U.S.G.S. Quads (east to west): Grand Portage, Minnesota; Mineral Center, Minnesota; The Cascades, Minnesota; all 7.5 minutes. Note that only a tiny section of the trail is on the Mineral Center quad.
Description: You'll get in some good climbing on this trail. Lake Superior is 602 feet and the high points on the trail are over 1,300 feet. In spite of the height, you'll find some wet ground along the way.

About a mile from the west end of the trail, a spur branches to the north. This leads to the Cascades, where the Pigeon River drops about 160 feet in a quarter mile. There is a Park Service campground at the site of Fort Charlotte.

TRAILS IN THE CHIPPEWA NATIONAL FOREST

The Chippewa National Forest lies in the northcentral part of the state in one of the greatest concentrations of lakes in Minnesota. The Mississippi's source is just northwest of the forest, and the young river flows through the Chippewa. The lakes are generally shallow and surrounded by vast marshes and substantial swamp areas.

This landscape is a creation of the last Ice Age. The dry ground between the lakes is glacial till, flat in some places and heaped into hills in others.

The forest is a mixture of northern types: pine woods, spruce-fir, hardwoods, swamp conifers, and the typical second-growth woodland of aspen and birch. Substantial areas have been planted with rows of trees as part of the reforestation efforts.

The Chippewa has been home to people for a long time. The Sioux lived here and then the Chippewa, attracted by the concentrations of waterfowl and other game and by the wild rice that still grows along the edges of the shallow lakes. Hikers will find that they are seldom very far from people. Road crossings are fairly common.

NORTH COUNTRY TRAIL

Location: Runs across the southern edge of the Chippewa. Completed portion as of October, 1979, runs from the western boundary of the forest southwest of Walker to Little Silver Lake northwest of Longville. Road crossings that provide access, west to east, are Minnesota Highway 12, 4 miles south of Walker; Minnesota Highway 34, 5 miles south of Walker; and U.S. Highway 371, 7 miles south of Walker. The trail crosses the Shingobee River on County Road 50. At the east end, a short dirt road runs south to County Road 5, about 4 miles west of Longville.

Length: 22 miles completed. Whole segment, when finished, will be 63 miles.

U.S.G.S. Quads (west to east): Akeley, Minnesota; Walker, Minnesota; Hackensack, Minnesota; Webb Lake, Minnesota; Jack Lake, Minnesota; Whipholt, Minnesota; Woman Lake, Minnesota; all 7.5 minutes. The trail just touches the northern edges of the Hackensack, Webb Lake, and Woman Lake quads. Quads for the unfinished part of the trail include Town Line Lake, Minnesota; Tobique, Minnesota; Remer, Minnesota; Goose Lake, Minnesota; and Shingle Mill Lake, Minnesota; all 7.5 minutes. All of these quads are aerial photo reproduced in color with contour lines and other information overprinted on them. They are very pretty, but we find them rather hard to read. The counters are printed in red and often quite hard to see.

Description: The trail winds through a rather interesting section of the Chippewa. It passes many lakes and the terrain is hilly enough to be interesting. The trail is marked in blue blazes with signs at road crossings.

SUOMI HILLS TRAILS

Location: On Minnesota Highway 38, 20 miles north of Grand Rapids. Parking area at Day Lake gives access to trailhead.

Length: 12.5 miles; 15 miles planned.

U.S.G.S. Quad: Little Bowstring Lake, Minnesota, 7.5 minutes.

Description: Doubtless some of the hilliest ground in the Chippewa with more than 150 feet of difference between lake levels and hilltops. The Suomi Hills are good examples of the sort of chaotic terrain left by the glaciers. The level of the surface of Day Lake is almost 60 feet above Balloon Lake, just a mile away.

There are very steep hills with views overlooking Kremer Lake and Beaver Lake. Wilderness campsites are available on Kremer, Spruce Island, and Adele lakes.

CUT FOOT SIOUX TRAIL

Location: A loop trail between Bowstring River and Cut Foot Sioux Lake. Best access is on Minnesota Highway 46 at the Cut Foot Sioux Visitor Information Center, 36 miles north of Grand Rapids, or at a roadside park 4 miles farther north on the same road.

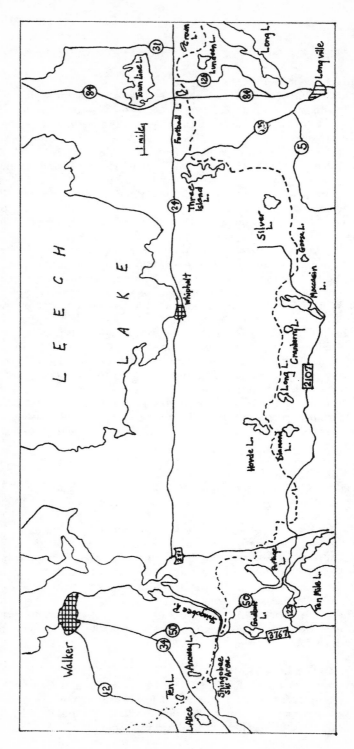

North Country Trail—west section

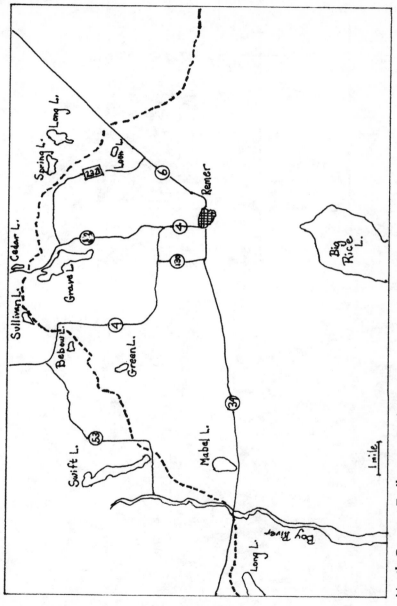

North Country Trail—east section

Suomi Hills Trails

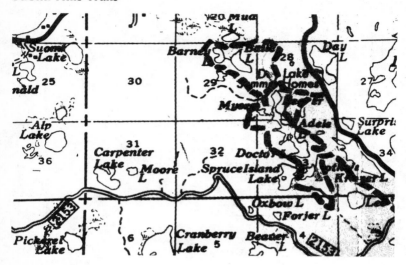

Cut Foot Sioux Trail

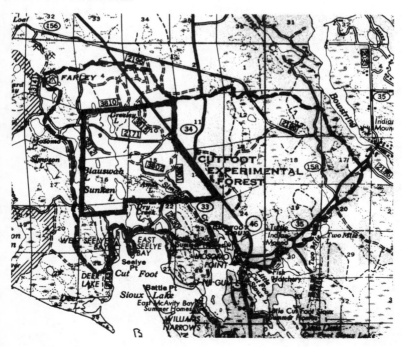

Length: 20 miles.

U.S.G.S. Quads: Max, Minnesota; Bowstring Lake, Minnesota; Pigeon Dam Lake, Minnesota; all 7.5 minutes.

Description: The water in Bowstring Lake will eventually flow into Hudson Bay. The water in Cut Foot Sioux Lake flows into the Mississippi. The trail follows the approximate route of an old portage used by Indians and voyageurs between the two watersheds.

The ground here is mostly quite flat with a good deal of marsh and swamp. Depressions are more common than hills. Lake Roosevelt is in a depression 60 feet deep. There are some good overlooks at West Seelye Bay and especially on Seelye Point.

There are four campgrounds along Seelye Bay and another on Mosomo Point near the visitor center. Backcountry campsites are available on Farley Lakes and Biauswah Lake.

One of the most interesting points on the trail is just east of Highway 46 near the visitor center. Here prehistoric Indians built a turtle-shaped mound that is still quite prominent.

TRAILS IN THE RICHARD J. DORER MEMORIAL HARDWOOD FOREST

The southeastern tip of Minnesota bears little resemblance to the wild northern counties. This is part of the Driftless Area, the region of Minnesota, Wisconsin, Iowa, and Illinois that, for reasons unknown, was never covered by ice. The landscape here is ancient. Instead of the lakes, swamps, and chaotic morainal hills of the north, the prominent features are rather flat ridges divided by deep, narrow canyons. Running water—not ice—has shaped the land.

The forest is different, too. You will see some trees—such as quaking aspen, paper birch, and basswood—that are found in the north, but you will also see black walnut and cottonwood, trees that reach the northern limit of their range south of the Superior National Forest.

Much of the land here has been farmed. The usual pattern is to plow the flat ridge tops and leave the steep canyon slopes covered with trees. In recent years, as the poorer ridge-top land became exhausted, the state has begun to buy it for inclusion in the forest. Extensive tree planting has been undertaken with hardwood species and with white and red pine. The pines are generally planted on the poorest soils, land so exhausted that it will not support the more demanding hardwood species.

The state has been developing multipurpose trails on several of the larger blocks of forest land. These trails are used by snowmobilers in the winter and hikers in the warmer seasons. They provide some interesting hiking, with elevation differences of as much as 500 feet between the creek bottoms and the ridges. The slopes are almost always wooded, but many of the ridge tops are still open, providing good views of the country.

Plan to carry water on these trails. Many of the smaller creeks are intermittent streams that are dry much of the time.

KRUGER RECREATION AREA

Location: Take Minnesota Highway 60 west from Wabasha for 5 miles. Turn south on County Road 81 a half mile to the parking area.

Length: 5 miles.

U.S.G.S. Quad: Wabasha, Minnesota, 15 minutes.

Description: The Department of Natural Resources supplies aerial photos of this area with the boundaries of the state land and the trail routes added. The photos are very pretty, and they provide a good look at the vegetation, at least as far as separating wooded and unwooded ground. However, they don't do a very good job of showing relief, and they are difficult to locate in relation to nearby towns without additional information. We have tried to transfer the trail routes onto the Wabasha quad, but you should be aware that our efforts are approximations.

There is a small eight-site campground in a red pine plantation near the parking area at the Kruger and a picnic area in a creek bottom. Camping is $3 per night. The main trail winds through forest and open ground with changes in elevation of as much as 400 feet. There are good views from some of the ridge tops.

Kruger Recreation Area

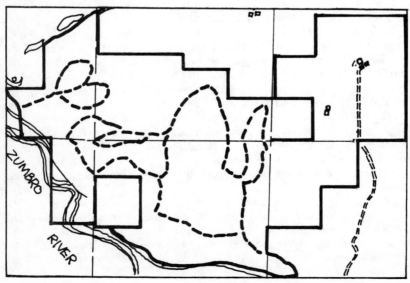

TROUT VALLEY DEMONSTRATION WOODLAND

Location: Just south of the village of Weaver. Take U.S. Highway 61 south from Weaver for a mile. Turn west on County Road 29, 1½ miles to the parking area.

Length: 8 miles.

U.S.G.S. Quad: Weaver, Minnesota, 7.5 minutes.

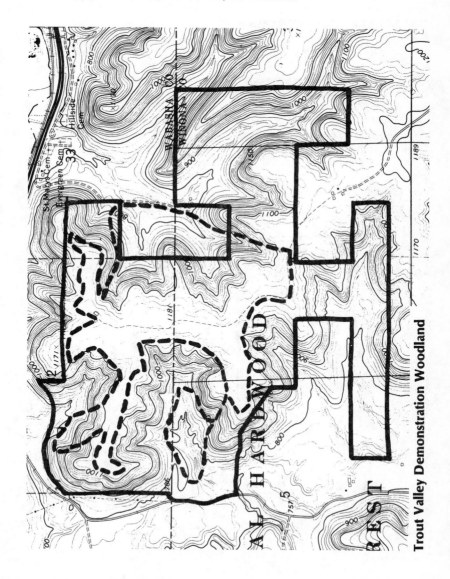

Description: Here again we have transferred information from an aerial photo to a quad sheet. The area is very hilly, with elevation differences of 500 feet. Again it follows the pattern of wooded slopes and open ridge tops, although pines have now been planted on some of the ridges. There are good views of the Mississippi from some of the ridge tops.

HAY CREEK RECREATION AREA

Location: Take Minnesota Highway 58 south 6 miles from Red Wing. Turn right at Dressen's Saloon and follow the road into the parking area.

Length: 6 miles in three interconnecting loops of about 2 miles each.

U.S.G.S. Quads: Red Wing, Minnesota, 15 minutes; Goodhue East, Minnesota, 7.5 minutes. You need both of these to cover the whole recreation area, but all of the trails are located on the Red Wing sheet.

Description: The Hay Creek area is about 2,000 acres of state-owned land. Its character is quite similar to the areas described above,

Hay Creek Recreation Area

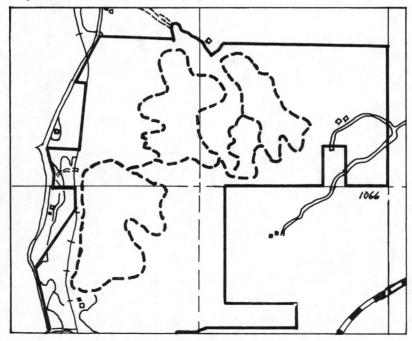

although there is less variation in elevation. There are open areas on the ridge tops and numerous young plantations of hardwoods.

SNAKE CREEK MANAGEMENT UNIT
Location: Off U.S. Highway 61, 3 miles south of Kellogg.
Length: Two trails, one 3 miles and one 8 miles.
U.S.G.S. Quads: Alma, Minnesota; Wabasha South, Minnesota; Beaver, Minnesota; Weaver, Minnesota; all 7.5 minutes.
Description: It is rather awkward to use quad sheets for these trails, since Snake Creek sits right on a corner where four separate sheets come together. The shorter of the two trails actually consists of two interconnecting loops, so you can make a 3-mile or a 2-mile hike. This trail is reserved for hikers. The long trail is multipurpose, so snowmobilers can use it too. The terrain is very like the trail described above, including views of the Mississippi from the ridge tops.

All of the trails above are under the jurisdiction of the Area Forest Supervisor for the Department of Natural Resources, Lake City Area #51, Box 69, Lake City, Minnesota 55041; (612) 345-3216.

RENO RECREATION AREA SNOWMOBILE TRAIL
Location: Trails begin at a parking area off a township road about a half mile west of the tiny village of Reno.
Length: 16.2 miles.
U.S.G.S. Quad: Brownsville, Minnesota, 15 minutes.

Reno Recreation Area Snowmobile Trail

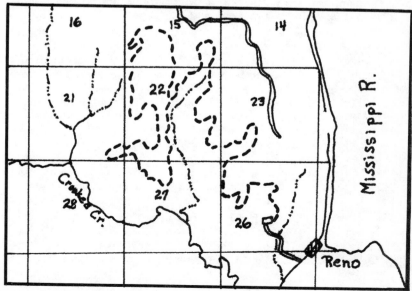

Description: Our map is again an approximation based on a sketch map provided by the Minnesota Department of Natural Resources. This trail is on typical driftless area terrain with 200- to 300-foot differences in elevation. At times the trail climbs hills steep enough to require switchbacks. The trail is long enough to make it attractive for backpacking, but the only water around is at a picnic area near the parking lot at the trailhead.

This trail is administered by the Lewiston District Forester, Box 278, Lewiston, Minnesota 55952; (507) 523-2224.

CASEY JONES TRAIL

Location: The southwest corner of the state, in Pipestone and Murray counties. The western terminus is at Pipestone, at the junction of state highways 30, 75, and 23. The trail follows an abandoned railway right-of-way east to the town of Slayton and then runs north cross-country to Lake Shetek State Park.

Length: Only the western 12½ miles of this trail was completely developed when we researched this book, but the rest of the 38-mile trek was under construction.

Public Transportation Access: None.

Description: This section of Minnesota is prairieland, so spring is an ideal time to go if you're interested in prairie grasses and wildflowers.

The town of Pipestone was named for the ceremonial pipes made of an unusual red stone found in the area and used by three centuries of Plains Indians. The early American artist, George Catlin, visited the site in 1836 and gave us the earliest published description. Explorer Joseph Nicolet also visited the quarries; his men carved an inscription into ledges which still can be seen.

Lake Shetek, at the eastern end of the trail, gets its name from a Sioux word for pelican. Before the white man came, and long before the lakeshore was made a state park campground, the spot was a campground for the Sioux. It was famous then for its abundant wildlife, fish, and waterfowl.

White trappers were later attracted for the same reason. Visitors today can observe dugout shelters built by early trappers on Loon Island.

Park facilities include campgrounds, pioneer group camp, a children's group camp, a picnic area, swimming beach, fishing, and boat rental.

DOUGLAS TRAIL

Location: The trail, recently completed, follows an abandoned railroad bed northwest from the town of Rochester (Olmsted County) in the

Casey Jones Trail

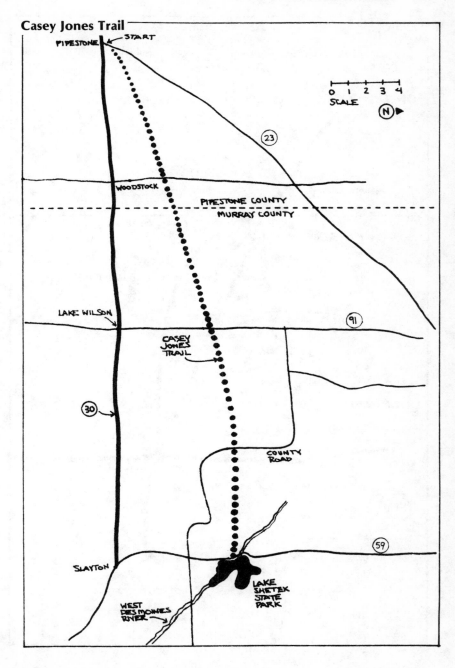

Douglas Trail

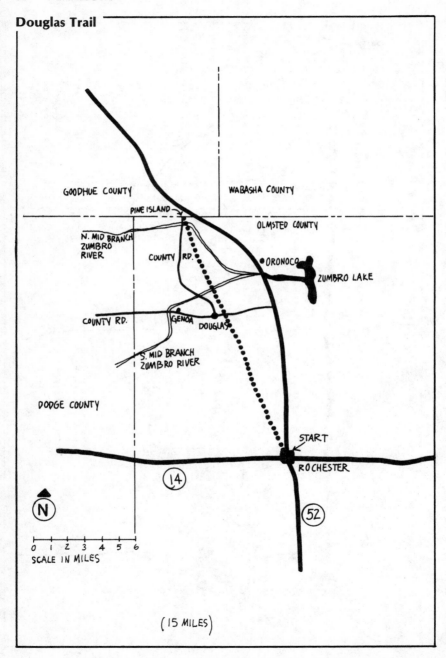

GOODHUE COUNTY

WABASHA COUNTY

PINE ISLAND

OLMSTED COUNTY

N. MID BRANCH
ZUMBRO
RIVER

COUNTY RD.

●ORONOCO

ZUMBRO LAKE

COUNTY RD.

GENOA

DOUGLAS

S. MID BRANCH
ZUMBRO RIVER

DODGE COUNTY

START

ROCHESTER

(14)

(52)

N

0 1 2 3 4 5 6
SCALE IN MILES

(15 MILES)

southeast corner of the state to Pine Island, at the county line between Olmsted and Goodhue counties.

Length: 15 miles.

Public Transportation Access: None.

Description: Small farms are frequent along this route. You will seldom be out of sight of a house. The countryside is gently rolling, with small streams and hardwood forests breaking up the pattern of cultivated fields.

There is some state-owned land adjacent to the path, but most of the property is private. No trespassing is allowed and certainly no camping. This is an easy one-day hike, however. Water pumps and picnic tables eventually will be provided by the state but have not been installed yet.

The trail runs roughly parallel to and within 5 miles of U.S. Route 52 at any point. An easy place to get on the trail for a short hike is at the point where it crosses the paved road that runs between U.S. Route 52 and the town of Douglas about 10 miles north of Rochester.

For more up-to-date information, contact Trail Coordinator, Division of Parks and Recreation, Department of Natural Resources, 320 Centennial Building, St. Paul, Minnesota 55155.

SAKATAH–SINGING HILLS TRAIL

Location: This trail follows an old railroad bed between the towns of North Mankato and Faribault in the lakes area about 40 miles south of Minneapolis.

Length: 42 miles.

Public Transportation Access: Buses from Minneapolis run both to Faribault on Interstate Highway 35 and to Mankato on U.S. Route 169. The Greyhound terminal in any major city will have current schedules.

Description: This trail was only completed and marked in 1973. Parking lots, litter barrels, water pumps and picnic tables eventually will be provided but have not yet been installed.

There is only one campground along the route, in Sakatah Lake State Park about 17 miles west of Faribault. However, food and lodging may be found in any of the towns near or adjacent to the path—at Morristown, Waterville, or Eagle Lake.

Rolling hills and farms along the way provide easy walking through bucolic countryside. Small lakes abound, but the water is not safe for drinking.

Much of the trail runs within a few miles of Minnesota Highway 60. North–south roads which cross both the trail and the state highway include a county road that runs north from Morristown, Minnesota, Highway 13 that crosses route 60 in Waterville, and another county highway a mile west of the hamlet of Elysian.

For more up-to-date information, contact Trail Coordinator, Division of Parks and Recreation, Department of Natural Resources, 320 Centennial Building, St. Paul, Minnesota 55155.

Sakatah–Singing Hills Trail

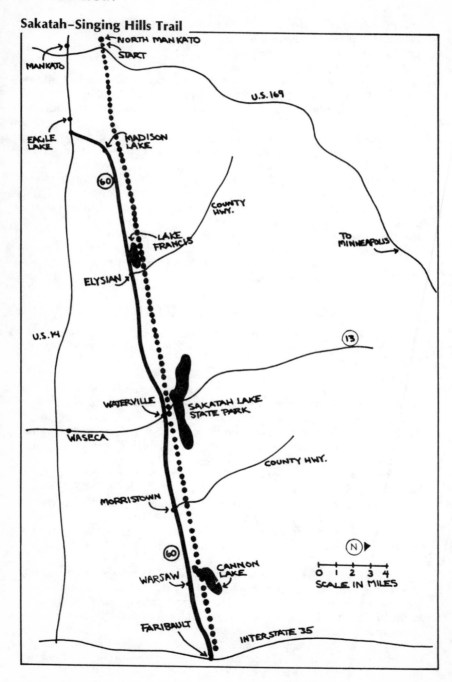

SOURCES

Other sources of information
  about hiking in Minnesota
  include:

Forest Supervisor
Superior National Forest
P. O. Box 338
Duluth, Minnesota 55801

Forest Supervisor
Chippewa National Forest
Cass Lake, Minnesota 56633

Trails Coordinator
Department of Natural Resources
Centennial Building
St. Paul, Minnesota 55155

For trails in the southeastern
  corner of the state:

District Forester
Red Wing District
Box 69
Lake City, Minnesota 55041

District Forester
Lewiston District
Box 278
Lewiston, Minnesota 55952

District Forester
Caledonia District
Box 72
Caledonia, Minnesota 55921

4

MICHIGAN

MICHIGAN—AN INTRODUCTION

Michigan can reasonably claim to offer more to Midwest hikers and backpackers than any other state in the region. Isle Royale National

Park and the Porcupine Mountains Wilderness State Park are the best known backpacking areas in the Midwest, a fact that makes them crowded at least part of the time.

But these two famous places are only the beginning. Two other national parks—Pictured Rocks and Sleeping Bear Dunes—provide backpacking trails as do the two national forests—Ottawa and Hiawatha—in the upper peninsula and the combined Huron–Manistee National Forests in Lower Michigan.

If that is not enough, consider a state forest system with a total of 3.8 million acres of land. Recently a number of trails have been developed in the state forests. This is partly a response to the growing interest in backpacking, but the main impetus comes from the foresters themselves. Many of them are anxious to show off the beauties of the land they administer, and they are hoping to see more backpackers using the facilities they have provided.

State and national forest lands are also great places to get away from marked trails and just explore. Old logging grades and fire breaks provide access to many areas for backpackers who know how to use a map and compass.

Michigan's upper peninsula is a huge, sparsely populated area that is nearly all covered with dense woods. The combination of poor soil and cold climate puts severe limits on agriculture. The economies of the towns are based chiefly on forest products and copper and iron mining.

The mining is concentrated in the western half of the peninsula, which is geologically part of the Canadian Shield. The bedrock here is extremely ancient. The oldest known rocks were formed about 3.5 billion years ago, and the youngest were laid down in the Early Cambrian Period, around 600 million years ago.

At times in the remote past, the western upper peninsula was covered with mountains as high as the Rockies. Even today, the remnants of those ancient ranges provide some of the most interesting backpacking country in the Midwest. See, in particular, the Porcupine Mountains, page 69, and the completed portion of the North Country Trail in the Ottawa National Forest, page 85.

The eastern portion of the upper peninsula and the entire lower peninsula are underlain by sedimentary rocks laid down during the Paleozoic Era, between 600 million and 220 million years ago. The terrain here is much less rugged and more commonly flat-to-rolling rather than hilly. Huge areas of the eastern upper peninsula are wetlands of various kinds.

While the ancient geologic history of the state has obviously played a central role in creating the geography, the most obvious influence on the terrain was exercised by the great continental ice sheets that covered the state during the Pleistocene Epoch. The most recent of the glaciers, the Wisconsinan, began receding from Michigan only 11,000 years ago and left the Superior Basin about 7,000 to 8,000 years ago.

Today nearly all of the state is covered by a layer of glacial till and outwash that is sometimes nearly 200 feet thick. Most of the many lakes occupy depressions in this debris. The large wetland areas are created by an immature and inefficient drainage system. The huge pine forests that drew the loggers to Michigan more than a century ago grew on sandy soils laid down in front of the ice sheets.

Nearly all the forests of Michigan have been cut at least once, although some virgin tracts remain—notably in the Porcupine Mountains and the Sylvania Tract. Repeated fires followed the loggers into many areas, and these fires often produced a radical change in the composition of the woods. In many areas that once supported forests of white and red (or Norway) pine, the fires gradually eliminated seed sources for new generations of these trees.

In the wake of the fires, trees that could send up sprouts fron roots far enough underground to survive the flames took over the ground. By the time effective fire control was established in the 1930s, species such as quaking and big-tooth aspen, paper birch, and red maple had taken over millions of acres of former pine lands. Today, second-growth forests dominated by these species and a few others are the most common woodland type in the upper peninsula and the northern half of the lower peninsula.

The richest soils are generally occupied by northern hardwood forests of beech, sugar maple, yellow birch, and basswood, with varying amounts of hemlock mixed in. Sandy ground is usually dominated by jack pine, a species that is adapted to areas in which fires are frequent.

Wet ground may be occupied by dense stands of northern white cedar, black spruce, or tamarack. The ground in these wet conditions is often the spongy peat called muskeg or quaking earth. Streams are often bordered with nearly impenetrable thickets of speckled alder, a shrub that sends up a dense clump of trunks.

In the north you will also find occasional stands of spruce-fir forest, here at the southernmost limits of the Boreal Forest that extends north to the edge of the tundra. In the central part of the lower peninsula, these northern forest types begin to give way to more southern types. You'll encounter sassafras and flowering dogwood growing under the forest canopy. Oak-hickory woods appear on dry ground, and tulip trees join the beeches and maples in the hardwood forests.

Michigan's state park system includes 207,000 acres of recreational land. There is a $2 daily use fee in these parks and more frequent users will want to buy an annual sticker for $7. Camping is allowed only in designated campgrounds in these parks. Many of these include such amenities as showers and flush toilets. Cost for these is $5 per night.

Some more primitive campsites are available in some parks for as little as $2. Information on the state parks is available from the Department of Natural Resources, Parks Divison, Lansing, Michigan 48926.

In both state forests and national forests, you can camp anywhere except where it is expressly forbidden, such as along roads and around forest campgrounds. National forest campgrounds are usually equipped with water pumps and pit toilets. Rates are $3 per night. All but a few state forest campgrounds are free. They are generally equipped like the national forest camps with pumps and pit toilets. Many of these state forest campgrounds are attractive places even for backpackers. They are often miles from the nearest paved road and quite small—some have as few as four campsites.

TRAILS IN UPPER MICHIGAN

ISLE ROYALE NATIONAL PARK TRAILS

Location: In Lake Superior about 50 miles from the upper peninsula of Michigan and 15 miles from the Minnesota shore.

If you have a boat more than 20 feet long or a plane outfitted with pontoons, you can make your own way to Isle Royale. Otherwise, you can take a ferry from Houghton or Copper Harbor, Michigan, or from Grand Portage, Minnesota. There is also air service from Houghton.

The Houghton ferry is run by the National Park Service. It operates twice a week, leaving Houghton Tuesdays and Fridays at 9:30 A.M. and returning from Rock Harbor Wednesdays and Saturdays at 9:30 A.M. from June 8 to September 8.

Round trip fares are $30 for adults, $15 for children under 12. Reservations must be paid in advance. For reservations and information, write Isle Royale National Park, 87 North Ripley Street, Houghton, Michigan 49931.

The Copper Harbor ferry departs daily at 8 A.M. from June 15 through Labor Day, and on Monday and Friday at 8 A.M. May 14 through June 11 and September 7 through September 28.

Fares are $28 round trip for adults, $22 for young people 12 to 17 years of age, $15 for children 11 years and under. For reservations, contact the Isle Royale Queen, Copper Harbor, Michigan 49918.

Two ferries operate from Grand Portage, Minnesota, to Windigo Lodge on the southwest side of the island.

The Wenonah, a 64-foot boat with a 150-person capacity, departs from Grand Portage at 9:30 A.M. daily from the third Saturday in June through Labor Day. Round trip fare for adults is $20, with children under 12 going at half price.

The Voyageur, a 60-foot boat equipped to carry 49 passengers, departs from Grand Portage at 9:30 A.M. Monday, Wednesday, and Saturday, from June through Labor Day. From mid-May until June, and

Isle Royale National Park Trails

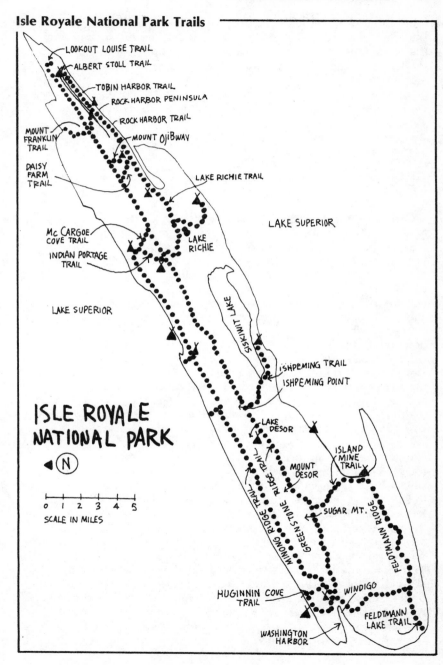

LOOKOUT LOUISE TRAIL
ALBERT STOLL TRAIL
TOBIN HARBOR TRAIL
ROCK HARBOR PENINSULA
ROCK HARBOR TRAIL
MOUNT FRANKLIN TRAIL
MOUNT OJIBWAY
DAISY FARM TRAIL
LAKE RICHIE TRAIL
LAKE SUPERIOR
Mc CARGOE COVE TRAIL
LAKE RICHIE
INDIAN PORTAGE TRAIL
LAKE SUPERIOR
SISKIWIT LAKE
ISHPEMING TRAIL
ISHPEMING POINT
LAKE DESOR
ISLAND MINE TRAIL
MOUNT DESOR

ISLE ROYALE NATIONAL PARK

◀ (N)

0 1 2 3 4 5
SCALE IN MILES

MINONG RIDGE TRAIL
GREENSTONE RIDGE TRAIL
FELDTMANN RIDGE
SUGAR MT.
HUGINNIN COVE TRAIL
WINDIGO
FELDTMANN LAKE TRAIL
WASHINGTON HARBOR

from Labor Day through October, it operates on Wednesdays and Saturdays only. Fares are $15 one way. The Voyageur circumnavigates Isle Royale, usually in clockwise direction, stopping overnight at Rock Harbor before returning to Grand Portage. The two-day round trip is $36.

For reservations and information, write Grand Portage–Isle Royale Transportation Line, Inc., 366 Lake Avenue South, Duluth, Minnesota 55802.

The air service leaves Houghton at 8:30 A.M. daily for Rock Harbor from mid-June through Labor Day. Round trip fares for adults are $50. For children under 10 the fee is half that.

Plane trips are also available from Rock Harbor to Windigo, at opposite ends of the island. The one-way fare is $20 for adults and $10 for children under 10.

Contact the Isle Royale Seaplane Service, P. O. Box 371, Houghton, Michigan 49931 in June and August. The winter address for the air taxi is 248 Airport Road, Shawano, Wisconsin 54166.

All the ferries will also carry canoes or boats up to 20 feet long with outboard motors. They do not carry gasoline, but it is available on the island.

Length: There are 26 named trails on the island with a total length of about 160 miles. Some of these trails are only a mile or less and do not connect with other trails, so we have not included them in the descriptions that follow.

U.S.G.S. Quad: Isle Royale National Park, Michigan.

Description: Isle Royale is a beautiful example of North Woods wilderness. The island is made up of a series of parallel basaltic ridges running from northeast to southwest. Between the ridges are low-lying areas of marshes, lakes, and streams. The shoreline is quite irregular, with many coves and harbors, and a number of small islands lie offshore.

The island is covered with a forest of hardwoods and conifers. It is an extremely interesting ecological laboratory, because different kinds of trees grow in different habitats on the island. Forests of maple and yellow birch predominate on the island's southern portion, giving way to spruce and fir in the north. Black spruce, tamarack, and alder thrive in the swamps while isolated white pines are the only trees on some of the higher and more exposed ridges.

Isle Royale is home to a moose herd of about 1,000. Their presence on the island is a bit of a mystery. No one saw a moose there before 1912. Since the mainland is so far away, the moose either swam out or crossed the ice during a winter freeze. There are reasons to dispute both of these theories, but there is no doubt that the beasts are there. Note: A moose of either sex can be dangerous. If you see one on the trail, enjoy the view, but don't try to get too close.

Isle Royale is also one of the few places left in the 48 contiguous states where timber wolves still run wild. The population is estimated at 40 to 50. They prey on the moose herd, culling out the weak and sick. You may hear a wolf at night, but your chances of seeing one are slim.

Isle Royale is a good spot for birders. An enormous fire devastated about a third of the island in 1936, so there are large tracts of young, scrubby forest alongside more mature woods. In additon, there are swamps, inland lakes, and the Lake Superior shore. With all these habitats in close proximity, the island harbors about 200 different species of birds.

There is one lodge on the island. Rates for two (American plan) are $62.50 a day at Rock Harbor. Housekeeping cabins are $32 for two with $3.50 additional for each extra person.

If you wish to stay at the lodge, contact Rock Harbor Lodge, P. O. Box 405, Houghton, Michigan 49931.

For hikers, Isle Royale offers considerable variety. There are short easy loop trails near the lodges for day hikes, and there are long, rugged trails through the wilderness that should be undertaken only by experienced hikers with the proper equipment. Trail heads along the shore away from the lodge are served by water taxis which will deliver hikers to the trail and pick them up later at the same spot or at any other trail head along the shore.

There are 24 campgrounds on the island, all but four along the shore. The camps are supplied with fireplaces, tables, and tent sites. You may not reserve a campsite, but if you cannot get space in a campground, wilderness camping is allowed, with certain restrictions:

First, no fires. Portable stoves must be used. Since gas cannot be carried on the ferries, it is necessary to buy fuel on the island.

Second, the campsite you choose must be out of sight of all trails or lake waters, and it must be at least half a mile from any established campground or developed area.

Third, camping is not allowed on any of the offshore islands.

Fourth, you cannot stay at any one site more than one night.

All campers, whether they use established sites or not, must get a camping permit when they arrive at the park.

A few additional points for hikers: Groceries and freeze-dried foods may be purchased on the island. No pets, other than seeing eye dogs, are allowed anywhere on the island. Disposable food or beverage containers cannot be taken into the backcountry. Wheeled vehicles are prohibited, and no outboard motors are allowed on inland lakes.

Water should be boiled for at least five minutes before drinking. Don't try to swim in Lake Superior. The water temperature seldom gets much above 40 degrees. If an inland lake seems warm enough to swim in, it is also warm enough to support leeches.

The trails of Isle Royale range in length from less than a mile to 40 miles. All the trails described here interconnect with each other, making trips of almost any length possible. Although visitors to the island are not allowed to stay more than 14 days, you can cover a lot of ground in that time.

You will need good boots for these trails. There is not much topsoil on the island, but there are many sharp rocks. The northwest faces of the ridges are frequently quite steep, and boots that give good traction will provide a bit more security.

The island's trails can be divided into four broad categories. First there is a group of trails—mainly short loops—near the Rock Harbor lodge and campground. A similar, but smaller, group is located near Windigo Harbor. Two long trails run on the ridge lines from southwest to northeast. Finally, there are trails branching off from these longer trails and connecting them to campsites.

The trails around Rock Harbor are:

The Albert Stoll, Jr., Memorial Trail (2.3 miles). The trail generally follows the shores of Rock Harbor and Tobin Harbor. The Indians used to mine copper on Isle Royale, and some remains of their activities still are visible.

Rock Harbor Trail (10.5 miles). Another shore line trail. This one passes the remains of copper mining done by whites in the 19th century. The Daisy Farm Campsite is 7 miles from the lodge, and the Moskey Basin campground is at the end of the trail.

The Mt. Franklin Trail branches off from the Rock Harbor Trail, making possible a loop trip of 6 miles from the lodge. At Suzy's Cave, a stone arch left behind by the retreating shoreline of Lake Superior, it is possible to cross from the Rock Harbor Trail to the Tobin Harbor Trail for a loop hike of 4 miles.

Tobin Harbor Trail (3 miles). The trail is mainly inland through woods, but the water often is visible. The trail joins the Mt. Franklin Trail at one end.

Mt. Franklin Trail (2.2 miles). The trail head is on Rock Harbor about 3 miles from the lodge. It is reachable by boat or by the Rock Harbor Trail. Three-Mile Campsite is near the trail head. The trail crosses the narrow peninsula dividing Rock and Tobin harbors and then climbs up again to the summit of Mt. Franklin, 1,074 feet above sea level. Mt. Franklin is a part of Greenstone Ridge, and the Greenstone Trail can be picked up here.

Lookout Louise Trail (1 mile). The trail head is on the northwest shore of Tobin Harbor, accessible by boat from the lodge. The trail passes a beaver pond called Hidden Lake as it climbs from the shore up to the lookout. Monument Rock is along the trail, a large, isolated stone that, like Suzy's Cave, is a remnant of a time when the lake waters were higher than they are now. This trail joins the northernmost section of the Greenstone Trail. This section is 5 miles long and carries its own name (Mt. Franklin–Lookout Louise Trail), but we will treat it as an extension of the Greenstone Trail.

Daisy Farm Trail (2 miles) and the Mount Ojibway Trail (1.7 miles) both begin at the Daisy Farm Campsite and head inland to Greenstone Ridge. The Daisy Farm Trail starts up Benson Creek, a brook trout stream. The creek flows out of Lake Benson, and near its headwaters is a swamp, which the trail crosses on a foot bridge. There are carnivorous pitcher plants here as well as the common bog trees, black spruce and tamarack.

The Mount Ojibway Trail ends at the mountain's summit, more than 1,100 feet up, where there is a lookout tower.

These two trails combine with a short section of the Greenstone to form a triangle about 5 miles long with the campground at one angle. The trails traverse both ridge and valley, offering views of bogs, stands of birch, white pine, and the northernmost examples of maples on the island.

Lake Richie Trail (2.3 miles). This begins at Moskey Basin at the head of Rock Harbor and travels through spruce and fir forests to Lake Richie, which is supposed to be a good spot to catch sight of a moose. The trail joins the Indian Portage Trail at the lake.

There are three main trails in the Windigo area at the southwestern tip of the island.

The Huginnin Cove Loop Trail (7 miles). It is 4 miles from Windigo to the campground at Huginnin Cove. The remainder of the loop is about 3 miles. Traces of mining once done along the first part of this trail include open shafts concealed by vegetation. Watch where you walk.

Two beaver ponds on the way to the cove, and two more on the way back, often are excellent spots to see other wildlife, including moose. There are bald eagle nests in the area too. The Superior shore around Huginnin Cove is made up of steep bluffs backed by aspens.

Feldtmann Ridge Trail (14.3 miles). This trail was opened less than 10 years ago. It provides access to some of the most rugged terrain on the island. Feldtmann Ridge itself rises to 1,173 feet, and its northwest face is a precipitous cliff nearly 400 feet high. The Big Siskiwit Swamp in this area is the largest on the island. It is virtually impossible to navigate on foot, and hikers are advised to stay on the trail and content themselves with gazing on the swamp from on top of the ridge. However, the trail crosses a bog near Feldtmann Lake that requires a boardwalk 1,200 feet long, and that stretch should satisfy most swamp enthusiasts.

The trail starts at the Windigo Ranger Station and hugs the south shore of Washington Harbor for about 1½ miles. It then turns inland over a low stretch of Greenstone Ridge to Grace Creek (brook trout). Beyond the creek, the boardwalks alternate with low ridges. Hardwoods predominate in the uplands, with black spruce and alder on the wet ground. A side trail leads to Feldtmann Lake (northern pike).

On the ridge, the woods give way to scattered white pine. There is a lookout tower and splendid views over much of the southern end of the island. The cliffs are undercut, so stay away from the edges.

From the ridge top it is downhill to Siskiwit Bay Campground about 5 miles away. About halfway along is a side trail to Lake Halloran. The Isle Royale Natural History Association recommends a visit to Lake Halloran in early summer when the rare ladyslipper orchid blooms along the southwest shore. The trail ends at Siskiwit Bay Campground where it joins the Island Mine Trail.

Feldtmann Lake Trail (2.5 miles). This connects the Feldtmann Ridge Trail with Lake Superior at Rainbow Cove on Isle Royale's southwest shore. It is about a mile long along a stream bank from the cove to Feldtmann Lake. The remainder of the trail skirts the lake to the Feldtmann Ridge Trail junction.

The two longest trails on the island are the Greenstone Ridge and the Minong Ridge trails. They are also the most difficult, and should be attempted only by experienced hikers.

Greenstone Ridge Trail (45 miles, including the piece from Mt. Franklin to Lookout Louise). This ridge is the backbone of the island. The highest peaks are along its length. The northwest face of the ridge tends to be quite steep, while to the southeast the slopes are gentler.

Water is available only at the inland lakes that occupy the low lands on either side of the ridge, and it must be boiled before it is drunk. There are three campsites on lakes along the way.

If you wish to start at Lookout Louise and hike the 5 miles to Mt. Franklin, you will get a chance to see some of the sites of prehistoric mining on the island. A few of these sites have been excavated to show their original form. Copper mined in the upper Great Lakes was traded by the Indians as far south as Alabama.

Starting from Rock Harbor, there are a number of ways to reach the trail. The most direct is via Rock Harbor Trail and the Mt. Franklin Trail. From Mt. Franklin, the trail crosses Mount Ojibway and then reaches a short side trail leading to the campsites at Chickenbone Lake.

A dip in the ridge beyond Chickenbone Lake precedes the climb to Mt. Siskiwit, 1,205 feet high. It still is possible in this area to see remnants of trees nearly destroyed in the fire of 1936.

Hatchet Lake Campground is on a spur trail 7 miles beyond Chickenbone. Then there is a climb to Ishpeming Point, 1,377 feet high, where there is a lookout tower. About 2 miles farther along the trail drops down to Lake Desor and the third campsite. From there it is a long climb to Mt. Desor, at 1,394 feet the highest point on the island.

From Mt. Desor, it is 4 miles to the junction with the Island Mine Trail. Six miles farther on through a forest of sugar maples and yellow birch is Washington Harbor.

Minong Ridge Trail (26 miles). This was originally constructed to provide access to the northwestern area of the island for fire fighting crews. It still is identified as a fire manway on our geological survey map. It is rugged hiking that will involve getting your feet wet at some stream crossings and low spots. Water generally is available only at a few points along the way, and it should be boiled before drinking.

The northern end of the trail is near McCargoe Cove and connects to the cove via the Minong Mine Trail, less than a mile in length. The Minong was the largest copper mine on the island 100 years ago, and there was a considerable settlement near it. Nothing remains now but a clearing, some pits and rock piles, and the remnants of the railway used to transport the ore from pit to dock.

Six miles along the trail, there is a campground at Todd Harbor, site of the old Haytown mine, and beyond it is a side trail leading to Hatchet Lake and Greenstone Ridge. A half mile beyond this junction is a short side trail to Pickett Bay where water can be obtained from Lake Superior. After 6 miles of hiking along the ridge through birches and aspens, another spur trail leads down to the shore of Little Todd Harbor.

There are steep grades between this junction and the Lake Desor spur trail about 6 miles farther on. This is the last good place to get water before the trail's end. There are swamps, streams, and beaver ponds to be waded in the final section of the trail. The last obstacle is Washington Creek. Once you have splashed through that, the Washington Creek Trail takes you into Windigo.

There are five trails more than a mile long running southeast–northwest along the island's short axis.

Indian Portage Trail (10.6 miles). This is the longest of these branch trails, its name stemming from the belief that Indians used to portage canoes across the island on this route. It should be a good trail for fishermen, since it skirts the shores of four inland lakes, while a short side trail leads to a fifth. Northern pike inhabit all these lakes.

The southern end of the trail is at Chippewa Harbor Campground. The spur trail to Lake Mason is a short distance inland, and beyond that the trail stays close to a stream that drains Lake Richie. The trail detours around the lake, meeting the Lake Richie Trail 4 miles from Chippewa Harbor.

There are no severe slopes on this trail, but the up-and-down pattern of the island is evident as the trail climbs to Greenstone Ridge past Lake LeSage and Lake Livermore. Beyond the ridge, it is downhill to Chickenbone Lake Campground. The trail follows first the shore of the lake and then Chickenbone Creek to McCargoe Cove.

Siskiwit Falls Trail and Ishpeming Trail (7.4 miles). These two trails can be treated together conveniently. The Siskiwit Falls Trail begins at Malone Bay at a campground and follows the stream that provides an outlet for Siskiwit Lake, passing Siskiwit Falls along the way. The Ishpeming Trail begins at the lake and climbs to Ishpeming Point on Greenstone Ridge, where it joins the Greenstone Trail.

The trail skirts the lake shore in a southerly direction, crossing a small swamp at the southern tip. Footbridges keep hikers dry during the crossing. Just beyond this swamp is a small stream that is the last reliable source of water for several miles. However, the water must be boiled.

Beyond the stream, the climbing begins. You will enter part of the burned over area from the 1936 fire, and as you go up the slopes, maples, oaks, and white pine will become more common. About three-quarters of a mile from the top of Ishpeming Point, you cross a stream on a footbridge. Beyond this, it really gets steep. At 1,377 feet, Ishpeming Point is the second highest spot on the island.

The Island Mine Trail (5 miles). The trail heads north from the Siskiwit Bay Campground, crossing the Big Siskiwit River, Senter Point, and Carnelian Beach before turning inland to climb to Sugar Mountain where it meets the Greenstone Trail. There are a number of interesting points along the way. For example, there is the Siskiwit River, which reverses its flow about every 20 minutes. Lake Superior, like the other Great Lakes, is subject to a phenomenon known as a seiche (pronounced "saysh"). The water in the lake basin sloshes from side to side like beer in a bucket, creating periodic reversals of flow in low-lying rivers such as the Siskiwit.

On Senter Point are the remains of a powder house used to store explosives in the 1870s when the Island Mine was in operation. The mine itself is located about 2 miles from the shore. Again, be cautious in exploring this area, since some open shafts are covered with vegetation.

The forests along the trail on the climb up to Sugar Mountain show some interesting changes. On the dry south slopes are maples and red oaks, while the ridge tops and the moist low places have spruce, fir, birch, and aspen. Near the end of the trail, the slightly warmer climate of the island's interior produces a forest of sugar maples and yellow birch.

It is possible to combine the Feldtmann Ridge, Island Mine, and Greenstone Trails into a loop trip starting and returning to Windigo. Total distance would be about 25 miles.

Lane Cove Trail (2.8 miles). This trail starts at Lane Cove on the island's north shore and ends at Mt. Franklin. Beavers have been active here, and you may see many trees that have been gnawed. Beavers are particularly fond of the stands of quaking aspen along the way.

McCargoe Cove Trail (2.2 miles). The trail provides a short route from the McCargoe Cove Campground to Greenstone Ridge. Along the way it passes the remains of a stamp mill. A spur trail about 100 yards long leads to a dam that used to provide power for the mill. The trail crosses directly over a beaver pond near Greenstone Ridge.

Additional information on Isle Royale is available from Isle Royale National Park, 87 North Ripley Street, Houghton, Michigan 49931. Ask especially for the list of publications of the Isle Royale Natural History Association. They sell a long list of low-priced books on flora, fauna, history, and geology of the island. They also offer guides to hiking trails, topographical maps, and lake survey charts.

PORCUPINE MOUNTAINS WILDERNESS STATE PARK

Location: The park is on Lake Superior about 17 miles west of Ontonagon. It comprises more than 58,000 acres of some of the wildest country in the Midwest.

The shoreline of Lake Superior forms the northern border of the park. The eastern edge is a few miles west of—and parallel to— Michigan Route 64. The southern border is irregular, running more or less west from the village of White Pine to the mouth of the Presque Isle River in Gogebic County.

The mountains are formed by a series of long ridges with valleys running roughly parallel to the Lake Superior shoreline. The approximate mean elevation of the lake is 602 feet, while the highest point in the "Porkies" is 1,958 feet. Elevations more than 1,500 feet are fairly common, and this makes the park demanding country to hike in. Trails may go up and down hundreds of feet within a few miles.

There are also streams to cross on many trails. The rivers are one of the glories of this park, and the trails frequently follow them. To get an idea why, consider this: A trail parallels the Little Carp River for 5½ miles. In that distance, the river drops nearly 700 feet. Only the most spectacular drops get named "falls," but rapids are more or less the ordinary condition of these rivers. There are lakes, too, in the valleys.

The park is virtually all wooded, with pine, hemlock, and northern hardwoods, and stands of virgin timber in various locations. There are only two paved roads. One is Michigan 107, which enters the park from the east. It ends a few miles into the park at a parking area which also is a trail head. The other road is South Boundary Road, which heads straight south from 107 just inside the eastern end of the park. It turns west at the southern edge to Presque Isle Campground. There are four other campgrounds scattered along the South Boundary Road, as well as one on Union Bay just off 107. Everything else in the park is accessible only on foot.

However, there are some rather plush facilities, principally nine cabins, eight with four bunks each and one with eight bunks. Four of the cabins are along the Superior shore at Speakers Creek, the Little Carp River, the Big Carp River, and Buckshot Point. Four are on the high lakes in the valleys of the Porcupine Mountains. They are Lake of

Porcupine Mountains Wilderness State Park

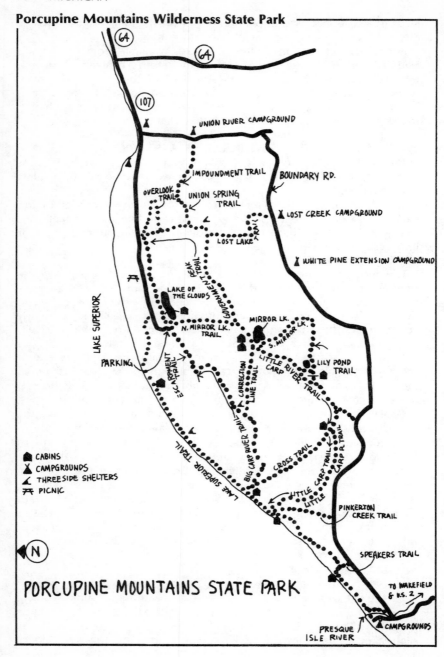

PORCUPINE MOUNTAINS STATE PARK

the Clouds, the Lily Pond, and Mirror Lake. Mirror Lake has two cabins, one with eight bunks. The last cabin—called the Section 17 cabin—is on the Little Carp River at Greenstone Falls, about 1,200 feet up. None of the cabins can be reached by road.

You can reserve a cabin by writing to the Park Supervisor, Porcupine Mountains State Park, Route #2, Ontonagon, Michigan 49953. Reservations are accepted for any year after January 1 of that year. The cost is $10 a night.

Half the rent has to be sent in with the request for reservations, and the other half is due when you pick up your key at the park office. Maximum stay at the Lake of the Clouds cabin is three days, seven at the others.

The bunks in these cabins have mattresses and springs, and the cabins also are equipped with wood stoves, a saw and axe, sink, cupboard, table and benches, cooking utensils, dishes, and tableware. The cabins on the lakes have free rowboats as well.

There are three Adirondack shelters available on a first come, first served basis for $2 a night. These are three-sided structures with bunks. Finally, you can camp beside the trail—for $2 a night—anywhere except within a quarter mile of a cabin or shelter.

Backpackers are required to register at the park office before setting out. Fires are allowed in the park, but be careful—especially in dry weather. Better yet, bring a stove.

Length: There are 17 named trails in the park with a total length of 85 miles. One of these—the Union Mine Trail—is only a mile long and does not connect with any of the others, so we will not describe it.

The others range in length from 2 miles to 16 miles. They interconnect in various ways, making it possible to put together a hike of almost any length. We will describe a few possible combinations after a brief look at the separate trails.

Keep in mind the nature of the terrain if you are planning a trip. Vertical miles take longer than horizontal ones, and nobody needs to spend his vacation doing a rerun of the Bataan Death March.

U.S.G.S. Quads: White Pine, Michigan; Carp River, Michigan; Thomaston, Michigan; Bergland, Michigan; all 15 minutes.

Lake Superior (16 miles). The trail follows the lake shore northwest from Presque Isle Campground to Buckshot Point. There it turns inland to end at Michigan 107. It starts atop high bluffs, but for most of its length the shoreline is somewhat less steep, and the trail usually is within 20 feet (elevation) of the water. There are four cabins and a shelter along this trail. Their locations—and distance from the Presque Isle River—are: Speakers Creek (2 miles), Little Carp River (6 miles), Big Carp River (7 miles), Buckshot Point (14 miles). The shelter is near Lone Rock about 12 miles from Presque Isle. Lone Rock is in the lake about 200 yards offshore. The trail from Buckshot Point to 107 climbs about

550 feet in 2 miles. For fishermen, this trail offers lake trout, rainbows, and salmon, especially around the mouths of the streams.

Pinkerton Trail (3 miles). This is near the western end of the park. It runs north from the South Boundary Road to the mouth of the Little Carp, passing through virgin hemlock along the way. It meets the Lake Superior Trail and the Little Carp Trail at its northern end.

Little Carp River Trail (11 miles). It begins at the river's mouth where there is a cabin as well as the junction with the Pinkerton and Lake Superior trails. It follows the river upstream for 5½ miles, and there are four falls big enough to have names in that span. In between are innumerable rapids. The Section 17 cabin is 6 miles from the trail's beginning, altitude about 1,200 feet. The Lily Pond cabin is 3 miles farther on—altitude 1,500 feet. The trail ends at Mirror Lake, altitude 1,531 feet, 2½ miles from the Lily Pond. There is brook trout fishing in the Little Carp and other trout in the Lily Pond and Mirror Lake. The Lily Pond has a soft bottom and fishermen should not try to wade it.

You can get to the Little Carp River Trail from the South Boundary Road via an access road called (oddly enough) Little Carp River Road. The road is quite short and gives way to a trail that joins the Little Carp River Trail between the Section 17 cabin and the Lily Pond.

Cross Trail (5 miles). This joins the Little Carp River Trail to the Big Carp River Trail and the Lake Superior Trail. The Section 17 cabin is at the south end and the Big Carp River cabin at the north.

Lost Lake Trail (4½ miles). It connects the South Boundary Road with the Government Peak Trail. It is 2 miles from the road to Lost Lake, and another 2½ miles to the junction. Lost Lake Trail joins Government Peak Trail between Union Spring Trail and North Mirror Lake Trail.

Correction Line Trail (3 miles). This runs between the Big and Little Carp River trails, crossing some extremely rugged terrain. It climbs about 500 feet in one mile and crosses Landlookers Creek and a small tributary of the Big Carp. The Mirror Lake cabins are at its west end, and there is an Adirondack shelter at its east end.

Lily Pond Trail (3 miles). This heads south briefly from the Little Carp River Trail at the Lily Pond and then turns east to end at Summit Peak Road, an unimproved road running north from the South Boundary Road. Highest point on the trail is more than 1,700 feet. The Lily Pond cabin is at one end, and parking is available on Summit Peak Road north of where this trail meets it.

South Mirror Lake Trail (2½ miles). This follows Summit Peak Road north from the South Boundary Road. You can leave your car in the parking area and continue on foot to Mirror Lake with its two cabins. A side trail a mile long leads west to Summit Peak (the mountain, not the road), the highest point in the park at 1,958 feet. You can see Lake Superior from there and get a magnificent view of the mountains as well.

Big Carp River Trail (9 miles). The trail begins at a parking area at the end of Michigan 107. For the first 2 miles, it follows a steep escarpment southwestward, providing excellent views of Lake Superior from a height of over 1,400 feet. It then turns south down into the fairly broad valley that divides the escarpment from the next ridge line south. The Big Carp River runs through this valley parallel to the lakeshore and then it—and the trail—turn toward the lake, tumbling through a narrow gorge. Shining Cloud Falls, the second highest in the park, is about a mile from the mouth of the river. It is 5 miles from the beginning of the trail to the shelter at the junction with the Correction Line Trail. At the end of the trail is the Big Carp River cabin. The trail crosses the river and a number of smaller streams as well.

North Mirror Lake Trail (4 miles). The trail begins at the end of 107, climbs over the escarpment to the valley of the Big Carp and then up again to the lake. Mirror Lake is at 1,431 feet, the highest lake in the state. This is probably the most physically demanding trail. In one stretch it climbs more than 300 feet in about half a mile.

Government Peak Trail (8 miles). This trail branches south from 107, following the Big Carp River as far as Trap Falls—about 2 miles. There is a shelter here. The trail then turns west to Government Peak which is 1,850 feet high and the second highest point in the park. This trail joins the North Mirror Lake Trail less than a mile from the Mirror Lake cabins.

Overlook Trail (3 miles). This is a side trail that forms a loop east off the Government Peak Trail. It begins a half mile south of 107, and returns to the main trail a mile south of the road. There are some good views from the high places as well as stands of virgin timber along the way.

Escarpment Trail (4 miles). This is a spectacular trail along the escarpment east from the end of 107. Lake of the Clouds is in a valley visible from the trail. Cloud Peak and Cuyahoga Peak are crossed along the way, and the trail ends at 107 where the Government Peak Trail joins it.

Union Springs Trail and Impoundment Trail (5½ miles). These are separate trails, but it is convenient to treat them together. The Union Springs Trail heads east from the Government Peak Trail to Union Springs, which produces 700 gallons of water a minute. The spring is 2 miles from the trail's beginning. From the spring, the Impoundment Trail goes east 3½ miles to South Boundary Road. The impoundment is an artificial lake in Union River where there are supposed to be brook trout.

Presque Isle (1 mile). From the Presque Isle Campground to the Lake Superior Trail. The Presque Isle is the largest and most spectacular of the park's many rivers.

SOME LOOP TRAILS:
Get a map of the "Porkies" from the park office and the U.S.

Geological Survey maps of the area (Carp River, Thomaston, White Pine, and Bergland quadrangles) and you'll have a great way to beguile the time on a winter evening. It is easy to conjure up enough trips to fill a summer. Out of many possibilities, we have picked five hikes ranging in length from 12 to 25 miles. All of these start at the tip of 107 and return there.

North Mirror Lake—Correction Line—Big Carp River (12 miles). Some spectacular scenery and some hard climbs. It is 4 miles to the Mirror Lake cabins, another 3 to the Correction Line shelter, and 5 back to the parking lot via the Big Carp River Trail.

Escarpment—Government Peak—North Mirror Lake (16 miles). It is 7 miles from the beginning of the Escarpment to the shelter near Trap Falls and 6 miles from there to the Mirror Lake cabins. If you turn north on North Mirror Lake Trail at its junction with the Government Peak Trail—instead of going on to the cabins—the loop is only 15 miles.

Lake Superior—Big Carp River (18 miles). It is 2½ miles to the Buckshot Cabin and another 6½ to the mouth of the Big Carp River. Four miles from the river's mouth, the Big Carp Trail meets the Correction Line Trail. There is a shelter at this point. Five miles from there back to 107.

Lake Superior—Little Carp River—North Mirror Lake (25 miles). This time, take the Lake Superior Trail 10 miles to the mouth of the Little Carp. Go up the Little Carp 11 miles to Mirror Lake, and from there it is 4 miles back to 107.

Lake Superior—Cross Trail—Little Carp—North Mirror Lake (23½ miles). The Cross Trail also branches off the Lake Superior at the mouth of the Big Carp. It joins the Little Carp Trail 5 miles inland, and from there it is 5½ miles to Mirror Lake. Again, it is 4 miles back to 107.

FOX RIVER PATHWAY

Location: The south end of the trail begins at the Seney Township Campground on Fox River Road about a mile northwest of the town of Seney. The north end is at the Kingston Lake State Forest Campground.
Length: 27.5 miles.
U.S.G.S. Quads (south to north): Seney, Michigan; Driggs Lake, Michigan; Sunken Lake, Michigan; Au Sable Point Southwest, Michigan; all 7.5 minutes.
Description: This pathway follows the Fox River and the Little Fox River upstream from Seney into a cluster of lakes around the headwaters of these streams. It continues north over the divide that separates the Lake Michigan watershed from the Lake Superior watershed to end just 3 miles south of the Superior shore.

Most of the country along the way is flat, sandy ground. Some of it is covered with jack pine, but extensive areas have never recovered from cutting and fires of the old logging days. The largest such area is on the Kingston Plains, a huge stump prairie just south of Kingston Lake. Grasses and bracken grow amid the stumps here, but those trees that do exist are scattered and small. A disease called scleroterris canker attacks the pines and helps keep the ground open.

The trail parallels the Fox River Road, a gravel route that receives fairly heavy use in summer from fishermen. The pathway is marked with blue paint blazes and the triangular "Pathway" signs used throughout the state.

Camping is allowed on state land anywhere along the trail, and three state forest campgrounds with water and pit toilets are available. The three and their distances from the south end of the trail are Fox River, 6.2 miles; Stanley Lake, 16.6 miles; and Kingston Lake, 27.5 miles.

The Department of Natural Resources has placed numbered posts along the routes that are keyed to interpretive material in a brochure they have published. Most of the posts refer to signs of human use of this land. For example, the ditches near the southern end of the trail (Post 3) were dug in 1914 as part of a scheme to turn the area into farmland. The soil—and climate—defeated that plan.

At Post 8, about 1.5 miles beyond the Fox River Campground, the foundations of a logging camp built in the 1880s are still visible. Post 11 marks an old logging dam, one of eight on the Fox and its tributaries. Loggers built these to form ponds to float the logs they cut during the winter logging season.

North of the confluence of the Fox and the Little Fox, the trail follows the latter stream, eventually climbing a slight hill and passing to the west of a small unnamed lake, the first of several lakes along the route. Near Clyde Lake, the trail enters the open ground of the Kingston Plains. It reenters the woods near the Baker Grade, an old two-track road that it parallels into the Kingston Lake Campground.

As of October, 1979, local foresters were working on an extension of the Fox River Pathway that would link it with the North Country Trail in Pictured Rocks National Lakeshore. If the link is not finished, you can reach the North Country by following the Au Sable Point Road, a gravel road, 4 miles north from Kingston Lake Campground.

NORTH COUNTRY TRAIL

The proposed North Country Trail would stretch all the way from Vermont to North Dakota through New York, Pennsylvania, Ohio, Michigan, Wisconsin, and Minnesota. When we did the first edition of this guide, the only completed section of the trail in the Midwest was in Wisconsin. But by fall, 1979, an 80-mile section had been completed through eastern Upper Michigan from the mouth of the Tahquamenon River to Munising. Another 17.5-mile section had been finished in the Ottawa National Forest south of the Porcupine Mountains. The latter trail connects with an 8.7-mile path that ends near the north shore of Lake Gogebic. And an 11-mile section has been completed in Hiawatha National Forest.

Work on additional sections of the trail is going on right now, so by

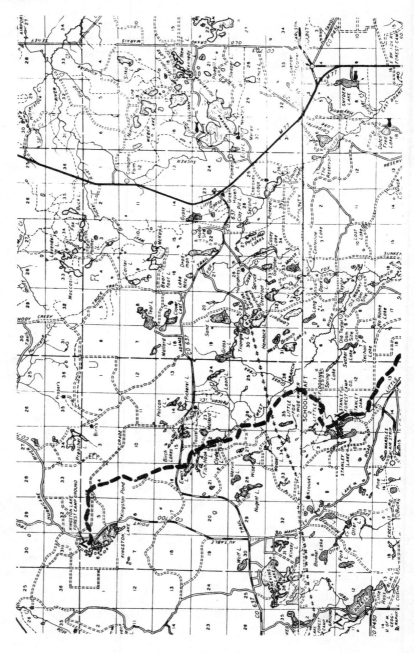

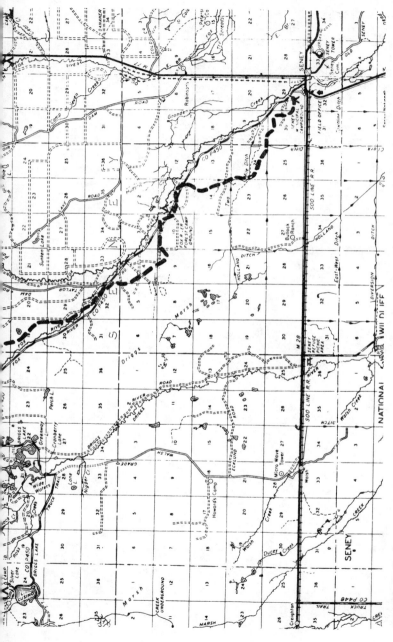

Fox River Pathway

the time you read this, many more miles may be open. The best sources of information about the trail are the Michigan Department of Natural Resources Information Services Center, Box 30028, Lansing, Michigan 48909, and the two national forests through which the trail will be routed: Hiawatha National Forest, Escanaba, Michigan 49829; and Ottawa National Forest, Box 468, Ironwood, Michigan 49938.

In order to keep our descriptions as clear as possible, we have divided the trail into sections. The first section runs from the mouth of the Tahquamenon to Little Lake, where the trail reaches the Lake Superior shore. The next section extends along the shore from Little Lake to the boundary of the Pictured Rocks National Lakeshore. The third includes all of the trail within the lakeshore, from Grand Marais to Munising. The fourth section is the portion within the Ottawa National Forest. The fifth is in the Hiawatha National Forest.

All sections of the trail are marked with blue paint blazes and the standard blue triangular "Pathway" markers.

THE MOUTH OF THE TAHQUAMENON TO LAKE SUPERIOR

Location: Begins at a campground on the south bank of the river, about 5 miles south of Paradise, Michigan. Crosses the river on Michigan Highway 123 and then goes west along the north bank. Little Lake is at the north end of Northwestern Road (Luce County Road 500). This road heads north from Michigan Highway 123 about 2½ miles west of the border of Tahquamenon Falls State Park. The trail also crosses Michigan Highway 123 near the lower falls of the Tahquamenon. A trail from the upper falls into Betsy Lake also connects with the North Country.

Length: 33 miles.

U.S.G.S. Quads (east to west): Emerson, Michigan; Timberlost, Michigan; Betsy Lake South, Michigan; Betsy Lake Southwest, Michigan; Betsy Lake Northwest, Michigan; all 7.5 minutes. We will indicate in the text where the trail leaves one quad and moves to the next.

Description: This portion of the trail is generally on low level ground, although there are a few moderately hilly sections and even some steep grades around the lower falls of the Tahquamenon. You'll find spruce and white cedar on the low ground, pine woods on the sand ridges, and a few areas of northern hardwood forest. South of Betsy Lake, you'll find some of the most difficult terrain in the North Country—a vast, open marshy area with a spongy muskeg soil. Hikers will have to wade here at any time of year. In early spring the water along the trail route may be over your head.

From the campground at river's mouth the trail crosses the Tahquamenon on the highway bridge and then briefly follows a gravel road west. This road parallels the river, and for the next 5½ miles, the trail is routed between the road and the river bank on flat ground. You'll pass

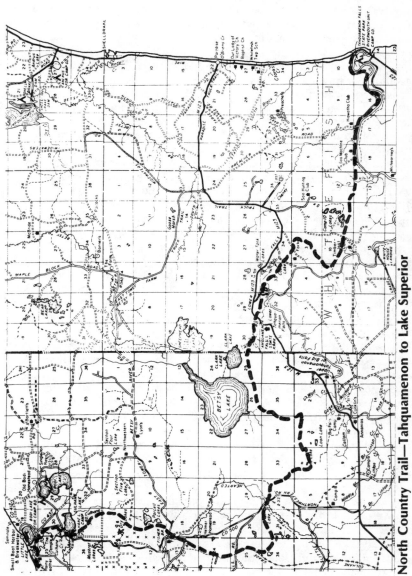

North Country Trail—Tahquamenon to Lake Superior

buildings belonging to private hunting and fishing clubs on this section. Past the Soo Machine Club the trail heads straight west away from the river—still on flat ground—crossing Lynch Creek after about a mile. **Timberlost.** Beyond Lynch Creek the ground begins to rise and the trail winds through a chaotic landscape with flat areas, depressions, and some steep slopes 50 to 60 feet high. There may be wet spots in the low ground.

The Tahquamenon here flows through a narrow valley bordered by steep bluffs as much as 100 feet high. The trail approaches the river and then turns back northeast over more jumbled terrain and then northwest again over terrain that gets somewhat more precipitous as the trail nears the lower falls.

The campground at the lower falls has flush toilets and hot showers. Campsites are $5 per night.

Beyond the campground, the trail crosses Michigan Highway 123 and then follows an old road through a hardwood forest toward Clark Lake. **Betsy Lake South.** The area around Clark Lake and Betsy Lake has been divided into two dedicated natural areas with a total area of 17,176 acres. Motorized vehicles are not allowed in these areas. Here the North Country Trail forms a part of an interlocking system of 13 miles of trails that would make a good backpacking trip all by themselves. On the North Country you will skirt the south edge of Clark Lake on a pathway that was noted as an Indian trail in the 1849 survey of the area. You'll also pass the remains of a logging camp dating from the days when the pines were cut off the sand ridges here. A side trail will take you to the upper falls of the Tahquamenon, the second highest waterfall in the eastern U.S.

The sand ridges around Betsy Lake are separated by low swales of muskeg, some covered with spruce, some open. The largest of these low spots forms the vast marsh we mentioned above.

Betsy and Clark lakes and the smaller lakes near them are quite shallow. Betsy Lake is only 7 feet deep. In cold years, these lakes freeze to the bottom, causing extensive fish kills, so this is not an area that would hold much interest for anglers.

The trail crosses the Little Two Hearted River on the Northwestern Road bridge, continues west through more swamps, muskeg, and marshes for about 1½ miles, and then turns north on an old railroad grade.

A short section of the trail on this old grade is on the Betsy Lake Southwest quad, but you can probably do without this map, since the pathway heads quickly into the Betsy Lake North sheet.

The trail stays on the grade for 2½ miles before cutting east to cross the Little Two Hearted River on another road bridge. It quickly leaves the road again to head north through pitted glacial outwash. It passes to the west of Parcell Lakes, through Dry Lakes and then to the campground on the west shore of Culhane Lake (22 sites). It crosses Culhane Creek on a road bridge and then parallels the road north and west to reach Lake Superior west of Little Lake.

About camping along the trail: Backcountry camping is not allowed in Tahquamenon Falls State Park. In Lake Superior State Forest you can camp where you like. However, please note that the trail crosses private land at various places along the route. The state has acquired easements for the trail route here, but you should not leave the trail or try to camp on private land. The Department of Natural Resources would prefer to have people camp in the state forest campgrounds, which are free.

LITTLE LAKE TO GRAND MARAIS
Location: The east end of this section, at Little Lake, is at the north end of Luce County Road 500. The west end, at Grand Marais, is at the northern tip of Michigan Highway 77. You can get to Muskallonge Lake State Park, about midway through this section, by following Luce County Road H-37 to its northern tip.
Length: 32 miles.
U.S.G.S. Quads (east to west): Betsy Lake North, Michigan; Betsy Lake Northwest, Michigan; Muskallonge Lake East, Michigan; Muskallonge Lake West, Michigan; Grand Marais Northeast, Michigan; Grand Marais, Michigan; all 7.5 minutes.
Description: This section follows the shore, except for brief detours inland to avoid private land. Sometimes you will be right on the beach, sometimes on low bluffs just back from the shore, and sometimes you will be on or just behind some of the extensive dunes along this coast. Where the bluffs are really steep, wooden steps have been built to take the trail up and down from the beach. The soil here is sandy, and the woods are preponderantly pine, especially jack pine.
Betsy Lake Northwest. Heading west from Little Lake, the trail crosses the Big Two Hearted River on a footbridge. There is a forest campground here with 45 sites. Beyond the river the trail skirts high dunes.
Muskallonge Lake East. About 8 miles past the river, note that the trail briefly follows a dirt road in three places. This routing was planned in order to avoid private property.

The trail follows a gravel road for about half a mile through Muskallonge Lake State Park.
Muskallonge Lake West. Beyond the lake, it heads north to the Superior shore again. The Blind Sucker River is about 30 feet across but shallow enough to be forded easily.
Grand Marais Northeast. The trail stays along the shore, passing through the Lake Superior Campground (18 sites).
Grand Marais. Near Grand Marais, the trail detours south around some

North Country Trail—Little Lake to Grand Marais

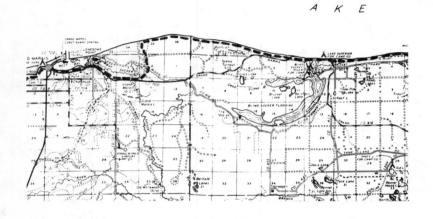

private land. There are two river crossings on road bridges. You cross the Sucker River on a dirt road and the Grand Marais Creek on the Grand Marais Truck Trail, Alger County Road 700. The trail goes right through the town of Grand Marais before continuing west into the Pictured Rocks National Lakeshore.

PICTURED ROCKS NATIONAL LAKESHORE
Location: The two ends of the trail are in Grand Marais and at the park headquarters just northeast of Munising. In between, there is road access at Miners Castle, Beaver Lake, near the east end of 12-Mile Beach, Hurricane River, and on the Grand Sable Banks.

Carl's Standard Service at 114 West Munising, Munising, Michigan 49862; (906) 387-3003, offers rides from Munising to points along the trail. In 1979, he was using a Blazer and a pickup truck and charging the same rate he charged for road service. That means you could leave your car in Munising, have him drive you to Grand Marais, and then walk back. Cost for this would be $55, with intermediate stops at proportionately lower fees. Note that this is the total cost for the vehicle, regardless of how many people are riding in it. Pat Carl is currently looking into the possibility of buying a van and establishing regularly scheduled runs between Munising and Grand Marais, so check with him if you need this service.
Length: 38 miles.

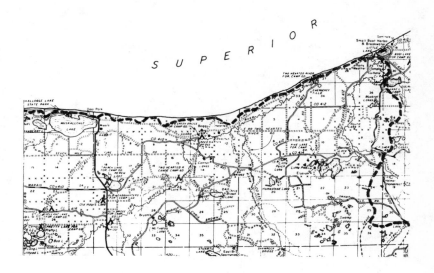

U.S.G.S. Quads (east to west): Grand Marais, Michigan; Grand Sable Lake, Michigan; both 7.5 minutes. Grand Portal Point, Michigan; Munising, Michigan; both 15 minutes.

Note: Camping is allowed only at designated sites at the lakeshore. You need a permit from the park headquarters, from a visitor center, or from any patrolling ranger. Note that the visitor center at Grand Marais is open only from mid-June to Labor Day. If you know when you are going to be there, you can get a permit in advance by mail. The backcountry sites have no water or latrine facilities. The park service requires hikers to use these campsites in order to avoid turning the whole lakeshore into a campground.

Description: This is a really spectacular section of the trail, taking you across dunes perched high over the lakeshore, along a broad beach that stretches for miles, and atop precipitous cliffs more than 200 feet high.

From Grand Marais, the trail parallels Alger County Road 700 west and south into the national lakeshore. After skirting the north shore of Grand Sable Lake, it heads directly across the Grand Sable Dunes to the shore of Superior. The dunes here are very impressive. Perched on high banks, their tops are more than 300 feet above the surface of Lake Superior, and they extend as much as a mile back from the shore.

Au Sable Point. Continuing west, the ground drops away to Au Sable

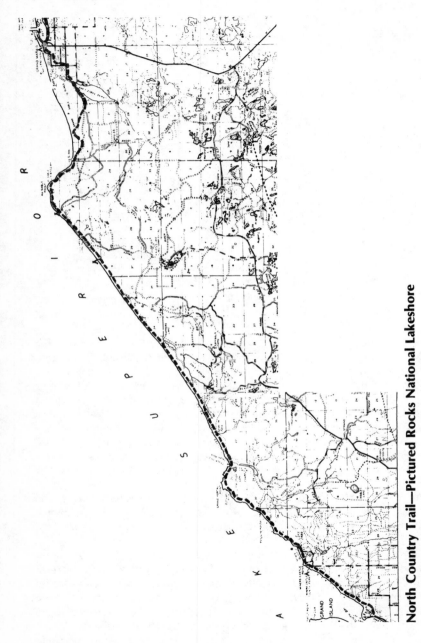

North Country Trail—Pictured Rocks National Lakeshore

Point and beyond. The trail crosses Hurricane River on a road bridge and then follows the shore along 12-Mile Beach.

Grand Portal Point. Heading southwest past Trappers Lake and Beaver Lake, the trail begins to climb onto the cliffs called Pictured Rocks. The "pictures" are color variations in the rocks of the cliff, and not human productions. By the time you reach Spray Creek and Spray Falls, the cliffs are 100 feet high. You cross Spray Creek on a footbridge.

Chapel Rock is a sea cave carved by wave action into the rock of the cliffs at the mouth of Chapel Creek. The trail drops into a gorge more than 100 feet deep, crosses the creek on a footbridge, and then climbs again.

The cliffs continue around Grand Portal Point until the trail drops into the valley of the Mosquito River (Munising), then it is back up before another drop into the Miners River gorge. Miners Castle is another spectacular rock formation at the mouth of the river.

After crossing Miners River on a footbridge, it's a steep climb back onto the cliffs that are more than 200 feet high along here. The trail ends at park headquarters near Sand Point.

NORTH COUNTRY TRAIL—OTTAWA NATIONAL FOREST

Location: The east end of the trail is currently at Whisky Hollow Creek, about 2½ miles—by trail—east of Norwich Road. As of October, 1979, an additional 2 miles of trail east of Whisky Hollow Creek had been marked but not cut. The closest road access is Norwich Road, about 8 miles north of the village of Matchwood. A large trail sign marks the trail head. There is no parking area as such, but you can park on the shoulder. The west end of the trail is along the South Boundary Road in Porcupine Mountains Wilderness State Park about 12 miles east of the Presque Isle River. A sign here marks the trail head.

Length: 33 miles completed.

U.S.G.S. Quads (east to west): Matchwood, Michigan; Bergland, Michigan; Thomaston, Michigan; all 15 minutes.

Description: There are some significant hills here, by midwestern standards, and the trail has been constructed to take full advantage of them. You will frequently follow the edges of steep escarpments that rise as high as 400 feet above the valleys below. These rocky promontories are open enough to provide good views of the valleys.

From Whisky Hollow Creek the trail climbs onto a high, steep escarpment and it stays high until it drops down to cross Norwich Road. Past the road it stays low, crossing Mason Creek, heading southwest, and then climbing again to the rugged hills overlooking Cascade Falls. There is no direct access from the trail to the falls because of some private property between them. The only way to get to the falls is by following the trail to its crossing of Forest Road 222. Go south on 222 for about a mile to the Cascade Falls Trail. Looking at the falls requires a total detour of 3 to 4 miles.

Past Forest Road 222, you cross Bush Creek and the Soo Line tracks, then the trail climbs up onto steep cliffs overlooking Cascade Creek. The junction with the Gogebic Ridge Trail is just after the trail turns north away from the creek. Bergland Fire Tower is about a mile east of Highway 64. From the top you can see about 20 miles in all directions.

There is another big trail sign where the North Country crosses 64. Note: 64 has been rerouted slightly to the west since the Bergland quad was published. North of 64, the ground is flatter and you will encounter some swampy ground. Substantial areas here have been logged relatively recently, and they are sparsely wooded and brushy.

About 2 miles north of Michigan Highway 64, the trail joins a badly rutted clay road and then crosses the Iron River. There are two crossings and only one is on a bridge. At high water the unbridged crossing may be over waist deep. Approach this with caution. The forest service may build a bridge here.

After the second river crossing, the trail parallels the west branch of the Iron to near the trail head. This is another scenic section, with the trail routed on hills overlooking the river.

GOGEBIC RIDGE TRAIL

Location: Beginning just north of Bergland off Michigan Highway 64. Joins the North Country Trail about 3 miles east of Michigan 64. Crosses 64 at a wayside area about 3 miles north of Bergland.

Length: 10 miles.

U.S.G.S. Quad: Bergland, Michigan, 15 minutes.

Description: This is a feeder trail to the North Country. From the south end the trail goes west about 1½ miles and then turns north. The Gogebic Ridge Trail originally began at Forest Road 789, south and west of Bergland. The current route meets the old route where the trail turns north. The old route comes in from the south. The northbound section follows, in part, an Indian trail at least 125 years old.

East of Michigan Highway 64 the ground is hillier. The trail crosses Cookout Mountain, passes Weidman Lake, crosses Forest Road 830, crosses Sandhill Creek on a bridge, and then joins the North Country Trail.

NORTH COUNTRY TRAIL—HIAWATHA NATIONAL FOREST

Location: The completed section of the trail begins about 4.5 miles south of Michigan Highway 28 and just east of Forest Road 3139. The north end is at the intersection of forest roads 3150 and 3156. Perhaps the easiest place to pick up the trail is near Soldier Lake Campground on Michigan Highway 28.

Length: 11 miles.

U.S.G.S. Quads (south to north): Sullivan Creek, Michigan; Strong, Michigan; McNearney Lake, Michigan; all 7.5 minutes.
Description: Construction is now underway on the south end of the trail, but for the moment, it just ends in the woods. You could pick it up by walking east from Forest Road 3139. There are a couple of logging roads heading in here, or you could strike a compass course due east through the woods.

South of Michigan Highway 28, the land is fairly flat and covered mainly with jack pine. From Soldier Lake north, it becomes progressively hillier and the forest contains increasing amounts of hardwood. Toward the north end it is predominantly pole-sized sugar maples.

Since construction is going on now on this section of the trail, it would be a good idea to check with the Hiawatha National Forest headquarters before you start hiking, since a lot more trail will be available soon.

An interesting section of the trail has been partially constructed near St. Ignace. This runs northwest from near Evergreen Shores to Brevoort Lake Road (County H-57). This country was once sand dunes. It is now covered by pine forest with spruce-fir forest in the low spots. The terrain is quite hilly, which makes for some interesting hiking. James Hooper, recreation forester for the Hiawatha, described it as "hikeable," although he said it needs more work to be finished.

A MICHIGAN ROADLESS AREA—STURGEON RIVER WILDERNESS STUDY AREA AND LITTLE SILVER ADDITION

Location: In the Ottawa National Forest near the town of Sidnaw. From Sidnaw, take Michigan Highway 28 east about half a mile to Forest Road 191. Follow 191 north. This road skirts the eastern edge of the roadless area. About 2 miles north of the highway, the road forks. Forest Road 191 goes northeast. Forest Road 192 goes west and provides access to the south end of the Little Silver Addition.
Nearby facilities: There is a small grocery store in Sidnaw. The forest service has a campground ($2 per night) where Forest Road 191 crosses the Sturgeon, about 7 miles north of Michigan Highway 28.
U.S.G.S. Quads: Sidnaw, Michigan (15 minutes), covers all but the western edge of the roadless area. Rousseau, Michigan, another 15-minute trail, covers that.
Description: The Sturgeon River Wilderness Study Area was created by the Eastern Wilderness Act of 1975. It includes 13,208 acres of rugged woods in and along the Sturgeon River Gorge. The forest service has added the Little Silver Addition to the original study area, creating a block of wild roadless land totalling 19,344 acres, just over 30 square miles. In 1979, the Carter administration recommended wilderness status for the entire area.

The Sturgeon flows north through a gorge that is often more than a

Sturgeon River Wilderness Study Area

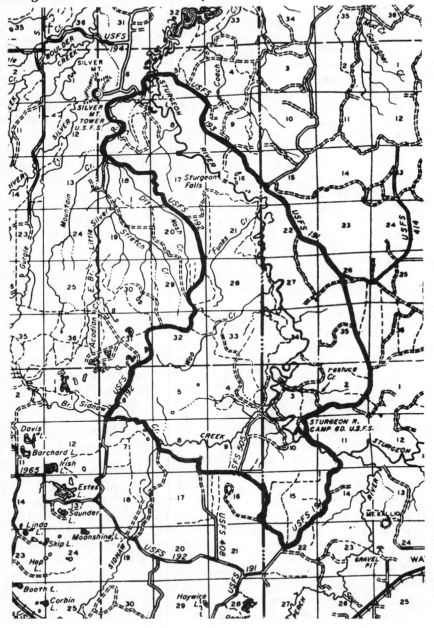

mile wide and 200 feet deep. The soil is apparently glacial outwash, extremely sandy and easily eroded. About the only significant bedrock outcrop is at Sturgeon Falls where the river drops 20 feet. The Little Silver River flows into the Sturgeon at the north end of the area. The Little Silver Addition includes a substantial part of the watershed of this stream, notably several north-flowing streams that have cut steep, narrow canyons on their way to the Little Silver.

The only routes through this land are the remains of old logging grades that have been closed to motor vehicles since the area attained wilderness study status. Even before that, these grades probably received little use other than occasional hunting parties. Today they are in various stages of regrowth. In some places, goldenrod and other herbs are thick by mid-summer. Elsewhere, dense growths of thimbleberry compete with seedlings of maple and balsam fir. On low ground, speckled alder—a shrub that typically grows in a dense clump of ascending trunks—sometimes blocks the trail completely. Deadfalls are common. You can climb over some of these; others require a detour.

However, the vegetation doesn't create as many problems as the maps. On a visit in July, 1979, Jerry and two friends did a lot of aimless wandering near the head of Funks Creek because a network of roads they were on simply did not appear on any maps of the area. It is easy to get lost under such circumstances, so hiking in the Sturgeon River wilderness is only for people who know how to navigate with map and compass.

Don't put yourself on too tight a schedule. The going is likely to be slow, and you won't enjoy it much if you are worried about getting somewhere in a hurry. The going is also likely to be strenuous. You don't have to be a marathon runner to hike this area, but you will have more fun if you are in fairly good physical condition.

It does take some effort to visit the Sturgeon River, but it is definitely worth it. The meandering river, cutting into sandy bluffs on the outer curve of its banks, has formed broad sand and gravel bars on the inner curves. The bars make great campsites, especially during the bug season when they catch whatever breeze is available.

The narrow canyons of the smaller creeks are quite beautiful, and the water in these streams runs icy cold even in mid-summer. We boiled water from the Sturgeon for drinking, but we drank directly from the tributary creeks. Anyone who wishes to do this should understand that there is always a risk involved in drinking water from any surface source. Animal wastes—or animal corpses—can pollute a stream as effectively as a human sewer system.

Most of the Sturgeon River area was logged off years ago, and the forest today is a fairly mature second growth, most of it sugar maple–yellow birch–hemlock forest with some cedar in the low ground and scattered red and white pines on the sandy uplands. Here and there, usually on ground too steep for cutting, small groves of virgin forest remain. The most impressive we saw was a grove of ancient hemlocks at the west edge of the gorge. We estimated one of these at 12 feet in circumference.

We came into the area from the south off Forest Road 191, following an old grade north to West Branch Creek and then east to the river. From there we followed the river north to the mouth of Woo Creek, where we camped on a sand bar. Some sections of the old grade between West Branch and Woo Creek were completely impassable. We had to leave the "trail" and hike on compass bearings through the woods, often on very steep grades.

Our second day, we started up Woo Creek, carrying only lunch. This was very slow difficult travel. Deadfalls, many of them produced by beavers, were very common, and thick brush make it hard to go around them.

The damp sand in the stream bed was covered with tracks—countless deer, as well as raccoon, mink (or weasel), muskrat, and some large doglike tracks we took to be coyote.

We left the creek after about 1.5 miles, heading northwest cross-country toward the heads of the creeks that feed the Little Silver River. This is where the "extra" logging roads got us into trouble. But we saw lots of pretty scenery—and some very large bear tracks—in our wanderings. The district ranger had told us that the campground around here had been the scene of 47 bear "incidents" in the past year, so the beasts were on our minds. We took the usual precautions, and the tracks were our closest encounter. (See the Introduction for advice on hiking in bear country.)

After several hours of aimless but pleasant meanderings, it became obvious that we simply couldn't be sure what trail we were following, so we just headed straight east through the woods, a course that would have to take us back to the river.

Our third day, we started returning south, camping at the mouth of West Branch Creek and then returning to the trail head the following morning.

Sturgeon River gave us marvelous backpacking, providing a sense of exploration that carefully marked trails just can't give. This is an area that should be treated with respect. The ground erodes easily, and hikers should pick their routes with care to avoid damaging the landscape. The streams will undercut steep banks soon enough; they don't need our help.

The Sturgeon's status as a Wilderness Study Area is, by definition, temporary, and depending on what happens in the near future, Sturgeon River could change. There may soon be maintained trails and even designated backcountry campsites, but at least for now it is as wild a piece of ground as the Midwest has to offer.

For current information on the status of Sturgeon River, contact the District Ranger, Ottawa National Forest, Kenton, Michigan 49943.

SYLVANIA RECREATION AREA

Location: In the Ottawa National Forest along the Michigan–Wisconsin border. Take U.S. Highway 2 west 5 miles from Watersmeet. Turn south on County Highway 535 and go 4 miles to the visitor center.

Length: About 17 miles total, although cross-country hiking is feasible here.

U.S.G.S. Quads: Starlake, Michigan; Thayer, Michigan; and Phelps, Michigan; all 15 minutes.

Description: The Sylvania is a very special place. One of the largest tracts of old-growth forest in the Midwest, its 21,000 acres are dotted with pristine lakes whose water is almost as pure as rain. This land was bought by a group of industrialists before its huge sugar maples, hemlocks, and yellow birches could be logged. They kept it as a summer playground, and it remained in private hands until the Forest Service bought it in 1966.

The maps show 36 named lakes in the Sylvania and probably at least that many smaller, anonymous ponds. During the years of private ownership, fishing pressure was very light, so the fish populations remained much as they were before settlement. A few large old predators—northern pike, walleyes, bass, and lake trout—at the top of the food chain, limit the numbers of smaller species such as bluegill and yellow perch.

If you want to fish in the area, you will need a Michigan license. Only artificial lures are allowed, and special trophy fishing rules are in effect. Minimum sizes are 30 inches for lake trout and northerns and 20 inches for walleyes, with a limit of one of each species. Bass must be returned to the water no matter how big they are. The rules may change, so fishermen should pick up a current guide at the Sylvania Information Center on U.S. Highway 45 just south of U.S. Highway 2 in Watersmeet.

The huge old trees of the Sylvania—the forest dates to the 17th century—will live up to your conception of a virgin forest. They keep the ground below them sufficiently shaded to lend an open character to the ground, a condition that makes cross-country hiking relatively easy for those who know how to use a map and compass.

All but two of the trails shown on our map follow the old two-track roads put in by the original owners. They are not marked, largely because markings are not needed. Signs at intersections give mileage to various destinations.

The Forest Service has opened two trails in the area that are both marked with blue diamonds on trees. One of these runs from the west edge of the tract to Whitefish Lake. The other is a 7-mile trail around

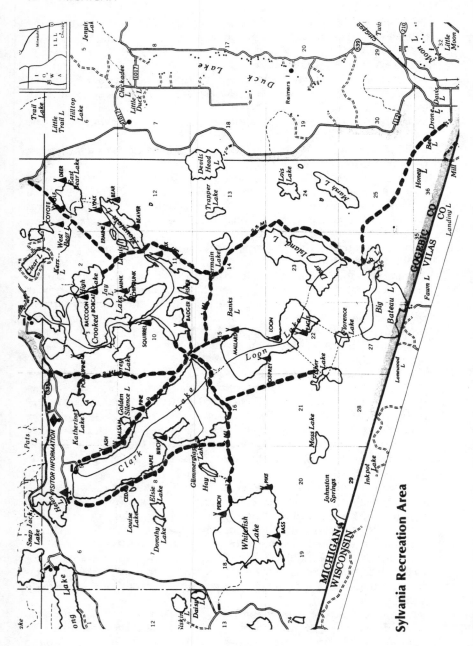

Sylvania Recreation Area

Clark Lake. The picnic area at the north end of the lake would make a good starting point for this one.

Camping is allowed only in designated sites, which are all outfitted with a table, tent pad, garbage can, fire grill, firewood, and toilet. The campsites are all on lakes—most visitors to the Sylvania are canoeists. Campers need a free permit—obtainable at the visitor information center at the north end of the tract—to stay at any site. Sites are assigned on a first come, first served basis, and 14 days is the maximum stay at any site.

Information on the Sylvania is available from the District Ranger, Ottawa National Forest, Watersmeet, Michigan 49969.

HIAWATHA NATIONAL FOREST

BAY DE NOC—GRAND ISLAND TRAIL

Location: Southern end is just east of Rapid River on Delta County Road H-5, also known as County 509. Take U.S. Highway 2 east out of Rapid River to County J-31, which forks to the left. H-5 is another left about a half mile farther on. The trail begins on the left about a mile north of J-31. The north end is at Michigan Highway 94 near Ackerman Lake, which is about 6 miles east of Chatham. Parking is available at the north and south ends of the trail and on H-5 at the Delta–Alger County Line.

Length: 40 miles.

U.S.G.S. Quads (south to north): Rapid River, Michigan; Trevary, Michigan; Au Train, Michigan; all 15 minutes.

Description: We described the southern two-thirds of this trail in our first edition. It has since been extended another 15 miles north. The long-term goal is to extend it all the way to Lake Superior. More immediately, an extension of just 4 miles north of Michigan Highway 94 would hook this trail into the proposed route of the North Country Trail west of Pictured Rocks National Lakeshore.

The trail parallels H-5 and actually crosses that road six times. The southern two-thirds goes over rolling country covered with jack pine and northern hardwood forest. A number of lakes are on or near the trail, and you will cross some small streams as well. A spur trail about 8 miles from the southern trail head leads to the forest service Hay-meadow Campground.

The new section north of Forest Road 2234 is routed mainly along the edge of a bluff overlooking the Au Train Basin, and there are some good views over the valley, particularly when the leaves are off the pole-sized sugar maples that make up a good part of the forest. The forest service is planning to build some spur trails to promontories along the way, and some trees have already been cut to provide vistas from the main trail.

Bay de Noc—Grand Island Trail—north section

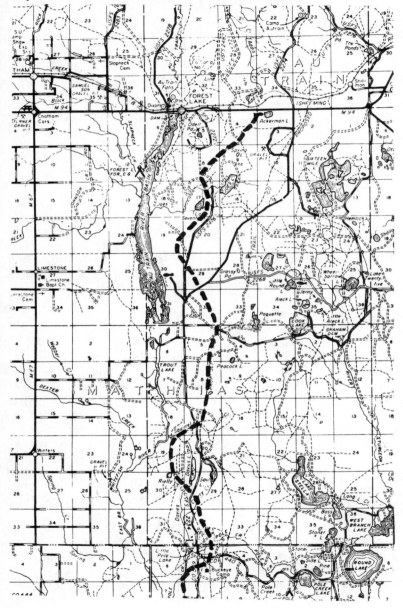

Bay de Noc—Grand Island Trail—south section

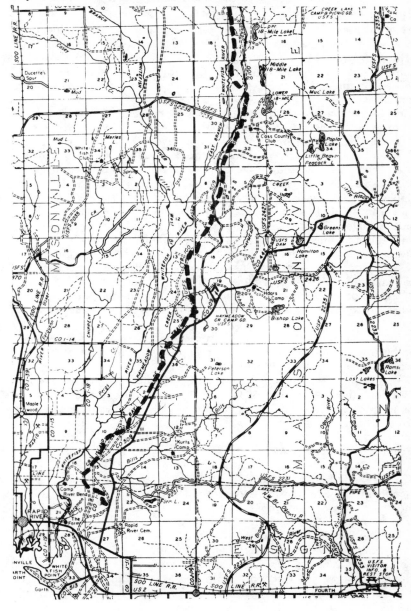

TRAILS IN LOWER MICHIGAN

SHINGLE MILL PATHWAY—HIGH COUNTRY TRAIL

Northcentral Lower Michigan is wild enough to support the only sizable elk herd east of the Rockies and to provide the best bear habitat in the lower peninsula. The state has set aside nearly half a million acres of state forest land in Otsego, Presque Isle, Cheboygan, and Montmorency counties, and the area has some rich opportunities for hikers.

We will describe two interconnecting loops here, a total of a little more than 60 miles of trail. This is only a portion of what is available. A local conservation organization called the Pigeon River Country Association has compiled a map and guidebook to 200 miles of trail in the area. The current schedule calls for publication in February, 1980, and a price of $2 a copy. Local people did all the research for the publication. Copies will be available from the association at Box 122, Gaylord, Michigan 49735. Both of the trails we will describe are marked with a blue triangle and blue paint blazes.

Portions of these trails pass through northern hardwood forests of beech and sugar maple, but most of the ground in this part of the state is sandy, a condition that favors pine. You'll find pine stands—particularly jack pine—as well as a mixed hardwood forest dominated by aspen, paper birch, and red maple. This combination is often found on sandy soil where clear-cut logging and repeated fires eliminated the pines.

The terrain is varied: Morainal hills surround broad swampy lowlands of cedar and spruce. The lakes were produced by glaciers and by groundwater dissolving the bedrock.

All the trails are on state forest land, so you can camp where you wish, but the Department of Natural Resources encourages hikers to camp in designated state forest campgrounds where water and latrines are provided.

SHINGLE MILL PATHWAY

Location: In Pigeon River Country State Forest east of Vanderbilt. From I-75 in Vanderbilt, take Sturgeon Valley Road east for 13 miles to the Pigeon Bridge State Forest Campground (10 sites). The trail begins at the north edge of the campground.

Length: Trail is a series of loops that allow hikes of ¾, 1¼, 6, 10, and 11 miles. The Shingle Mill connects with the High Country Pathway.

U.S.G.S. Quad: Hetherton, Michigan, 15 minutes.

Description: The Shingle Mill Pathway covers the heart of the elk range, so this is where to go if you hope to catch a glimpse of one of these animals. The trail heads northeast from the Pigeon Bridge campground through a forest of pines and hardwoods. It follows a low hill

Shingle Mill Pathway

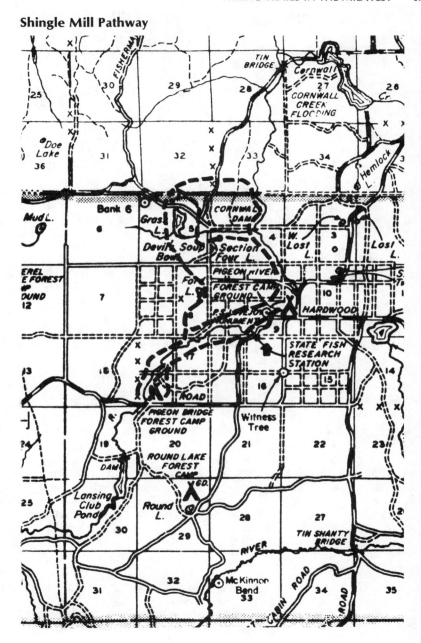

that overlooks a beaver meadow, then drops down to low ground next to the river before climbing again—about 60 feet—over another hill just southwest of the forest headquarters. The two shortest loops branch to the left along the way. Past the headquarters, the trail stays on the hillside that goes into the Pigeon River Campground (19 sites). Just beyond the campground, it crosses the Pigeon on a road bridge. The 6-mile loop turns off to the left just past the bridge. The longer loops turn northeast following the edge of a steep bluff about 60 feet above the river.

Two miles north of the bridge the trail forks again. The left fork is the 10-mile loop; the right, the 11-mile loop. The 10-mile loop turns west on a hill above a small tributary to the Pigeon and about half a mile farther on passes the tiny sinkhole lake romantically dubbed Section Four Lake. There are a number of sinkhole lakes in this part of the state. They are formed when limestone bedrock is dissolved by ground-water. If the overlying rock and surface deposits are strong enough, this process produces caves. If they are weak, they collapse into the hollow left by the dissolved rock, producing a deep, steep-sided depression called a sinkhole. Sinkholes fill with water up to the level of the regional water table. In Section Four Lake, the surface is more than 40 feet below the level of the surrounding land.

The 10-mile loop continues west to the southwest tip of Grass Lake and then turns north. It crosses two small creeks and two gravel roads before climbing about 120 feet to an overlook that gives a good view of Grass Lake and the surrounding woods.

The 11-mile loop continues north, staying in the river valley for a little more than a mile before turning west and climbing onto high ground. The section of this loop in the valley passes through an old logging settlement called Cornwall that was active around the turn of the century. Not much remains now but the foundations of the sawmill and an apple tree.

The 10-mile and 11-mile loops come together again at the overlook near Grass Lake. From there, the trail goes southwest downhill to cross Grass Lake Road. The High Country Pathway heads north just short of the road crossing. The Shingle Mill Pathway heads south over low to slightly rolling country back to the Pigeon Bridge Campground. The last mile or so runs through a huge cedar swamp that is a major deer yard in winter.

HIGH COUNTRY TRAIL

Location: From the Shingle Mill Pathway, runs north, then east, south, west, and north again to form a huge loop ending at the Pigeon Bridge Campground. (See Shingle Mill Pathway for directions.) Other good starting points are the Shoepac Lake and Tomahawk Lake State Forest campgrounds on Tomahawk Lake Road east of Michigan Highway 33, 10 miles south of Onaway. Or start at Clear Lake State Park, on Michigan Highway 33, 10 miles north of Atlanta; or at Jackson Lake State Forest Campground, 3 miles south of Clear Lake.

Length: 50 miles.

U.S.G.S. Quads: Hetherton, Michigan; Tower, Michigan; Atlanta, Michigan; all 15 minutes.

Description: From its junction with the Shingle Mill Pathway, the High Country heads north 3.5 miles over hilly ground, fording one creek, then crossing Pigeon River on a road bridge at Pine Grove Campground (eight sites).

Tower. It then proceeds north and west 5 miles to a road crossing north of Dog Lake Flooding. The last part of this is on low ground, something you will see more of as the trail continues south and east between McLavey Lake and Duby Lake. A short side trail leads to the former. The latter is surrounded by swampy ground. You'll see more of the same in Sections 5 and 4, then it is high ground until you reach the valley of the Black River, which the trail crosses on a road bridge.

Atlanta. You will pass through more low ground near Canada Creek. Cross Michigan Highway 33 north of Long Lake, then head across Tomahawk Creek on a road bridge. Then proceed to Shoepac Lake Campground (50 sites) and Tomahawk Lake Campground (42 sites).

Shoepac, Francis, Tomahawk, and Little Tomahawk lakes are all sinkholes. A string of five sinkholes runs east from Shoepac. All of these are dry, even though the bottom of the hole nearest Shoepac is more than 100 feet below the surface of the lake. The reason for this apparent anomaly is that the collapsed bedrock is overlain by 100 to 140 feet of glacial overburden. The water does not have sufficient pressure to get through this. A short loop trail (1.5 miles) from the east end of Shoepac Lake provides a good look at the four dry sinkholes. This area is still active. A portion of the east shore of Shoepac collapsed in 1976.

The High Country continues south, skirting the east side of the Tomahawk Creek flooding. This is one of many projects the Department of Natural Resources has undertaken to improve game habitats. The Flooding combines Little Mud Lake, Mud Lake, and Spring Lake along with the low ground that used to surround these lakes. The trail continues south through jack pine woods, skirting low ground south of the Millersburg Road and then climbing 160 feet to a hill topped by a TV tower in Section 26. From here, you get a good view of the countryside.

The trail crosses Highway 33 and skirts the north shore of Clear Lake. The spur trail from Jackson Lake State Forest Campground (24 sites)

High Country Trail—west section

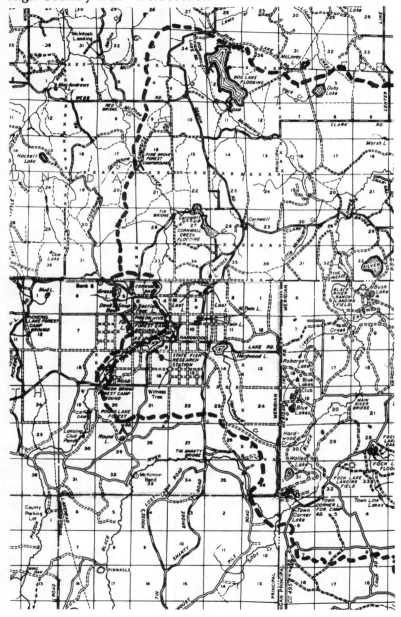

High Country Trail—east section

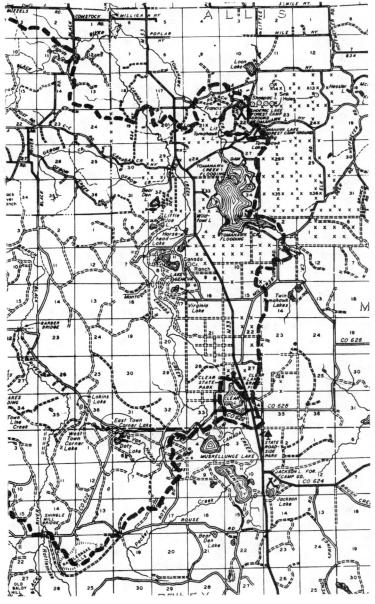

joins it here. The spur trail is 3 miles long. It parallels Highway 33, often quite closely.

From Clear Lake, the trail goes southwest through some private property—and more low ground—before climbing over a knobby hill in Section 18.

Hetherton. It climbs again, almost 250 feet, to the top of Rattlesnake Hills. The origin of this name is obscure, although the small, shy, seldom seen Massassauga rattler does live in these parts.

The trail drops back to low ground to cross the east branch of the Black River on the Shingle Mill Bridge, then climbs to high ground again.

After the crossing of Tubbs Creek and the Black River, a spur trail leads to Town Corner Lake Campground (six sites). Then you climb to the Pigeon River Lookout Tower in Section 36—for another good view. From there the trail stays on high ground to its end at Pigeon Bridge. A spur trail leads to Round Lake Campground (six sites).

SAND LAKES QUIET AREA

Location: From Kalkaska, take Island Lake Road west 7 miles, then turn south and go on Campground Road a mile to Guernsey Lake State Forest Campground at the east end of the quiet area.

Length: 10 miles.

U.S.G.S. Quad: Fife Lake, Michigan, 15 minutes.

Description: The state of Michigan has set aside several parcels of forestland as quiet areas where motor vehicles are not allowed. Travel is by foot or horseback, and in winter by ski and snowshoe. Sand Lakes includes 2,800 acres of rolling wooded country—mostly aspen and scrub oak—with 11 lakes of various sizes. The trails are primarily on old logging roads or firebreaks. Most are marked with blue paint blazes. Those designated as cross-country ski trails are marked with a blue plastic marker with a silhouette of a skier.

The Shore-to-Shore Trail crosses the southern edge of the quiet area. The trail mileage listed above includes the length of this trail within the area as well as all the access trails.

Starting from Guernsey Lake, a logging road across from the parking lot provides access. The loop shown on our map from Guernsey Lake around the Sand Lakes would total 7 miles, counting the short access trail. It would make a good day hike or an easy overnighter. A campsite with a well and toilets is provided near Sand Lake 1, but you are not required to camp there. Camping is allowed anywhere in the quiet area, except within 100 feet of a lake. If you can use map and compass, you can travel cross-country. It is a good idea to carry water, since water from the lakes—even though boiling will purify it—is not very palatable.

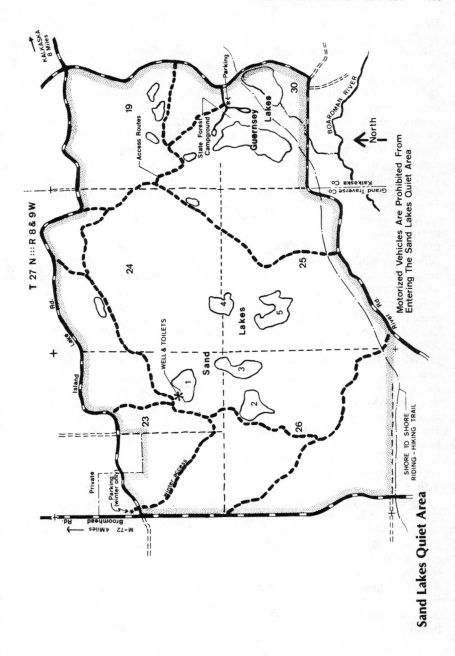

Sand Lakes Quiet Area

JORDAN RIVER PATHWAY

Location: In Jordan River State Forest. Take U.S. Highway 131 north from Alba 6 miles to Dead Man's Hill Road. Go east 1½ miles to parking lot.

Length: 18-mile loop.

U.S.G.S. Quads: Boyne Falls, Michigan; Boyne City, Michigan; Mancelona, Michigan; Alba, Michigan; all 15 minutes.

Description: This trail roughly follows the Jordan River, a beautiful clear stream that was designated a Natural Scenic River in 1972. The stream is surrounded by hills formed by the Wisconsinan glaciation. A gravel road also parallels the river. The road gets fairly heavy use during autumn when people come to see the fall colors. The trail makes four road crossings, but most of the time trail and road are far enough apart to keep the traffic out of hikers' eyes and ears.

The Michigan Department of Natural Resources has placed 25 numbered posts along the trail, each designed to point up some aspect of the history and ecology of the region. A brochure available from the Department of Natural Resources offers a planographic map of the trail and its surroundings, along with interpretive information coded to these numbered posts.

The trail, marked with the triangular blue "Pathway" signs, begins at a parking area atop Dead Man's Hill. It heads north along the top of the ridge, then drops down into the river valley and loops back to the south.

The trail follows the river for the next several miles, staying in the valley a good part of the way and occasionally climbing the hills. There are a lot of beavers in the valley, so you will have lots of chances to see dams, floodings, lodges, and with a bit of luck, maybe an animal. The biggest, most elaborate flooding appears as a small lake on the map. The trail follows a boardwalk across part of this pond, so you can get a good look at it.

The trail forks before you arrive at this flooding. The left fork goes back to the parking lot, forming a 3-mile loop. The right fork is the main trail.

Note the river crossing downstream from the beaver flooding. The trail is on the north side of the river until you reach Pinney Bridge Campground. It is about 5.5 miles from the crossing to the campground. Just before the campground, you will climb a hill that takes you 200 feet above the river, providing good views of the valley and the surrounding hills.

The campground has a pump and pit toilets, and camping there is free.

After crossing the river again, the trail climbs nearly 200 feet and heads south into what may be the most beautiful section of the loop.

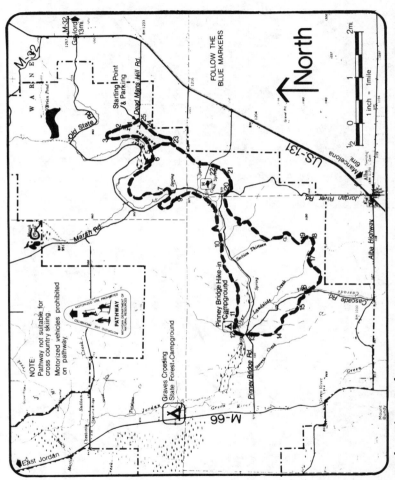

Jordan River Pathway

Sleeping Bear Dunes National Lakeshore Trails

(above) northeastern section

(below) southwestern section

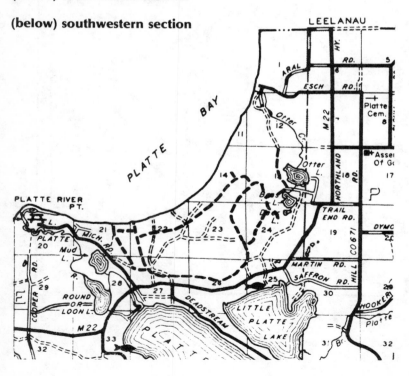

(below) central section

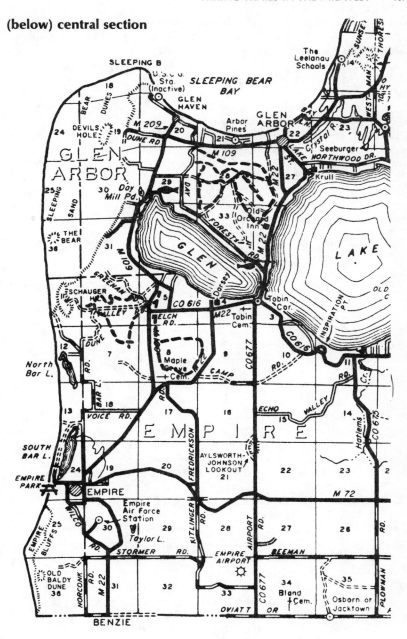

You'll be on high ground amid northern hardwoods—sugar maple, basswood, beech—occasionally dropping into narrow, steep ravines to cross creeks on footbridges. Near Landslide Creek, the grade is so steep that steps have been laid out. The ravines are usually covered with conifers—fir, spruce, cedar, and hemlock.

The loop ends back at Dead Man's Hill.

SLEEPING BEAR DUNES NATIONAL LAKESHORE TRAILS

Location: Park headquarters is at 400½ Main Street, Frankfort, Michigan 49635. The park extends north from the headquarters along the shore and also includes North and South Manitou islands. Ferry service to these islands leaves from Leland, Michigan.

Day hikers can enjoy four separate trail networks on the mainland:

Platte Plains: access from the Platte River Campground; about 10 miles of interconnecting loops.

U.S.G.S. Quad: Frankfort, Michigan, 15 minutes.

Schauger Hill and Windy Moraine: access from the visitor center. Two loops, 3 miles and 1.5 miles, respectively.

U.S.G.S. Quad: Empire, Michigan, 15 minutes.

Good Harbor Bay: access from Good Harbor Bay Picnic Area. One 2.5-mile loop.

U.S.G.S. Quad: Maple City, Michigan, 15 minutes.

Alligator Hill: access from the D. H. Day Campground. About 8 miles of interconnecting loops.

U.S.G.S. Quads: Empire, Michigan; Maple City, Michigan; both 15 minutes.

South Manitou Island: For backpackers this is the best bet. You will need a reservation for the ferry, which runs year-round in ordinary winters. Several times in recent years, however, the lake has frozen over between Leland and the islands. You can be certain of service between April and December. Monday through Saturday, the boat leaves Leland at 10 A.M. On Sundays, departure is at 1 P.M. Adult fare is $8.50. Children under age 12 ride for $6.50. For reservations, call (616) 256-9061.

U.S.G.S. Quad: for both North and South Manitou islands, North Manitou, Michigan, 15 minutes.

South Manitou Island is only about 3 miles on a side, so you can walk around it in a day. The park service has three walk-in campgrounds on the island. The Bay Campground is right by the boat dock. The Weather Station Campground is on the south coast, just a bit over a mile from the dock. The third campground, Popple, is on the north shore about 2½ miles from the dock. The campgrounds have pit toilets and communal fire rings. Water is available at the Bay Campground and near the weather station, but it is a half-mile hike for water from the Popple Campground.

A Park Service information center at the dock supplies camping permits and information. There is also a small restaurant and grocery store that sells a few staples.

The best way to see the island is to bring along a day pack. Set up on a tent site and leave your backpack there. Put some water and your lunch in the day pack and take off.

The limestone bedrock of the island has been overlaid by a thick deposit of glacial till that is thickest at the west edge of the island and slopes down to the east. The winds have added sands that at the western edge have created perched dunes. These extensive dunes sit on top of the glacial till. The whole sequence of bedrock, till, and sand creates cliffs 200 feet high, topped by a spectacular dune landscape that the winds are constantly rearranging.

Behind the dunes is a rich beech–maple forest. There are no deer or grouse on this island, and their absence affects the vegetation rather dramatically. American yew, a low evergreen shrub that grows in dense thickets, is a favorite deer browse. Heavy deer populations have made this plant rather scarce over much of the upper Midwest. Here it is abundant, a fact that helps make off-trail travel rather difficult.

We visited South Manitou in September and found berries of all kinds extremely abundant. Spikenard, yew, juniper, baneberry, and many others seemed to be everywhere. A good grouse population would reduce the numbers somewhat, but these poor fliers have never made it from the mainland.

South Manitou used to be inhabited before the Park Service bought the land, and a substantial amount of the interior of the island is open fields now beginning to return to woodland. Poison ivy is very common in these old fields and in the woods as well, so beware.

In the southwest corner of the island, an ancient grove of northern white cedars is worth a look. These trees are over 500 years old and include the largest tree of this species in North America. This giant is 17 feet 2 inches in circumference and 111 feet tall.

The much larger North Manitou Island has just been bought by the park service, but as of the fall of 1979, it is not available for public use. Plans call for reserving this island for backpackers—possibly with unrestricted backcountry camping. The island may be open as early as spring, 1980, so if you are interested, call park headquarters.

SHORE-TO-SHORE TRAIL

This trail was created by a group of horsemen called the Michigan Trail Riders Association, and it is set up primarily with the needs of riders in mind. The trail is frequently on roads, often for miles at a stretch—a situation that hikers are likely to find less than exciting.

However, sections of the trail through public land would be interesting to hike. This is particularly true of the area east of Grayling, the

Shore-to-Shore Trail

TRAIL USE

1. Do not litter trail or destroy trees.

2. Fires to be built only under safe conditions.

3. Cut only dead or down timber for firewood.

4. Stick to the trail. If you plan to leave the trail, obtain Department of Natural Resources maps and stay on state land and established rights of way.

5. Have a good time.

HORSEBACK RIDERS

1. Horses are not to be tied directly to trees — use a picket line.

2. When watering horses in streams, approach where banks will not be broken down.

3. Approach horse watering places with caution. Many lakes and streams are surrounded by soft and boggy ground that could mire a horse.

4. Do not use forest campground sites for horses. Special sites are prepared for horses.

5. Horses should not be ridden up and down streams.

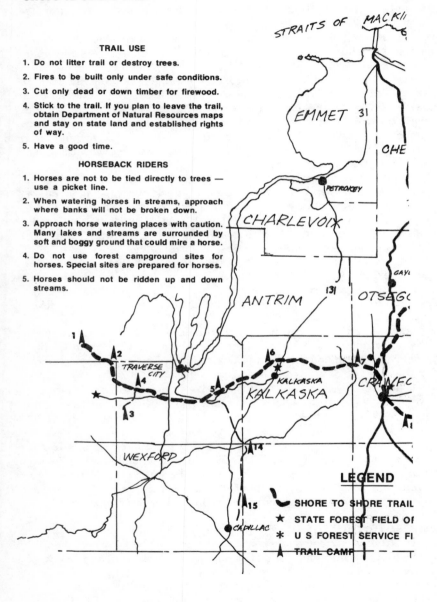

LEGEND

 SHORE TO SHORE TRAIL

★ STATE FOREST FIELD OI

✳ U S FOREST SERVICE FI

▲ TRAIL CAMP

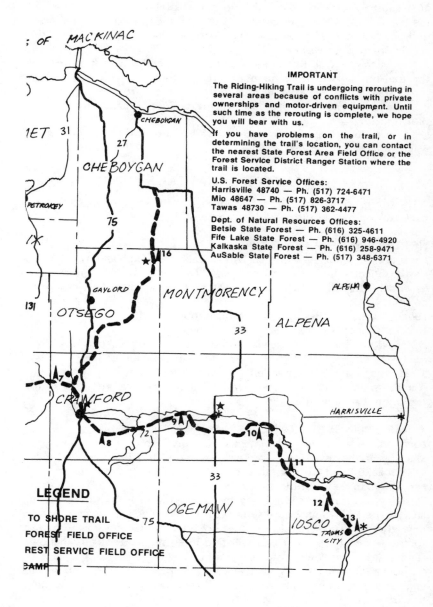

IMPORTANT

The Riding-Hiking Trail is undergoing rerouting in several areas because of conflicts with private ownerships and motor-driven equipment. Until such time as the rerouting is complete, we hope you will bear with us.

If you have problems on the trail, or in determining the trail's location, you can contact the nearest State Forest Area Field Office or the Forest Service District Ranger Station where the trail is located.

U.S. Forest Service Offices:
Harrisville 48740 — Ph. (517) 724-6471
Mio 48647 — Ph. (517) 826-3717
Tawas 48730 — Ph. (517) 362-4477

Dept. of Natural Resources Offices:
Betsie State Forest — Ph. (616) 325-4611
Fife Lake State Forest — Ph. (616) 946-4920
Kalkaska State Forest — Ph. (616) 258-9471
AuSable State Forest — Ph. (517) 348-6371

LEGEND

TO SHORE TRAIL
FOREST FIELD OFFICE
REST SERVICE FIELD OFFICE
CAMP

area south of Traverse City, and portions of the north leg of the trail east of Gaylord. The trail crosses through the Sand Lakes Quiet Area, described in this chapter, and just east of there, follows along the scenic Boardman River.

The Michigan Trail Riders Association sells a complete set of maps of the trail but only to their members. To get the maps you have to join the association. The cost is $10, and the maps are thrown in as a premium. The maps are standard Michigan County maps with the trail drawn in.

To join, write the association at 1179 Garn Road, Traverse City, Michigan 49684.

BRIEFLY NOTED TRAILS

Here are some trails intended primarily for day hiking, although backpacking of a sort is possible in some of them.

NORDHOUSE DUNES
Location: In Manistee National Forest. Take U.S. Highway 31, 11 miles north of Scottville. Turn west on Forest Road 5629. Follow it 10 miles to its end at the Lake Michigan Recreation Area, a Forest Service campground.
Length: About 7 miles of trail in various loops.
U.S.G.S. Quad: Manistee, Michigan, 15 minutes.
Description: This is an excellent example of Great Lakes dunes in a relatively untouched state. Nordhouse Dunes includes 3,000 roadless acres and was recommended for wilderness status by the Carter Administration in 1979. The campground makes a good base for exploring it on day trips.

YANKEE SPRINGS RECREATION AREA
Location: Near Middleville in Barry County. From U.S. Highway 131 take the Bradley exit. From Bradley go east on Metz Road about 8 miles to Gun Lake Road. Turn south about 2 miles to area headquarters.
Length: 18 miles in various loops.
Description: Yankee Springs is a morainal landscape of steep, irregularly shaped hills and depressions with many lakes and swamps in the low ground. This area is on the boundary between northern and southern forest types, so you will find interesting plant combinations, such as sassafras growing under white pine.

The various trail loops give a good sample of all the terrain and vegetation, including pine woods, hardwood forest, old fields returning to woods, and bogs.

You can get a good map at the headquarters or by writing Yankee Springs Recreation Area, Gun Lake Road, RFD 3, Middleville, Michigan 49333.

ALLEGAN STATE GAME AREA

Location: In Allegan County. Exit I-196 at Glenn, go north to 118th Avenue, and then east 11 miles to area headquarters.

Length: 30 miles.

U.S.G.S. Quads: Allegan, Michigan; Fennville, Michigan; both 15 minutes.

Description: Much of this game area is on the bed of an extinct glacial lake. The ground is flat and quite sandy, so you can expect lots of scrub oak. The Department of Natural Resources has planted pines, and there are a few older pines that are fairly tall.

The main backpacking trail is a large loop that begins and ends at Swan Creek Pond. Allegan also has 18 miles of cross-country ski trails, but hikers are not allowed to use these in the summer.

In winter, between October 1 and April 1, trailside camping is allowed, but in summer months you must camp in one of the five campgrounds. These are now free, although some thought is being given to charging for them.

A number of gravel roads form a grid on the game area, and you are never more than a mile from one of them. This is one of the few areas offering any sort of backpacking experience that is within a reasonable weekend's drive from Chicago.

PINCKNEY RECREATION AREA

Location: Near Dexter, northwest of Ann Arbor. Take the Dexter exit from I-94. Go north on Dexter-Pinckney Road to Territorial Road. Go west on Territorial Road to Dexter Townhall Road, then north to Silver Lake Road and northwest to area headquarters.

Length: 25 miles in various loops.

Description: Another interlobate moraine with hills and lakes. The forest is mostly hardwoods with some pine plantations. A portion of this park has been designated a quiet area where no motor vehicles are allowed. There are four campgrounds in the area.

Maps and information are available from Pinckney Recreation Area, 8555 Silver Hill Road, Pinckney, Michigan 48169.

LOST LAKE NATURE PATHWAY

Location: At the north end of Wildwood Road, north of U.S. Highway 31, 12 miles east of Honor.

Length: 5.5 miles.

U.S.G.S. Quad: Thompsonville, Michigan, 15 minutes.

Description: There used to be a small body of water here called Mud Lake. The Department of Natural Resources built a dam that submerged Mud Lake in a much larger creation called Lake Dubonnet. The nature trail here gives some good looks at a variety of northern landscapes, including aspen stands, pine plantations, and bogs. Beaver activity is also much in evidence. The trail has 28 numbered posts along the way, and you can get information about the things each post is pointing out by writing to the Department of Natural Resources, Information Services Center, Box 30028, Lansing, Michigan 48909.

The Shore-to-Shore Hiking and Riding Trail crosses the south end of this area and connects with the nature pathway.

URBAN TRAILS

The Huron/Clinton Metro Parks Authority administers a park system in the five-county area around Detroit. The system includes 20,000 acres in 10 separate parks, with four more parks totalling 15,000 acres now under development. There are more than 80 miles of trails in the parks. Information and maps are available from Huron/Clinton Metro Parks, 3050 Penobscot Building, Detroit, Michigan 48226.

The biggest parks with the most trails are:

Stony Creek Metropark, 4300 Main Park Road, Washington, Michigan 48094, a 4,500-acre park with 5½ miles of marked trails.
Hudson Mills, 8800 North Territorial Road, Dexter, Michigan 48130.
Metro Beach Metro Park, P. O. Box 1037, Mt. Clemens, Michigan 48043, a footpath through an excellent marsh.
Kensington Metropark, 2240 West Bruno Road, Milford, Michigan 48042. You can get a look at tamarack bogs here.
Lower Huron Metropark, 17845 Savage Road, Belleville, Michigan 48111.
Oakwoods Metropark, P. O. Box 332, Flat Rock, Michigan 48134.

SOURCES

For more information on hiking in Michigan, contact the following sources:

Department of Natural Resources
Information Services Center
Box 30028
Lansing, Michigan 48909
(For "State Forest Pathways" directory to trails in state forests and for maps of individual trails. Limit map requests to five at a time.)

Shore-to-Shore Hiking Trail
Michigan Trail Riders Association
1179 Gran Road
Traverse City, Michigan 49864
(Complete set of maps of Shore-to-Shore Trail is $10)

Sleeping Bear Dunes National
  Lakeshore
400½ Main Street
Frankfort, Michigan 49635
(616) 334-4017

Pictured Rocks National Lakeshore
Munising, Michigan 49862
(906) 387-2607

Isle Royale National Park
87 North Ripley Street
Houghton, Michigan 49931
(906) 482-2890

Porcupine Mountains Wilderness
  State Park
Star Route
Ontonagon, Michigan 49950
(906) 885-5798

Forest Supervisor
Ottawa National Forest
Box 468
Ironwood, Michigan 49938
(906) 932-1330

Forest Supervisor
Hiawatha National Forest
Escanaba, Michigan 49829
(906) 786-4062

Forest Supervisor
Huron–Manistee National Forest
421 South Mitchell Street
Cadillac, Michigan 49601
(616) 775-2421

The state of Michigan publishes a
  guide called "Michigan Hiking
  Opportunities" that includes
  information on nearly all the
  trails in this guide, plus maps of
  shorter trails good for day
  hiking. It costs $4.95 and is
  available from Michigan Natural
  Resources Reference Library,
  Box 30034, Lansing, Michigan
  48909.

5

WISCONSIN

WISCONSIN—AN INTRODUCTION

The southern half of Wisconsin is a patchwork of small farms and woodlots on gently undulating hills. Hiking trails have a pastoral aura. As one proceeds north, though, the farms gradually give way to forest and lake country. Trails penetrate real wilderness, sometimes wandering up to 10 miles without crossing a road.

The northwestern part of the state lies on the Canadian shield, bedrock that dates from the Precambrian period; the southwestern quarter of Wisconsin is part of what geologists call the "Driftless Area." It was never covered by glaciers.

The glacier that melted from the state as recently as 12,000 years ago had the most dramatic effect on the state's present topography. It created the thousands of small depressions that became lakes, marshes, and bogs; it left the vast expanses of sandy outwash plains and the jumbled morainal hills along its frontier. Drainage patterns are still primitive. There are hilltop swamps. You can't count on following a river downstream to civilization if you get lost, as you can in the more southern states of our region.

Boreal spruce-fir forests, more typical of Canada and northeastern Minnesota, are found in a small corner of northwestern Wisconsin in Douglas and Bayfield counties. White pines once covered large sections of northern Wisconsin. Nearly all of them were cut down within a few years at the turn of the century by timber companies. Quaking aspen, a pioneer species, is now the most common tree, although sugar maple is also typical, along with northern red oak, white and green ash, white birch and yellow birch, basswood, hemlock, and—in the eastern counties along Lake Michigan—American beech. Oaks and hickories dominate the Driftless Area.

When the timber companies finished harvesting the state's virgin forests in the early 1900s, they either allowed the lands they had owned to be sold for taxes or made outright donations to county, state, or federal governments. As a result, the bulk of public land in the state is now in the northern half. There are two national forests, the Nicolet and the Chequamegon; an unusually large state forest, the Northern Highland; and extensive county and school forests. Trails have been laid out and wilderness areas designated on many of the public lands.

The only other major trail development is along the terminal moraine of the Woodfordian glacier and is managed by a coalition of volunteers working through an organization called the Ice Age Park and Trail Foundation, Inc.

In our trail descriptions, we have listed the names and addresses of groups involved with trail building and maintenance throughout the state.

There are also outings clubs at various branches of the University of Wisconsin, and several Sierra Club groups sponsor group backpacking trips. Chairperson for the Sierra Club's statewide John Muir Chapter is Spencer Black, 3001 Harvey, Madison, Wisconsin 53705.

TRAILS IN NICOLET NATIONAL FOREST

This forest spreads over a six-county area encompassing nearly 650,000 acres in northeastern Wisconsin. The headwaters of six major rivers—the Wolf, the Pine, the Wisconsin, the Peshtigo, the Popple, and the Oconto—lie within its boundaries.

Trees and wildflowers in Nicolet are similar to those found in Chequamegon National Forest, except that the Chequamegon contains a few more western and southern species. White pine is more common here, possibly because the Nicolet has served as a major experimental area for breeding genetically superior strains of this tree. It is hoped the new varieties will withstand blister rust, a disease that has destroyed huge numbers of pines across the northern United States.

Other common trees are red pine and jack pine, white and yellow birch, hemlock, sugar maple, red maple, white and black ash, northern red oak, quaking aspen and bigtooth aspen.

The terrain is either slightly elevated with gentle rolling hills or, in places, quite flat. Northern bogs, with their exotic insect-eating plants and profusion of early summer wildflowers, are scattered in patches between the sections of high ground.

Trail building has been slow in the Nicolet. Administrators in the past have not been sensitive to the fact that backpackers prefer trails to two-lane roads for hiking and that snowmobile trails are not always easily adaptable to summer use. That attitude has begun to change, so we expect to see more good trails in this forest in the future. We have supplemented descriptions of a few formal trails with descriptions of areas that are suitable for cross-country navigation with map and compass.

Write Forest Supervisor, Nicolet National Forest, Federal Building, 68 South Stevens Street, Rhinelander, Wisconsin 54501.

ANVIL TRAIL

Location: Nicolet National Forest. Access is from a parking area on Wisconsin Highway 70 about 8.5 miles east of Eagle River.

Length: 25-mile series of loops.

U.S.G.S. Quad: Anvil Lake, 7.5 minutes.

Description: This series of three interconnecting loops was designed as a cross-country ski trail but works well for a weekend backpack trip in the warmer seasons. The terrain is gently rolling over most of the route. It was built by the Civilian Conservation Corps in the 1930s but fell into disuse until the cross-country ski boom of the 1970s.

The forest primarily consists of upland hardwoods, mainly sugar maple, although there are fine stands of large hemlocks and balsam fir. A new shelter—meant mainly as a warming hut for skiers but adaptable for packpackers—was built in 1978. It is about 2¾ miles south of the parking lot on Highway 70 on the westernmost trail fork.

Anvil Trail

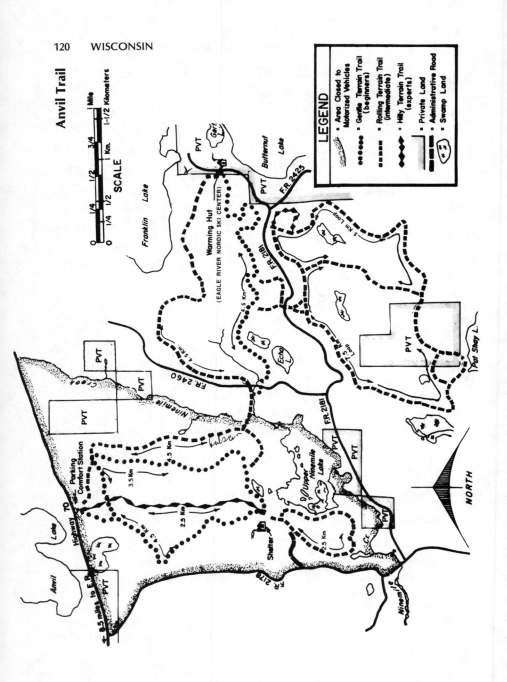

The trail passes by several small lakes. There is a developed Forest Service campground on the east shore of Franklin Lake.

Bert Kleerup of the Eagle River Nordic Ski Center supervises maintenance of the Anvil Trail both in winter and in summer. He has a warming hut where the trail touches Forest Road 2181 between Franklin and Butternut lakes.

KIMBALL CREEK TRAIL

Location: Nicolet National Forest. Access to the north end of the trail is from a parking area on Wisconsin Highway 70 about 14 miles east of Eagle River. There is also a parking area at the south end of the trail on Wisconsin Highway 32 just south of Forest Road 2183, about 8 miles southeast of Three Lakes.

Length: 19 miles.

U.S.G.S. Quads: Alvin Northwest, Alvin Southwest, Julia Lake; all 7.5 minutes.

Description: This trail was designed for snowmobiles but works reasonably well for hikers. It follows the abandoned roadbed of the Thunder Lake narrow-gauge railroad over most of its route. The railroad track was constructed in 1893 to haul white pine to sawmills in Rhinelander. The rails were removed in 1941.

It parallels but remains out of sight of Forest Road 2176 most of the way, through a forest of maple, basswood, white birch, and other hardwoods. It passes by a small but attractive lake called Indian Camp Lake, comes near several other lakes, and crosses a small tributary of the Pine River as it flows from Butternut Lake.

The trail branches near the southern end. The westernmost fork (right as you're heading south) ends at a parking area on Forest Road 2182. The easternmost fork, a portion of it rerouted around boggy areas for hikers, passes on the east side of Woodbury Lake, through a plantation of red pines, and across a black spruce swamp on a 500-foot boardwalk before reaching the parking area on Highway 32.

AREAS TO EXPLORE CROSS-COUNTRY

BLACKJACK SPRINGS WILDERNESS

Location: Nicolet National Forest. Wisconsin Highway 70 just east of Anvil Lake (just over 8 miles east of Eagle River) forms the southern boundary of this wilderness tract. Forest Road 2178 forms the eastern boundary from Highway 70 north to the Deerskin River.

Length: No formal trails, but cross-country navigation with map and compass is allowed. There are several old logging roads. One may also hike along the banks of Blackjack Creek to Blackjack Springs or south up Goldigger Creek.

U.S.G.S. Quads: Anvil Lake, Eagle River East, Phelps, all 7.5 minutes.

Description: The topography of this newly declared 6,145-acre wilder-

Kimball Creek Trail

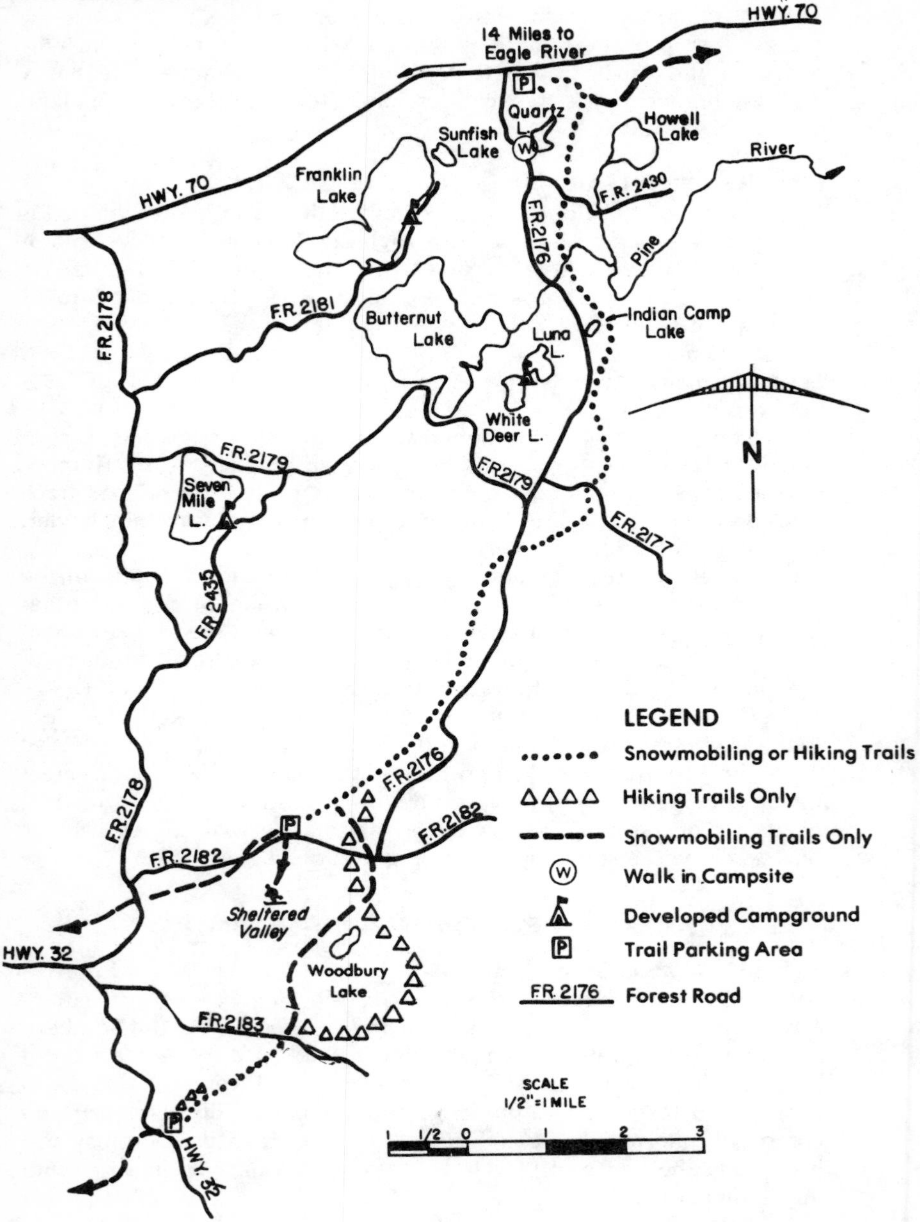

Blackjack Springs Wilderness (circles denote entry points)

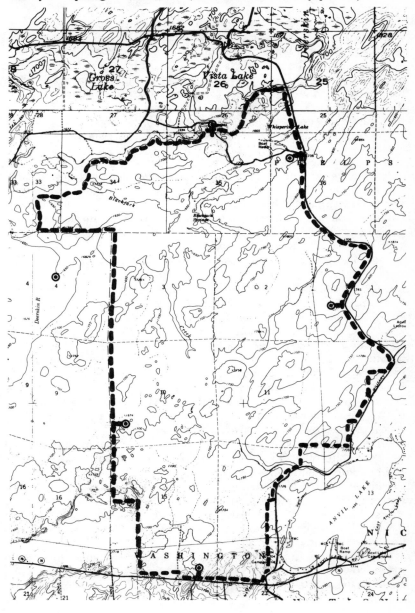

ness is gently rolling. Forest cover includes stands of mature white and red pine.

Major water sources in the tract include the streams named above—Blackjack Creek, Goldigger Creek, and Deerskin River—and also Whispering Lake, near the northern boundary but accessible only on foot.

The section of the wilderness east of Goldigger Creek is the hilliest; the trees there are mainly white and red pines. There are more hardwoods such as sugar maple along the banks of Blackjack Creek, at Blackjack Springs, and between Blackjack Creek and the northern boundary at Deerskin River. The area west of Goldigger Creek to the forest boundary is flatter, planted mainly in jack pine by the Forest Service.

There are privately owned lands along the east side of Forest Road 2178 from Deerskin River south to about 3 miles north of Highway 70.

WHISKER LAKE WILDERNESS

Location: Nicolet National Forest. There are several official wilderness entry points on Forest Road 2150 north of Wisconsin Highway 70 about 12 miles west of Florence.

Length: There are two short trails—each about 3 miles long—extending from west to east across the wilderness from entry points on Forest Road 2150. Hikers are free to wander wherever they like on the tract, however. Riley Creek runs diagonally from southwest to northeast across the wilderness; it is also a potential hiking route.

U.S.G.S. Quad: Nault, 7.5 minutes.

Description: Whisker Lake Wilderness contains 7,765 acres within its boundaries; 250 of them are privately owned. It is bounded on the south by Wisconsin Highway 70; on the west by Forest Road 2150 (called the Rainbow Trail); on the north by the Brule River, which is also the state line between Wisconsin and Michigan. Its east boundary is also the Nicolet National Forest boundary and passes from north to south just west of Pickerel Lake and Boot Lake.

Terrain is gently rolling. The forest cover includes natural and planted red and white pine, sugar maple and other hardwoods, quaking aspen and bigtooth aspen, and white spruce.

Whisker Lake gets its name from scattered virgin red pine on the shores of that lake (accessible only on foot). Seen from a distance, they are said to resemble "chin whiskers," and they somehow escaped burning by the wildfires that ravaged the area after it was railroad-logged in the early 1900s.

There are five small lakes within the wilderness boundaries. Riley Creek flows north from Riley Lake to the Brule River. It is clear, cold, and contains native brook trout.

Whisker Lake Wilderness (circles denote entry points)

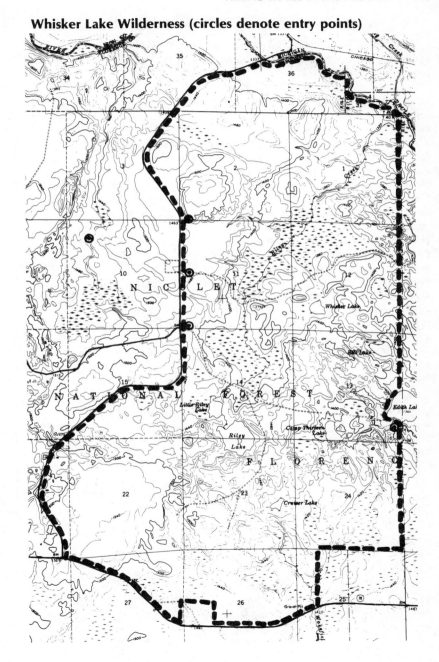

BRIEFLY NOTED TRAILS

LAONA RANGER DISTRICT BACKCOUNTRY AREAS
Location: Nicolet National Forest, Laona District.
Length: No formal trails, but networks of logging roads and fire lanes.
Description: This ranger district has set aside three areas for use mainly by hunters in autumn; the areas can be used by hikers in nonhunting season.
Little Star Lake Area. Bound by County Highway W on the south, Forest Road 2144 on the east, Mayflower Lake on the north, and Eds Lake on the west. The 100-mile Nicolet Snow Safari Trail passes through the area; there are also numerous old logging grades now cleared and clover-seeded for easy walking. A square plot of private land occupies the center of the area. There are four small lakes—Mayflower, Midget, Little Star, and Eds Lake—within the tract. All are accessible only on foot.
U.S.G.S. Quads: Roberts Lake and Lake Lucerne, both 7.5 minutes.
Catwillow Creek Area. Lies north of Forest Road 2131, east of the Peshtigo River, and (mainly) south of Catwillow Creek. There are numerous skid trails and woods roads in the tract. To stray off them may be to step off into a bog. Catwillow Creek, the Peshtigo River, and Rock Creek provide the drainage for the area.
U.S.G.S. Quad: Blackwell, 7.5 minutes.
Colburn Creek Area. Lies north of Forest Road 2361 and west of Forest Road 2363. It is heavily crisscrossed by old clover-seeded roads; there are also numerous small wildlife ponds and openings created by the Forest Service to attract ruffed grouse and deer.
U.S.G.S. Quad: Otter Lake, 7.5 minutes.
    A brochure of the Laona district with detailed maps of the above area is available from the district ranger in Laona or from the Forest Supervisor, Nicolet National Forest, Federal Building, Rhinelander, Wisconsin 54501.

TRAILS IN CHEQUAMEGON NATIONAL FOREST

    This forest, established in 1933, stretches from just south of Lake Superior near Bayfield down to Park Falls and Phillips in northcentral Wisconsin. It contains more than 838,000 public acres, more than 400 lakes, and more than 460 miles of streams. Its major waterways are the Flambeau, the Yellow, the Chippewa, and the Namekegon.
    The forest cover is typically North Woods: birches, aspens, sugar maple, balsam fir and various pines—mainly jack pine, white pine, and red pine—with white cedar in swampy areas, tamaracks and spruces in bogs.

In far northern sections, such boreal forest plants as spruce and fir trees, along with the tiny delicate twinflowers, pipsissewa, and pyrola species become more common. Prairie wildflowers creep into the forest on its western edge, and more southern plant species can be seen in the southernmost unit near Medford.

Pine barrens—scattered jack pines among acres of blueberries—are special attractions in the northeast section of the forest, not far west of the Mt. Valhalla Trail.

For more information about the forest, write to the Forest Supervisor, Chequamegon National Forest, Park Falls, Wisconsin 54552.

NORTH COUNTRY TRAIL
Location: This trail is located within the boundaries of the Chequamegon National Forest in northern Wisconsin. Its eastern end is just west of Mellen—a town on Wisconsin Route 13—and its western end is 3 miles south of Iron River, Wisconsin, which is on U.S. Route 2. To reach the western end of the trail, take Bayfield County A south from Iron River to Lake Ruth. The trail starts at County A just south of the lake. Its beginning is marked by a large wooden sign.

The eastern terminus can be reached by taking Hillcrest Avenue west from Mellen. This street becomes Forest Road 390 about 2½ miles west of Mellen, and the trail branches off to the left from the road about 3 miles from town. This end of the trail is also marked with a large wooden sign.

Length: 60 miles.

U.S.G.S. Quads: Mellen, 7.5 minutes; Marengo, 15 minutes; Grandview, 7.5 minutes; Diamond Lake, 7.5 minutes; Drummond, 7.5 minutes; Delta, 7.5 minutes; Iron Lake, 15 minutes.

Description: The trail is marked with either orange or yellow diamond-shaped blazes, and there are frequent signs giving the distance to the next notable landmark along the way. The eastern two-thirds of the trail is marked with numbered posts every mile.

The land here is heavily forested with fairly mature second-growth timber. In a couple of places, there are remnants of the virgin forest. A ranger told us that the lumber companies had apparently had a fit of conscience and decided to leave a few trees standing. These trees are mainly white pine, and they are more fully described below in the sections dealing with Lake Owen and Drummond.

The landscape ranges from rolling to rather rugged. In the Penokee Mountains, some of the upgrades get pretty long and steep, but generally speaking the walking is not especially difficult. There is no place where you would have to do any scrambling.

We walked the trail in June of a very wet year, and there were a few spots where we had to hop from high spot to high spot in order to

North Country Trail—west section

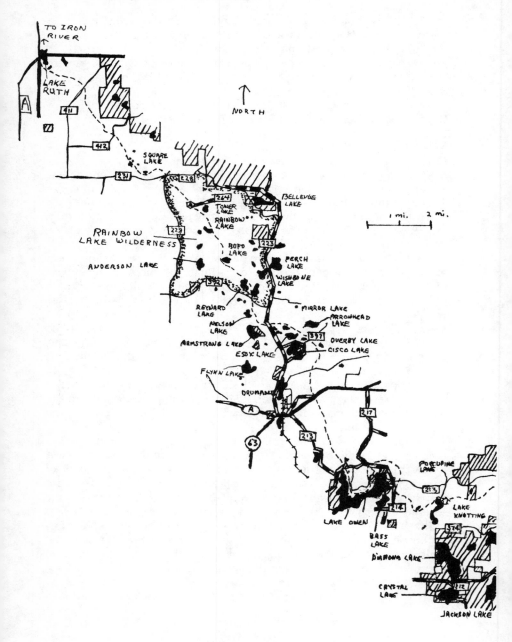

North Country Trail—east section

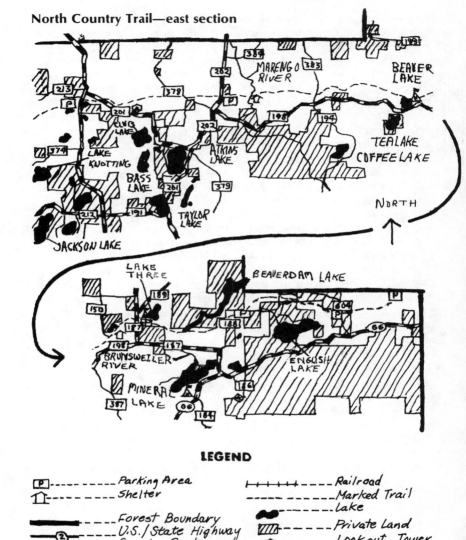

LEGEND

keep our feet dry. However, all of the larger streams are bridged, and it is likely that later in the year much of the standing water we encountered would be dried up.

Bugs—mosquitoes, deer flies, and wood ticks—can be a problem. However, it is possible to minimize this problem by picking the right time of year. The woods are really beautiful in late spring and early summer. There are wildflowers everywhere. The birds are nesting about this time, and the males seem to sing constantly. But if you want to avoid giving a pint of blood to the mosquitoes, come earlier in the spring, later in the summer, or best of all, in fall. The number of bugs declines as the summer goes on, so they will not be as bad in August as they are in June. In the early spring, the weather is always uncertain, but there is a magical quality about early spring that can go a long way toward making you forget cloudy skies or a persistent drizzle.

Fall is incredibly beautiful in this area. The hardwoods of the forest are mainly maple, the aspen that is known locally as popple, and birch. Their fall colors are punctuated by the occasional conifer. The bugs are gone, and for birders, the fall migration is in full swing.

Of course, you do have hunters. September is bear season. In October it is grouse and partridge, and toward the end of November it's deer. Actually the deer hunters are probably the only ones you have to worry about. Bear are hunted from baited stands in this area, so you do not have hunters with rifles roaming around in the woods. Birds are hunted with shotguns, so you would have to be close to a hunter to be in any danger.

By November, winter has set in. This is deep snow country, and snowshoes or cross-country skis are needed to navigate the trail.

There are several Forest Service campgrounds on or just off the trail. These have pit toilets, wells, fireplaces, and access by road. You can lay out a trip that will allow you to stay at one of these every night, but the Forest Service will not object if backpackers camp anywhere they like along the trail.

Fires can be built along the trail with the usual precautions. Keep the fire confined to a ring of stones (you can put these back where you found them when you are through). Use only dead wood, and be sure the fire is out before you leave it.

Human wastes should be buried (shallowly) away from the trail and away from water. Garbage can be carried out.

Water in most of the streams that cross the trail probably is drinkable, but Halazone tablets should be used just to be on the safe side.

It is a good idea to check with the rangers before you start out on the trail. They have current information that can often be very helpful. A ranger's good advice steered us around a beaver pond some 6 feet deep.

What follows is a detailed description of the trail beginning at the east end. The trail heads southwest from Forest Road 390, but this is the section that the beavers have dammed. If you want to avoid the pond created by these industrious rodents, continue west on 390 to Forest Road 604. Turn south on 604 and follow it until you pick up the trail 2½ miles from its beginning. There are plans to put a bridge across the pond, but check with the rangers to find out whether this has been done before you start walking.

The country here is heavily forested rolling hills. Just over 8 miles from the trail's beginning you will cross the Brunsweiler River. The river widens out into a beaver pond where the trail crosses it, and local residents come here to fish for muskies.

There is a campground at Three Lake, 10 miles from the beginning of the trail, and an Adirondack Shelter just beyond it. There is another campground at Beaver Lake (13 miles). The trail splits here, with the right fork continuing on, while the left fork leads to the campground.

The Marengo River is 18½ miles from the trail's beginning. This beautiful fast-rushing stream flows through a gorge in the Penokee Mountains. There is another shelter on the eastern side of the gorge, and on the ridge that forms the western side, there is an outcrop that gives a beautiful view of the mountains.

The Penokees ain't exactly the Rockies. Their tallest summits are only 1,600 feet above sea level. But to flatlanders, all mountains are a surprise and a delight, even the little ones.

Moving west from the Marengo, the rugged country gradually gives way to more rolling land. Thirty miles from trail's beginning is Porcupine Lake, where there is another shelter. Two and a half miles farther on, you strike a side trail that leads to Twin Lakes Campground, about half a mile away. The campground is located on a narrow piece of land between two lakes. It has almost 100 sites. We saw our first bald eagle soaring over the trail less than a mile from this campground. There were about 20 active nests of our national bird in various sections of the Chequamegon in the spring of 1973.

Three miles beyond the Two Lakes turnoff is one that goes to the picnic grounds at Lake Owen. The section of the trail between Two Lakes and Lake Owen contains some virgin white pine.

There is more virgin pine—one tree is about 51 inches in diameter— just north of Wisconsin Route 63, which the trail crosses 40 miles from its beginning. About a mile west on 63 is the tiny hamlet of Drummond (general store, restaurant, motel, and three bars).

Beyond 63, you cross the Long Branch River as well as about a dozen small lakes. One of these, Perch Lake, has a campground. To get to it, turn off the trail at Forest Road 223 (45 miles). The camp is about 3 miles from the trail.

The sections between Drummond and trail's end are possibly the most attractive of the whole trail. They also get the heaviest use. The trail passes numerous small lakes, accessible only on foot. Several of them lie within the Rainbow Lake Wilderness, through which the main trail passes. Old railroad grades crossing the trail provide access to several more lakes. Among our own favorites are Rainbow Lake itself, Anderson Lake, and Bufo Lake. There is a fine natural campsite at Anderson Lake, which is used by canoeists as well as hikers. (Access to Anderson is by one of the railroad grades. Check your topo map.)

The trail ends at Lake Ruth where there is a privately owned resort with spaces for tent campers, a nice beach, and a small bar and store where you can buy a few food items—bread, milk, butter, eggs—as well as soft drinks and beer.

The Chief Ranger, Chequamegon National Forest, Park Falls, Wisconsin 54552, can supply a planometric map of the forest that shows the trail. The scale is ¼ inch to 1 mile. He also can send you a mimeographed map of the North Country Trail, a detailed list of points of interest along the trail, and some advice for hikers.

MT. VALHALLA TRAIL

Location: In far northern Wisconsin roughly straight west of Washburn, a town on the shore of Lake Superior. To reach it from Washburn, take Bayfield County Route C west to the Mt. Valhalla Recreation Area. The trail is entirely within the Chequamegon National Forest.
Length: 17 miles. The trail is a loop beginning and ending at Mt. Valhalla.
U.S.G.S. Quads: Mt. Ashwabay and Washburn, both 7.5 minutes.
Description: This marked trail is part of a network of snowmobile trails that the forest service has opened up in this area. When there is no snow on the ground, hikers can use the facilities. The countryside is hilly, with the typical northern forest cover of jack pine, aspen, and birch.

There is a chalet at Mt. Valhalla (the area has been used for training the U.S. Olympic Ski Team) with drinking water available. Leaving the chalet, the trail climbs to a high hill from which you can see Lake Superior. The Birch Grove Campground is 4.7 miles south of Mt. Valhalla. It offers pit toilets, drinking water, and fire rings. There are 16 campsites, and the daily use fee is $2.

Beyond Birch Grove, the Long Lake Picnic Ground (6.5 miles from Mt. Valhalla) has drinking water and toilets, a beach with change houses, and picnic facilities.

From Long Lake, the trail heads west and then north again, through a forest that is mainly jack pine. To reach the Birch Grove Campground from this western leg of the loop, turn right off the trail onto Forest Road 435 and follow it for about a mile. The main trail continues north across Forest Road 236 and, before turning south again to Mt. Valhalla,

Mt. Valhalla Trail

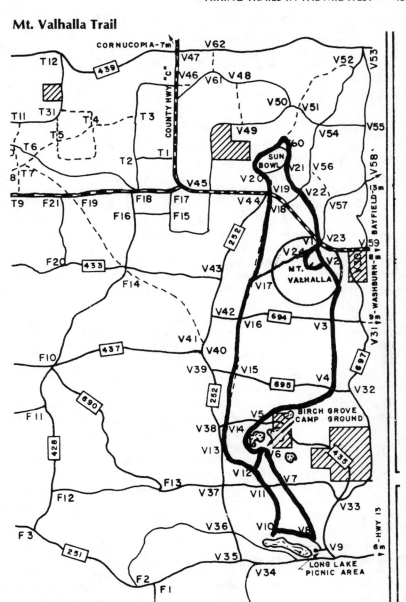

it circles a valley called the Sun Bowl because, for reasons unknown, it has never supported much vegetation.

In addition to the trail markers, each intersection of the trail with other trails or with forest roads is numbered. The number at the intersection corresponds to a number on a sketch map of the area which is available from the Forest Service Office, Park Falls, Wisconsin 54552, or from the District Ranger, Washburn, Wisconsin 54891. The district office can also supply a planometric map on a scale of ½ inch to 1 mile.

FLAMBEAU TRAILS

Location: There are 11 different interconnecting trails in the Flambeau system, all located in the Park Falls Section of the Chequamegon National Forest. There is an access point with a parking lot just off Wisconsin Route 70, about 5 miles east of Fifield. Most of the trails in the system begin at this point, branching out to the north, south, and east.

The longest of the trails, Number 111, does not begin at the access point. Its western end is at Blockhouse Lake and can be reached by taking Wisconsin 182 east from Park Falls to Forest Road 648. Go north on 648 for about 2 miles. The trail intersects 648 at Forest Road 153.

Length: The trail numbers and lengths are as follows—101, 15.4 miles; 102, 10.6 miles; 103, 2.2 miles; 104, 6 miles; 106, 0.6 miles; 107, 0.1 miles; 108, 0.8 miles; 109, 1.2 miles; 110, 0.5 miles; 111, 24.8 miles; 119, 0.6 miles.

U.S.G.S. Quads: Park Falls, 15 minutes; Pike Lake Northwest, 7.5 minutes; Pike Lake, 7.5 minutes; Pike Lake Southwest, 7.5 minutes.

Description: These trails were originally cut to restrain meandering snowmobilers, but the forest service has added bridges over streams so they can be used all year. A warning note in the words of the forest service: "The Flambeau Trails are managed for multiple use: snowmobiling, hiking, hunting, walking, horseback riding, trail bike riding, etc." A trail bike driven by an idiot is a menace to life and limb. This is not meant to suggest that all trail bike riders are idiots, but it does mean that it is a good idea to regard them as idiots until they have proven otherwise. If you hear one of the things coming, get off to one side of the trail and wait for it to pass.

This is rolling to flat country covered with a typical northern forest vegetation—birch, aspen, spruce, and jack pine. There are numerous lakes, ponds, and small streams, and the South Fork of the Flambeau River also flows through the area. There are also extensive areas of marshy land, some of which has been set aside as waterfowl refuges.

In this kind of country, it is a good idea to stay on the trails. There are no landmarks to speak of, and it is easy to get lost.

Trail 101 begins at the access point and winds eastward for 15.4 miles,

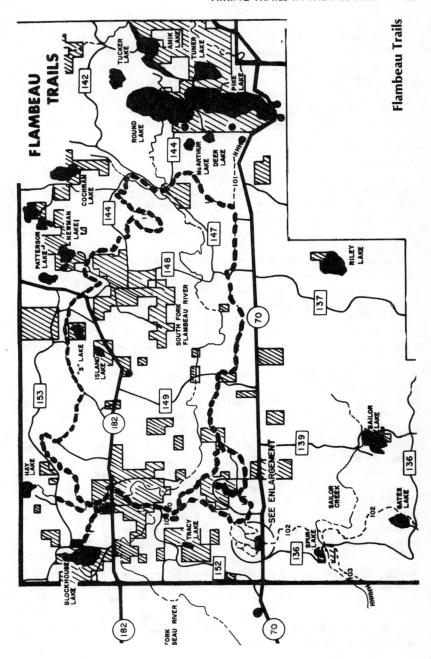

FLAMBEAU TRAILS

Flambeau Trails

ending just west of Pike Lake. There are two Forest Service camp-grounds north of the trail. A bit more than halfway along the trail you can turn off north on Forest Road 148 to the Smith Rapids Camp-ground, which is between 1 and 2 miles from the trail. Two miles beyond 148, you can turn north on Trail 111 approximately 3 miles to Fishtrap camp (Note: there is no water at this camp). Both of these campgrounds are along the Flambeau River.

The land around Pike Lake is privately owned, but there is a campground on the northeast shore called Stein's Oak Grove. Camp-sites are $2.50 per night and there is a beach, boat launching facilities, and boats for rent.

Trail 102 heads south from the access point past Spur Lake (2–3 miles), Sailor Creek (3 miles), Gates Lake (4–5 miles), Nichols Lake (6 miles), and the Squaw Creek Flowage (8–10 miles), ending at the Forest Boundary. The Squaw Creek Waterfowl Area is near this trail. From the Squaw Creek dam, take Forest Road south 2–3 miles to a county campground on Solberg Lake.

Trail 103 branches off 102 just south of Sailor Creek. It follows the creek westward, ending at the forest boundary. Beyond the boundary, there is a poor road that leads to the Sailor Creek Flowage Camp-ground approximately 2 to 3 miles away.

Trail 104 begins at the western edge of the access point, meandering northeast and then looping back southeast to join Trail 101 about 3 to 4 miles east of the access point. The entire 104-101 loop is about 10 miles long.

Trails 106 through 110 are very short, serving mainly to connect some of the larger trails; 106 runs north from the access to 104. If you want to take the 104-101 loop, starting out on 106 would shorten things slightly. Trail 107 joins 104 and 106 just north of the access. Trail 108 branches north from 101 about a mile east of the access and heads northeast to join 104. This is another alternate that could shorten the 104-101 loop. Trails 109 and 110 are best considered together. They head north from the northernmost point of trail 104 and end at Forest Road 152.

Trail 111, the longest in the system, starts 2 to 3 miles from the east end of 101. It meanders north and then east, ending at Blockhouse Lake. Along the way it crosses the Flambeau near Fishtrap Camp-ground. While it does not touch any lakes until trail's end at Block-house Lake, it passes within a mile or two of more than a dozen.

It is possible to make a complete loop of just under 50 miles by taking trail 101 east from the access point to trail 111. Then take 111 to its end. From there, walk south along Forest Road 648 about 1.5 miles, then east on Wisconsin Route 182 for another mile and a half to Forest Road 152. Take 152 south about 1.5 miles, then east a few hundred yards to where trail 109 hits it. Trail 109 connects to 104 which takes you back to the access point.

Finally, trail 119 is a short north-south walk connecting trails 101 and 108 just east of the access point.

Additional information: It is rather difficult to describe a trail network like this one in words. With a map, the whole thing becomes immediately clear. The District Ranger, Park Falls Ranger District, City Hall Building, Park Falls, Wisconsin 54552, can supply you with a planometric map of the entire Chequamegon National Forest (scale ¼-inch to the mile). This map shows the three longest trails (101, 102, and 111), as well as information on campsites. The Ranger also will supply a rough sketch map of all the trails, and some information on the trails and their use.

The City Hall building in Park Falls is right on Route 13, and it might be a good idea to check in there for any last minute information before you start hiking.

(See the following Ice Age Trail section of this chapter for description of a 41-mile segment of that trail which passes through the Medford district of Chequamegon National Forest in Taylor County.)

THE ICE AGE TRAIL

For more than a million years and as recently as 12,000 years ago, ice covered much of Canada and the northern United States. In this country, four separate glacial stages—the Nebraskan, the Kansan, the Illinoisan, and the Wisconsinan, are named for their most southerly advances.

Because evidence of the glaciers is preserved especially well in Wisconsin, scientists have been interested for years in establishing some kind of linear park or "scientific reserve," as it came to be known, to study that evidence without worrying that unique and fragile landforms would be destroyed by development.

In October, 1964, thanks mainly to the long-time efforts of a Milwaukee attorney and outdoorsman named Ray Zillmer, the Ice Age National Scientific Reserve was made official by federal legislation. Nine separate research areas were established, and to complement and connect these areas, a 600-mile hiking and bicycle trail was proposed to run diagonally across the state along the hills that mark the farthest advance of the Wisconsinan glacier.

The trail was to begin on the Door County Peninsula and proceed south along the Lake Michigan lobe of the glacier to Kettle Moraine State Forest. From the southern end of Kettle Moraine, the trail would turn sharply northwest and continue diagonally across the state—along terminal moraines of the Green Bay, Chippewa, and Superior lobes of the glacier—to the interstate park at the border with Minnesota in Polk County.

Parts of the trail are still a dream, but many sections have been completed—some under the supervision of local hiking clubs, others by state, county, and national forest personnel. We have chosen to describe only those sections we feel are particularly well adapted for backpackers. Other sections are designed mainly for bicyclists and either follow roads or hard-surfaced paths. Still other sections—for the moment at least—lend themselves best to car touring.

For maps and more information about the entire trail project, along with the names of volunteer groups coordinating trail-building in different counties, write the Ice Age Park and Trail Foundation of Wisconsin, Inc., 780 North Water Street, Milwaukee, Wisconsin 53202.

AHNAPEE TRAIL, DOOR COUNTY

Location: The Ahnapee Trail follows an abandoned railroad bed from the town of Algoma, 11 miles north of Kewaunee on the shores of Lake Michigan, to Sturgeon Bay at the southern end of the Door County peninsula. The southern terminus is about a mile north of Algoma on County M. Watch for a small sign on the right identifying the trail. The northern end is at County U near the southern city limits of Sturgeon Bay. You can also get on by taking County J east out of Forestville or by driving to Maplewood where State Route 42 crosses Kewaunee County H.

Length: 15 miles.

U.S.G.S. Quads: Algoma, Wisconsin; Casco, Wisconsin; Sturgeon Bay, Wisconsin; all 15 minutes.

Description: The Ahnapee Trail makes a pleasant day hike if you camp at nearby state parks and drive over early in the morning. Potawatomie State Park is only 20 minutes by car from the Sturgeon Bay Trail access, and Point Beach State Park at Two Rivers is about a 40-minute drive from Algoma.

The countryside is level to gently rolling with a mixture of farms and small patches of woods, mainly hardwoods. There are small dairy and beef herds as well as swine, and several corn fields and apple and cherry orchards. Apples grow wild along the trailside, too, so in season you can eat your fill.

About 5 miles of the trail between Algoma and Forestville runs along—and at one point across—the Ahnapee River, a scenic, meandering stream. There is a reservoir behind a small dam at Forestville, and marshy ground along the trailside for part of the way. We saw a great blue heron wading there one fall day.

The tiny hamlet of Maplewood is located almost exactly halfway and it makes a good stopping point. There are a couple of bars and a grocery store where food, corn plasters, and moleskin are available for hungry and blistered hikers.

North of Maplewood, the route crosses County O a mile or so past County H and meets County S about 3 miles south of Sturgeon Bay.

Ahnapee Trail, Door County

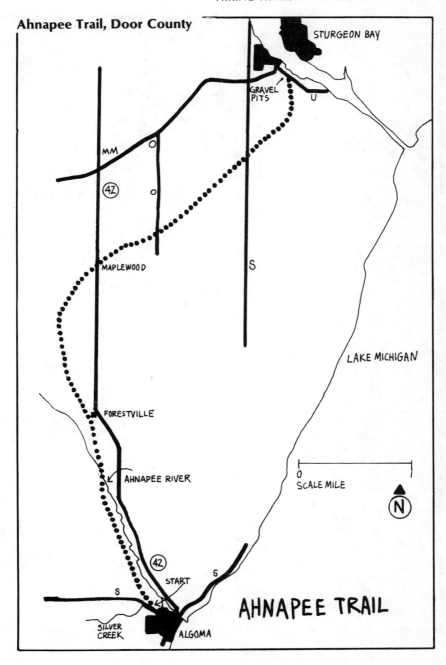

STURGEON BAY

GRAVEL PITS

U

MM

O

42

O

MAPLEWOOD

S

LAKE MICHIGAN

FORESTVILLE

AHNAPEE RIVER

0
SCALE MILE

N

42

START

S

S

SILVER CREEK

ALGOMA

AHNAPEE TRAIL

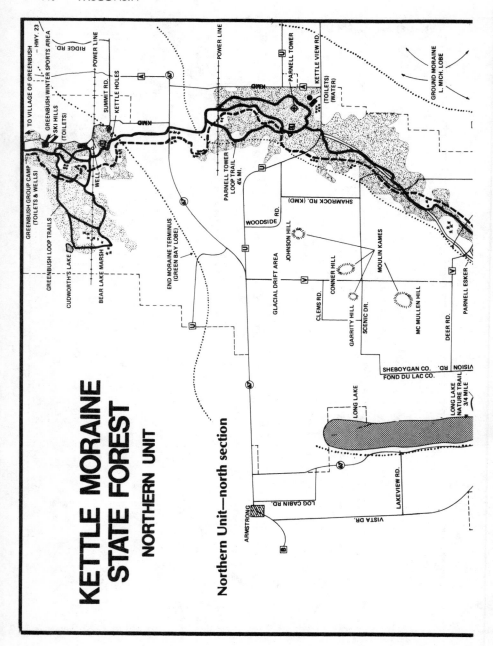

KETTLE MORAINE STATE FOREST
NORTHERN UNIT

Northern Unit—north section

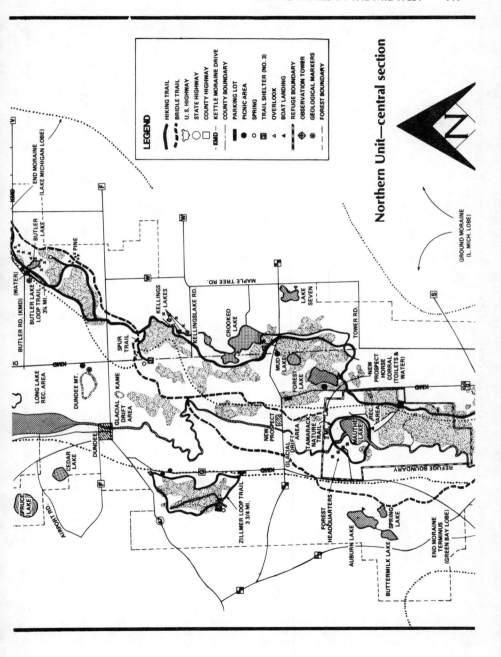

Northern Unit—central section

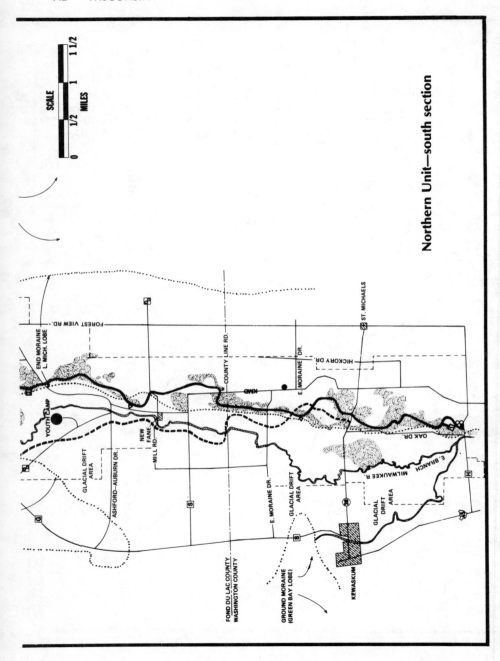

Northern Unit—south section

KETTLE MORAINE STATE FOREST, NORTHERN UNIT

Location: This long narrow unit of the state forest stretches from just east of Kewaskum in Washington County north to the ski hills of the Greenbush winter sports area. Major developed recreation areas for the forest are on the shores of Long Lake and in the Mauthe Lake area.

To reach the southern end of the trail, drive south from Kewaskum on U.S. 45 for 1.8 miles to Washington County H. Turn east on H for 1.5 miles to a parking area on Kettle Moraine Drive at the trail head.

Access to the northernmost point of the trail (recently extended) is on Highway T a quarter mile south of the village of Greenbush. The former northern trail terminus—and still a good access point—is 4 miles south of the town at the Greenbush winter sports area. Take County T to Kettle Moraine Drive and follow it south 1.3 miles to the ski area.

Length: 29 miles.

U.S.G.S. Quads: Dundee, St. Cloud, Cascade, and Elkhart Lake; all 7.5 minutes.

Description: Some of the state's most extreme glacial topography is found along the Ice Age Trail in this state forest. Two great lobes of ice jostled each other here, and the glacial hills are steep and high. Between them are marshes and lakes large and small.

Special scenic attractions include the Parnell Esker, a sinuous ridge formed by a river that once flowed under the ice; rounded hills called "kames," which look like inverted salad bowls (or on topographic maps like a series of circles so perfect in shape you'd swear they couldn't occur in nature); numerous kettlehole depressions, some of them containing small lakes; and the series of elongated hills known to geologists as the Campbellsport Drumlins.

The trail is marked with blue blazes. Five three-sided Adirondack-type trail shelters are scattered along the route; reservations are required to use them. The trail passes through hardwood forests in which northern red oak is the most common species. Basswood, sugar maple, shagbark hickory, white oak, and red maple are also common. Tamaracks are the most common naturally occurring conifers, but red pine, white pine, and white spruce trees have been planted on the forest over the last 30 years.

For more information, write Forest Supervisor, Kettle Moraine State Forest, Northern Unit, P. O. Box 426, Campbellsport, Wisconsin 53010.

KETTLE MORAINE STATE FOREST, SOUTHERN UNIT

Location: East of Whitewater, west of Milwaukee in Walworth and Waukesha counties. Access to the southern end of the trail is at the ranger station near the Whitewater Lake Campground. Drive southeast from Whitewater on U.S. 12 for 1.6 miles to Walworth County P. Follow P south 3.5 miles to Kettle Moraine Drive. Turn west on the drive to the Forest Ranger Contact Station.

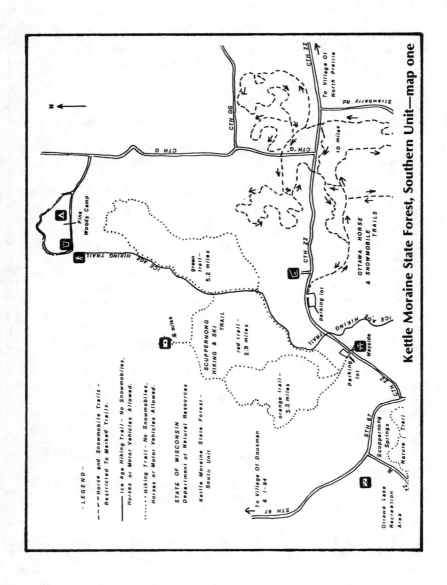

Kettle Moraine State Forest, Southern Unit—map one

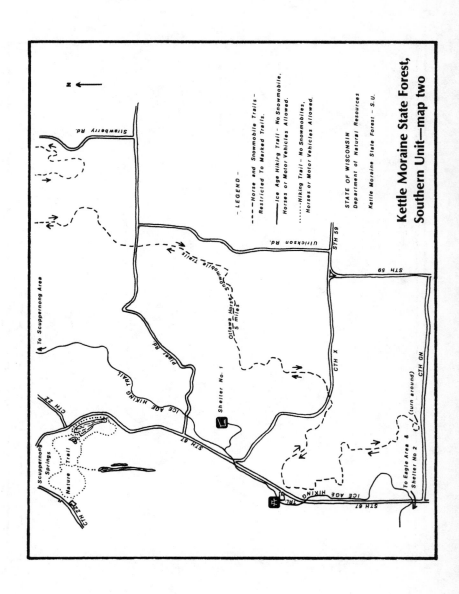

Kettle Moraine State Forest,
Southern Unit—map two

STATE OF WISCONSIN
Department of Natural Resources

Kettle Moraine State Forest – S.U.

– LEGEND –

––– Horse and Snowmobile Trails –
Restricted To Marked Trails.

——— Ice Age Hiking Trail – No Snowmobile,
Horses or Motor Vehicles Allowed.

······· Hiking Trail – No Snowmobiles,
Horses or Motor Vehicles Allowed.

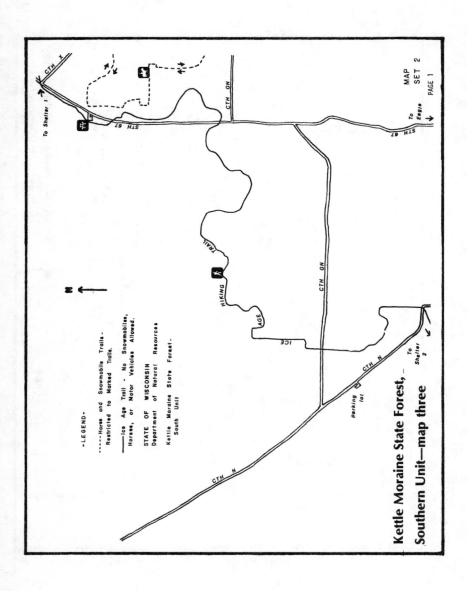

-LEGEND-

·····Horse and Snowmobile Trails -
Restricted to Marked Trails.

——Ice Age Trail - No Snowmobiles,
Horses, or Motor Vehicles Allowed.

STATE OF WISCONSIN
Department of Natural Resources

Kettle Moraine State Forest-
South Unit

**Kettle Moraine State Forest,-
Southern Unit—map three**

MAP SET 2

PAGE 1

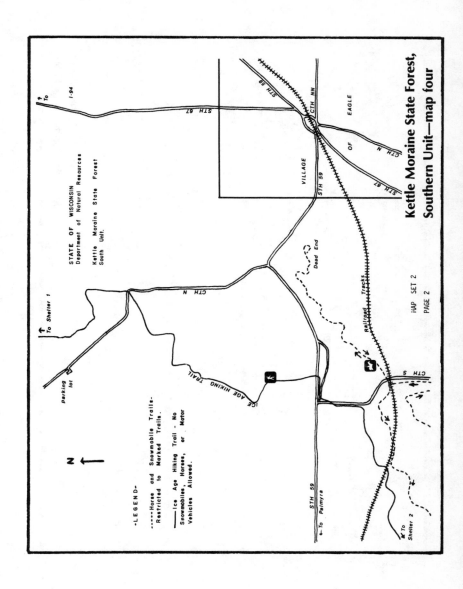

STATE OF WISCONSIN
Department of Natural Resources

Kettle Moraine State Forest
South Unit.

Kettle Moraine State Forest,
Southern Unit—map four

MAP SET 2
PAGE 2

-LEGEND-

----Horse and Snowmobile Trails-
Restricted to Marked Trails.

——Ice Age Hiking Trail - No
Snowmobiles, Horses, or Motor
Vehicles Allowed.

N

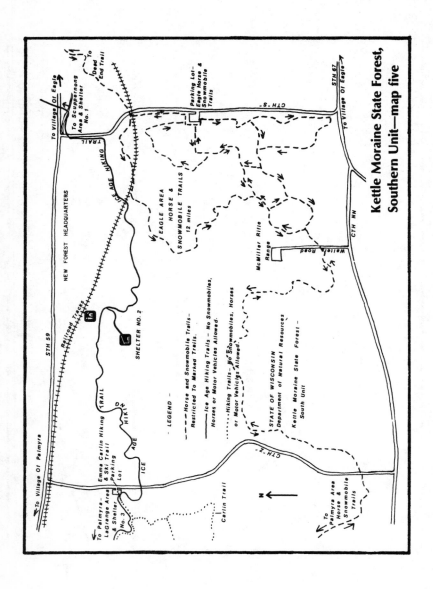

Kettle Moraine State Forest,
Southern Unit—map five

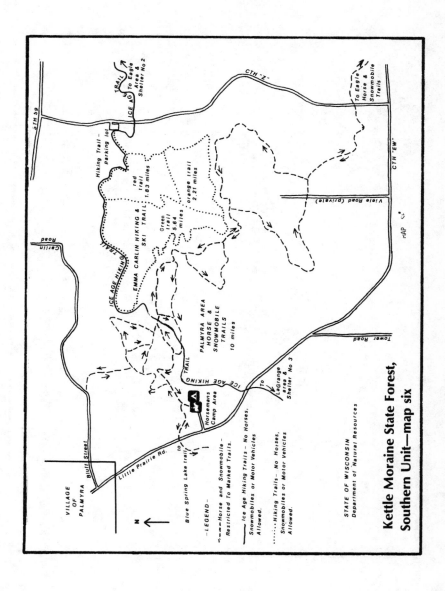

Kettle Moraine State Forest,
Southern Unit—map six

STATE OF WISCONSIN
Department of Natural Resources

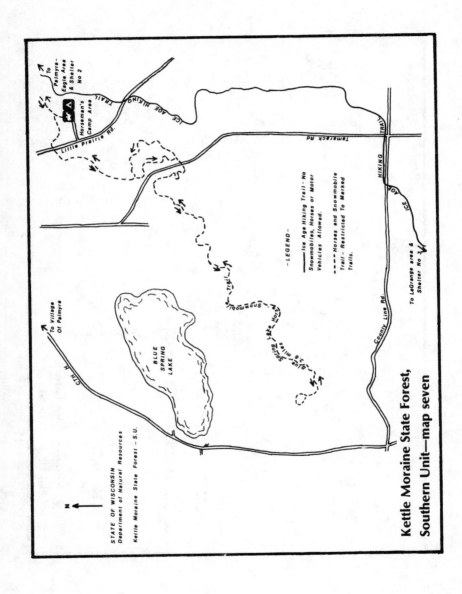

**Kettle Moraine State Forest,
Southern Unit—map seven**

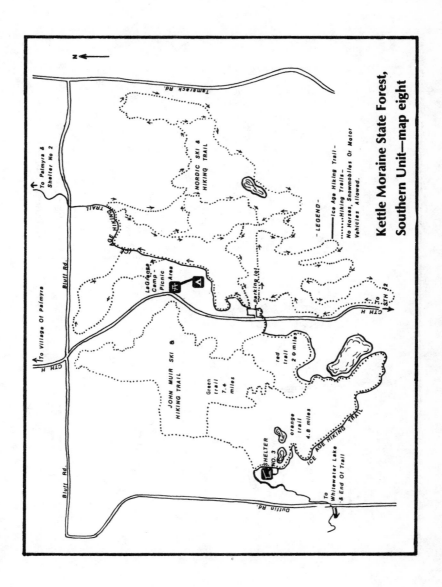

Kettle Moraine State Forest,
Southern Unit—map eight

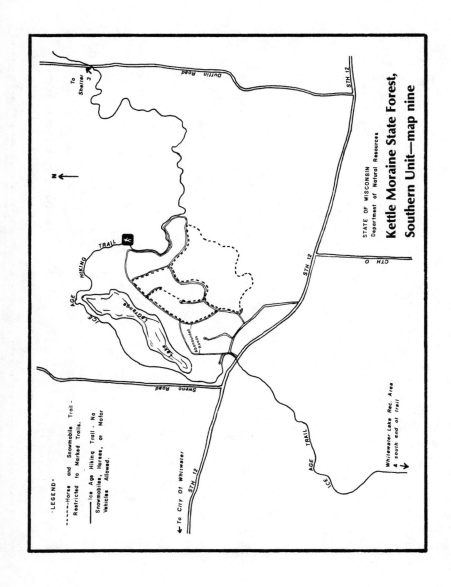

-LEGEND-

-----Horse and Snowmobile Trail - Restricted to Marked Trails.

——Ice Age Hiking Trail - No Snowmobiles, Horses, or Motor Vehicles Allowed.

STATE OF WISCONSIN
Department of Natural Resources

Kettle Moraine State Forest, Southern Unit—map nine

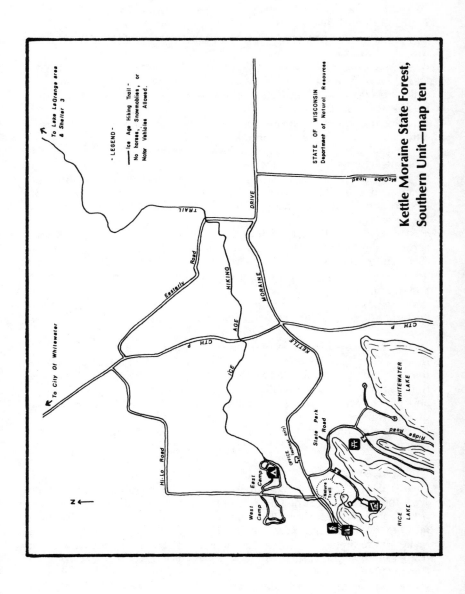

To Lake LaGrange area
& Shelter 3

- LEGEND -

Ice Age Hiking Trail -
No horses, Snowmobiles, or
Motor Vehicles Allowed.

STATE OF WISCONSIN
Department of Natural Resources

Kettle Moraine State Forest,
Southern Unit—map ten

McCabe Road

TRAIL

DRIVE

Easterly Road

HIKING

MORAINE

ICE AGE

KETTLE

CTH P

CTH P

To City Of Whitewater

WHITEWATER
LAKE

Hi-Lo Road

OFFICE
(summer only)

State Park Road

Nature
Trail

West
Camp

East
Camp

Ridge Road

RICE
LAKE

N

The north end of the trail is at the Pine Woods Family Campground. To reach it, take Wisconsin Highway 67 north from Eagle to County Z. Turn right (east) on Z to County G, then left (north) on G to a dirt lane where signs direct you west into the group camp.

Length: 25 miles.

U.S.G.S. Quads: Whitewater, Little Prairie, and Palmyra; all 7.5 minutes.

Description: The trail through this unit of the state forest is marked by yellow blazes with black dots in the center. Reservations are required to use any of the three Adirondack-type shelters along the trail. Hunters use the trail during fall deer season; check hunting season dates before you make autumn hiking plans.

The trail alternates between following the ridgelines of the glacial moraine to crossing flat, sandy outwash plains. Glacial features visible from the trail include knobs, kettles, kames, springs and a pond, an esker, and a postglacial lake bed. There are also outcroppings of the Niagara limestone that once divided the Green Bay ice lob from that of Lake Michigan.

Most of the trail route is forested, but there also are long sections across open fields. Posts have been inserted in the ground as blazes along these open field stretches. There are wet prairie wildflowers such as blue-eyed grasses and shooting star in some of the open areas; don't pick them, please.

White oaks, bur oaks, and pines prosper on the sandy outwash plains. Sugar maples and hickories become more common along the ridge slopes.

Two developed car campgrounds, in addition to the Adirondack shelters, lie along the trail route. La Grange Camp is just east of where the trail crosses County H. The Whitewater Lake Campground is at the trail's south end. There is also an equestrian camp, with water, toilets, and picnic facilities along the trail just north of Little Prairie Road east of Palmyra.

For more information and a map, write Forest Supervisor, Kettle Moraine, South Unit, Box 87, Eagle, Wisconsin 53119.

LANGLADE COUNTY

Location: The local hiking club that built and maintains the Ice Age Trail through this county has divided the trail into five segments for organizational purposes and for developing access points with parking facilities for one-day hikes. The sections are contiguous, however, and make for a single linear trail 56 miles long. To reach the west point from the town of Parrish, drive south on Wisconsin 17 to One Lake Road. Drive west on One Lake Road 1½ miles until pink blazes are visible on the right. Park along the road. The trail begins on the east side of the road.

The easternmost access of the trail in Langlade County is on Wiscon-

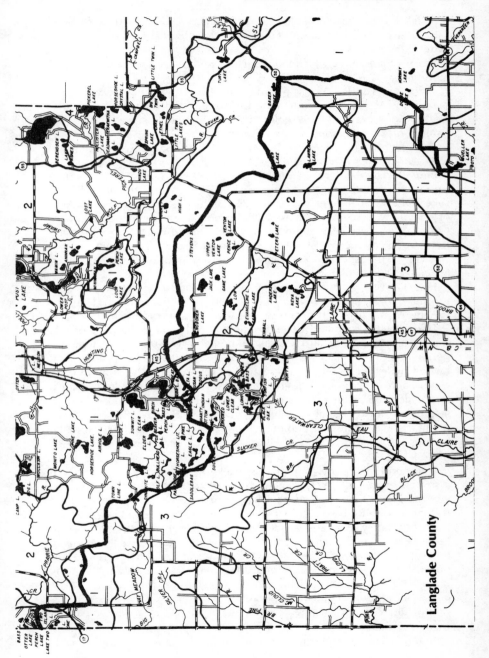

Langlade County

sin Highway 64 about 10 miles east of Antigo at Polar Road by Mueller Lake. There is a small parking area on the Mueller Lake access road.
Length: 56 miles.
U.S.G.S. Quads: Polar, Pickerel, Pearson, Kempster, and Bavaria; all 7.5 minutes.
Description: The Ice Age Trail in Langlade County is marked with pink blazes. Joe Jopek, the county extension agent and coordinator for trail work, said it was the only color they could find that wasn't used by county foresters for some other purposes.

The sections, as labeled by the local hiking clubs, are as follows (from west to east): Parrish Segment, 10.4 miles, Parrish to Townline Lake on County T; Highland Lakes Segment, 12.7 miles, County T at Townline Lake to a parking area in a field on U.S. 45 a mile north of Noboken Lake; Old Railroad Segment, 9.3 miles, Highway 45 east to the junction of County A and Squaw Creek Road; Lumber Camp Segment, 9.2 miles, County A to Wisconsin Highway 52 at Baker Lake Road across from the Kettlebowl commercial ski area; Kettlebowl Segment, 14.5 miles, Highway 52 at the ski area east and south to Wisconsin Highway 64 by Mueller Lake at Polar Road.

The Parrish Segment is relatively uninteresting, passing mainly through flat, sandy outwash plains, forested but with no lakes or streams of any size. Part of the route follows a snowmobile trail.

The adjacent Highland Lakes Segment, on the other hand, is one of the most attractive of all Ice Age segments in the state. Unfortunately, permission is still lacking to cross one small patch of private land owned by a hunting club. The section starts on outwash plain but soon climbs onto a terminal moraine and passes through a maple, hemlock, and yellow birch forest, interspersed with several white cedar swamps and featuring several perched lakes (a North Woods glacial phenomenon—lakes in kettlebowl depressions on top of wide flat hilltops). We had to climb uphill from the trail at several points to see these lakes.

Trail coordinator Joe Jopek is especially proud, almost gleeful, about a stretch of the trail in this section that is actually located on top of a very long beaver dam. The dam has to be seen to be believed; these rodents could not be outdone by any Army Corps of Engineers crew.

Unfortunately, camping is not encouraged along the route at present because of trail easement problems. The local hiking club also tends to think in terms of day hikes rather than longer trips; when a trail is just outside your back door you aren't interested in spending nights in the open. There is a somewhat messy group campsite on Alta Lake at the end of a road that is gated and therefore accessible only on foot.

The Old Railroad Segment east of U.S. 45 follows a railroad grade that is apparently also used by logging trucks or other vehicles; although somewhat muddy after rains, it has no grass growing over the ruts. This segment, like the Parrish Segment, runs mainly through flat and sometimes marshy country. A small side loop heads north around Stevens Springs, which empties into the Wolf River not far north of the trail.

The Lumber Camp Segment also follows an old railroad grade through country that is flat along the western half and grows gradually hilly as it approaches Baker Lake near Highway 52 and the Kettlebowl Ski Area. Snowmobile trails crisscross the area; one of them leads south about a quarter mile to an attractive woodland lake called Fischer Lake. It is easy to get confused and pick the wrong side trail, however. One advantage of staying on the railroad grade is that it's impossible to get lost.

The forest in this section is mainly aspen with some maple. There are white cedar stands in wet areas.

The Kettlebowl Segment of the trail vies with the Highland Lakes Segment for scenic beauty. There are few lakes—none right on the trail. But the terrain is hilly, even offering occasional vistas. The forest is mature sugar maple and other hardwoods, and the forest floor in many areas is quite open, with nothing but grasses and ferns to cover it. Much of this land is owned by a private timber firm, but camping is allowed.

Maps and up-to-date information on trail conditions and rerouting is available from Joe Jopek, County Extension Agent, P. O. Box 460, Antigo, Wisconsin 54409.

CHEQUAMEGON NATIONAL FOREST SECTION, TAYLOR COUNTY

Location: In the Medford district of Chequamegon National Forest. To reach the eastern terminus from the town of Chelsea on U.S. 13, take Forest Road 102 west 4 miles to Forest Road 101. Take Forest Road 101 north 1.5 miles to Forest Road 563.

To reach the western terminus, take County F from Lublin 3.6 miles north to Wisconsin 64. Turn east on 64 for 3 miles to the junction with Forest Road 119. Take 119 north 3.2 miles to the trail crossing, about 100 yards north of the intersection of roads 119 and 554.

Length: 41 miles.

U.S.G.S. Quads: Westboro, Mondeaux Dam, Perkinstown, Lublin Northwest, and Lublin; all 7.5 minutes.

Description: Because this trail follows the terminal moraine—rocky hills deposited on the landscape by a glacier some 12,000 years ago—along most of its route, it offers something unusual in North Woods scenery—hilltop vistas. The trail is marked by yellow diamond-shaped plastic blazes.

The easternmost section, which leads to and around a manmade lake called the Mondeaux Flowage, features flat-topped hills that geologists call "perched lake plains." Other glacial features include small kettle

Chequamegon National Forest Section, Taylor County—west section

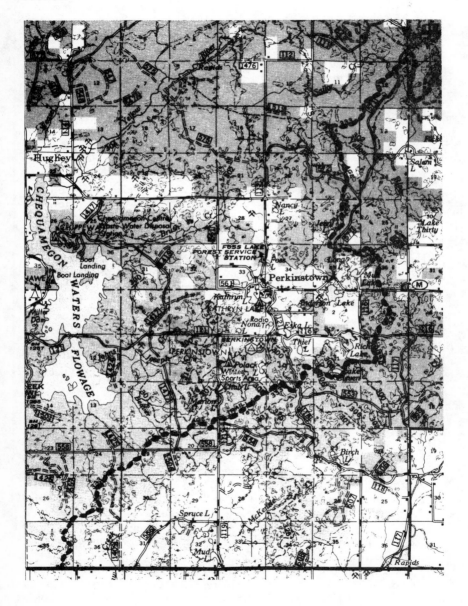

Chequamegon National Forest Section, Taylor County—east section

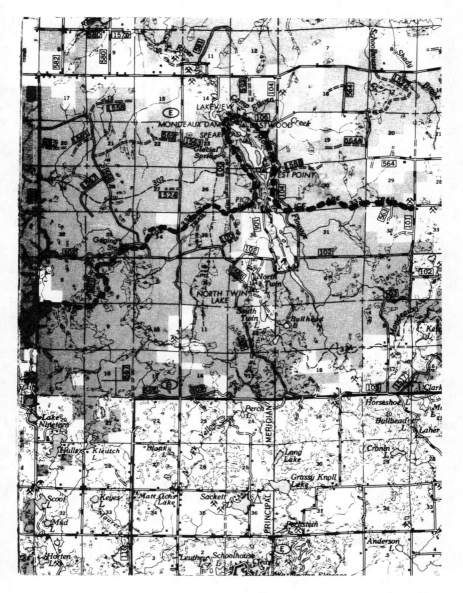

holes (depressions that sometimes contain lakes), and forest-covered kames and knobs. Unusually numerous in the area are "crevasse-fill" ridges, whose hogsback characteristics make for curious vistas and plenty of up-and-down hiking.

The forest on the high sandy kames and knobs is mainly red, white, and jack pine; on the perched lake plains, it is mainly sugar maple and other hardwoods. There are also occasional hilltop marshes, a North Woods oddity that is an indication of how recently (in geological terms) the glacier passed this way.

There are four developed campgrounds along the trail route around Mondeaux Flowage where water and toilets are available. West of the flowage, the trail cuts through a younger forest of aspens and birches in the Yellow River area. There are more perched lake plains, kames, kettles, and knobs.

Car access points are at Forest Road 102 just south of Forest Road 568, and also at Forest Road 107 about 3½ miles south of County D.

Jerry Lake, 1.2 miles south of Forest Road 572, is an excellent backcountry campsite. The lake is 33 feet deep at its center and about 10 acres in area. Locals catch northern pike, bass, and sunfish there.

The trail crosses County M about 3 miles east of Perkinstown and continues south past Lake Eleven (another good camping area) and then west through hilly country that is mainly covered today with hardwood forest. You may notice the giant stumps of white pines that covered the area before heavy logging in the early 1900s.

The trail crosses numerous small streams, so there is no shortage of water. All of it (except water from the pumps at developed campgrounds) should be boiled before drinking. The trail ends at Wisconsin Highway 64.

Trail brochures and maps are available from the Medford District, Chequamegon National Forest, Box 150, 304 South Main, Medford, Wisconsin 54451.

RIB LAKE SECTION, TAYLOR COUNTY

Location: North and west of Rib Lake, through county forest lands in Taylor County. To reach the east end of the trail, drive north from Rib Lake 1.5 miles on a town road to an intersection. Turn left (west) .2 miles to the trail head sign on the south side of the road.

Access to the west end of the trail is from a wayside on Wisconsin 13 north of Chelsea (14 miles north of Medford).

Length: 5 miles.

U.S.G.S. Quads: Rib Lake, 15 minutes; Westboro, 7.5 minutes.

Description: This trail is short but perfect in its way. It is also so little used that one gets a greater sense of isolation than you would suspect on a trail of this length.

It starts uphill, crosses a power line clearing and then plunges into a

Rib Lake Section, Taylor County

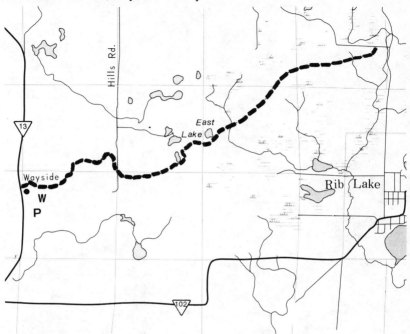

beautiful maple forest which continues unbroken for a least 3 miles. The terrain is hilly, but there are no steep grades to climb.

When we last hiked this trail about three years ago, there was a tricky log crossing over a stream that had been widened by beaver. The precarious balancing act was made worthwhile when we feasted our eyes on East Lake, a small secluded body of water banded by hemlocks and with cranberries ripening on its shores in September. This is probably the best natural campsite along the route unless you visit at the height of the mosquito season. There is an open field farther down the trail where the breezes can get at you to keep the bug population down.

The trail crosses Hills Road after about 3½ miles, then passes a second, smaller lake half a mile past East Lake before coming out on the aforementioned open field. It heads west for a mile to a dead-end town road which it follows north for about 50 yards before heading west again into the forest. The trail follows logging roads for brief segments along this section; keep an eye on the yellow blazes.

Just east of the wayside, the trail joins a marked nature trail.

The wayside has drinking water, toilets, and picnic tables.

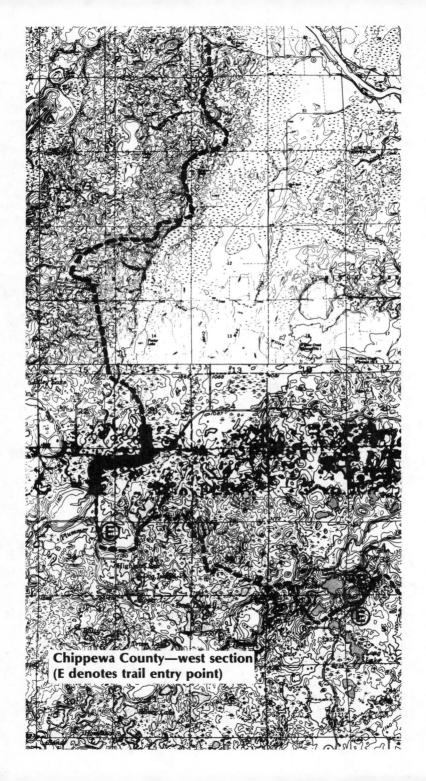

**Chippewa County—west section
(E denotes trail entry point)**

CHIPPEWA COUNTY

Location: The Ice Age Trail segment in this county begins at an orange gate on an old farm road off County CC directly across the Chipppewa River from Brunet Island State Park north of Cornell. It heads west through private and county forestlands to Plummer Lake, then north across the Rusk County line to end at old County Highway D south of the Fireside Lakes.

Length: 25 miles.

U.S.G.S. Quads: Cornell, 15 minutes; Bloomer, 15 minutes; Fireside Lakes, 7.5 minutes.

Description: The Chippewa Moraine hills left by the Wisconsinan glacier are not as high or as dramatic in appearance as those of the Kettle Moraine in southeastern Wisconsin. These were created while the ice remained still for long periods rather than when it moved. Some of the ridges here were formed when debris filled crevasses. Ice-walled lake plains, flat-topped areas formed by interglacial lakebeds, are peculiar to this area. There are also more small shallow kettles and swales alternating with knobs than in most sections of the state.

Chippewa County—east section

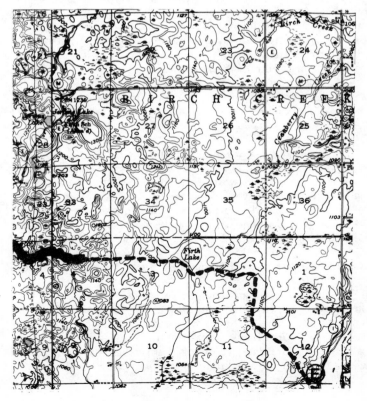

Some of the irregularity in the landscape features here in Chippewa County can be explained by the fact that the bedrock, acted on first by the glacier and later by wind and water, is unusually resistant, a hard quartzite.

The trail is marked with yellow blazes. Camping is allowed only on county forest lands.

The trail cuts cross-country on a single-lane brushed trail for part of the route, but it also uses logging roads, snowmobile and hunter trails, and even gravel county and township roads for short distances. It crosses Firth Lake on a beaver dam about 4 feet high and 100 feet long.

Most of the trail passes through hardwood forest, although it winds through a stand of large red pines along the Moon Ridge Trail, a gravel-surfaced county forest road that it follows for about half a mile. At one point it crosses a swamp on log corduroy.

Scenic attractions include Old Baldy Mountain, a kame that is a local landmark; more beaver dams; and numerous small kettlehole lakes. Most of the lakes have boggy edges, but some have clear sand or gravel bottoms and are ideal for swimming. The trail also crosses several creeks.

At Plummer Lake, the path turns sharply north, across County M and then a township road along the east side of Bradley Lake. It continues north past several more small lakes to end just across the county border in Rusk County at County Highway D 3 miles east of Wisconsin 40. (Old Highway D intersects Highway 40 about a mile south of Island Lake. It runs east and west just south of the Fireside Lakes.)

For up-to-date information (routes tend to change periodically), write to the Ice Age Trail chairperson for this area—Professor Adam Cahow, Box 222, Route 2, Eau Claire, Wisconsin 54701.

RUSK COUNTY

Location: This section of the Ice Age Trail begins on a town road $2\frac{1}{2}$ miles west of Weyerhauser and proceeds north, crossing Rusk County F (an alternate access point) just west of that road's junction with County O, angling northwest, then west along the south side of the Murphy Flowage. The trail proceeds north from the flowage to Wisconsin Highway 48 east of Red Cedar Lake $1\frac{1}{2}$ miles west of Birchwood. The trail connects here with the Tuscobia Trail (see separate listing).
Length: 27 miles.
U.S.G.S. Quads: Weyerhauser, 7.5 minutes; Bucks Lake, 7.5 minutes; Rice Lake, 15 minutes.
Description: More than perhaps any other section of the Ice Age Trail in Wisconsin, this trail through the Blue Hills has an air of real wilderness about it. There is one 9-mile stretch and another 7-mile stretch in the Rusk County Forest where the trail crosses no roads.

There are hardwood ridges, some of them eskers (sinuous ridges formed where rivers once flowed under the glacier); scattered stands of

Rusk County—north section (E denotes trail entry point)

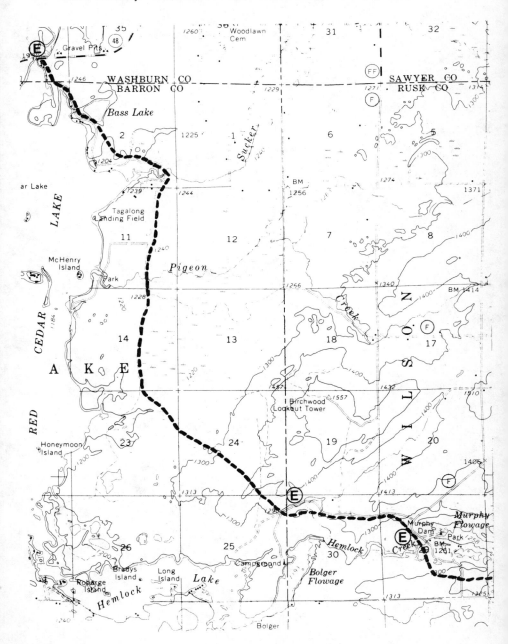

Rusk County—central section

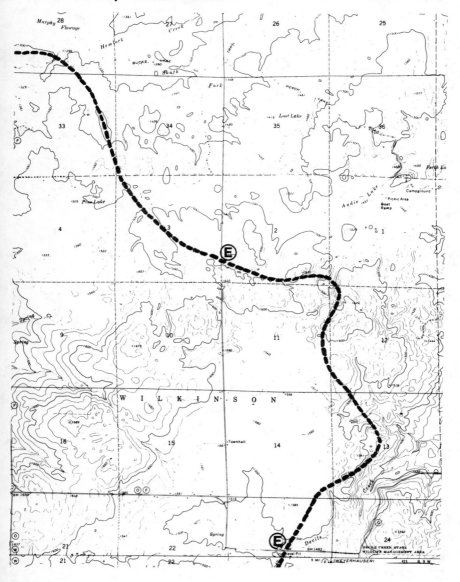

Rusk County—south section

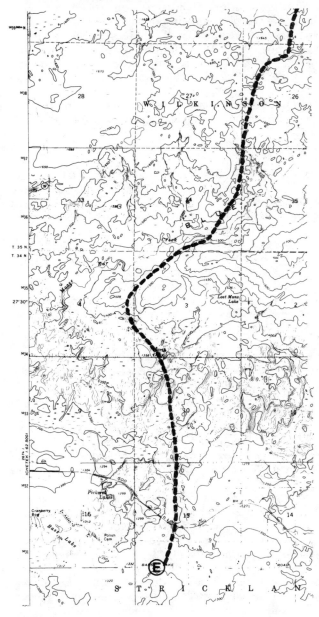

hemlocks, balsam fir, and spruce; and small lakes so remote you could swear no one had ever laid eyes on them before you arrived.

Yellow blazes mark the trail at frequent intervals. Backcountry camping is allowed only on county forest lands. There are also developed campgrounds at Murphy Dam Park on the Murphy Flowage and another at nearby Perch Lake (take Bucks Lake Road east from the trail at the Murphy Flowage for 1½ miles, then turn right on Perch Lake Road for 2 miles).

For up-to-date information, contact the Ice Age Trail chairperson for northwestern Wisconsin—Professor Adam Cahow, Box 222, Route 2, Eau Claire, Wisconsin 54701.

TUSCOBIA TRAIL

Location: The Tuscobia Trail is another of the state-maintained trails that follows an old railroad bed. It runs from Park Falls on State Route 13 in northern Wisconsin (about 50 miles south of Lake Superior) west on a meandering line cross-country to Tuscobia, a tiny hamlet 4 miles north of Rice Lake on State Route 53.

Length: 74 miles. Most of the trail's eastern half, however, runs adjacent to, or very near, county highways E and EE and State Highway 70. So hikers can arrange a walk of any length they choose.

U.S.G.S. Quads: Rice Lake, 15 minutes; Edgewater, 7.5 minutes; Couderay, 7.5 minutes; Radisson, 7.5 minutes; Winter, 7.5 minutes; Lake Winter, 7.5 minutes; Blaisdell Lake, 7.5 minutes; Loretta, 7.5 minutes; Kennedy, 7.5 minutes; Butternut Lake, 7.5 minutes; Park Falls, 15 minutes.

Description: The western part of the trail contains the most spectacular scenery, since you will be passing through the Meteor Hills country. The elevation is more than 1,800 feet, almost as high as it gets in Wisconsin, but since the trail does follow an old railroad bed you will not encounter grades steeper than five to six percent.

About 2 miles from the western end of the trail you will cross Tuscobia Creek; if the weather is dry, you might miss it. Two miles farther on, however, you may have to detour a few hundred feet to the north and cross the Brill River on a highway bridge of a town road leading into the village of Brill.

From Brill the trail angles northeastward toward State Highway 48 and the town of Angus. Shortly after passing through Angus you will detour again, this time to a highway bridge on 48, to get across a narrow stream of water connecting Balsam and Red Cedar Lakes. The next small town is Birchwood; it's approximately 7½ miles between Brill and Birchwood.

After Birchwood there are no more detours for 17 miles. The few streams that cross your path will be easily fordable—Malviney Creek, 33 Creek, Knuteson Creek just past the town of Yarnell, and Swift Creek at

Tuscobia Trail

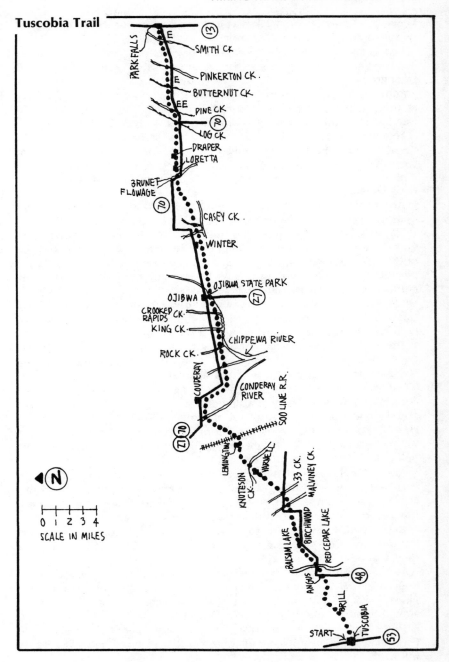

Lemington. This segment takes you through some of the wildest, most remote land in northern Wisconsin.

Just before reaching the town of Couderay, you will have to detour south on town roads to avoid having to swim the Couderay River and Eddy Creek.

Some day, officials hope to build bridges on the trail itself. They recently completed culverts but Wes Johnson, the forest ranger in charge of the trail, says a single bridge can cost up to $30,000.

The trail parallels state highways 27 and 70 for 5 miles between Couderay and the town of Radisson (named for the first white man to visit the area—in 1659). Rock Creek crosses the trail just before Radisson, but since you are immediately adjacent to the highway there is no inconvenience.

At Radisson you will have to hike Highway 70 east 2 miles to a town road, then south a half mile to intersect the trail again.

Six miles east of Radisson is the town of Ojibwa, another—you guessed it—detour across the Chippewa River highway bridge, and the only authorized campground you will encounter along the trail ($2.25 per night). Camping is allowed anywhere beside the trail for your other nights out, but rangers caution hikers to leave each site as they found it when leaving in the morning. Carry out empty all containers you carried in full. Campfires are allowed but small stoves are preferred (and Primus stoves are lighter in weight than axes anyway).

The six-unit Ojibwa Campground is a mile east of the town. Toilets and drinking water are available (for drinking along the trail take Halazone tablets for purification, if available).

The trail runs adjacent to Highway 70 again for the 5 miles between Ojibwa and Winter. There is a ranger station at Winter, and the ranger there is the man in charge of maintaining the trail. You might want to consult him about current conditions on the trail ahead of you. At Winter you will be hiking right on the highway for about three quarters of a mile.

About 2 miles east of Winter you will encounter the Brunet River, an excellent place to fish for walleye, as are many of the streams in this area. To get around the river, take Highway 70 north a quarter mile to a town road, then walk a half mile east to intersect the trail again.

After about 7 more miles you will cross Fly Blow Creek (small detour), and then come upon the twin towns of Loretta and Draper, a mile apart.

The last stretch of the trail, 19½ miles between Draper and Park Falls, is occasionally marshy and crisscrossed with creeks—Thornapple, Log, Pine, and Butternut. So for most of this distance, it is best just to walk along the edge of county highways EE and E.

When you encounter a private property sign about 2 miles west of Park Falls, take the town road there north to County Highway B and follow that on in to town.

MARATHON COUNTY

Location: The local hiking club that maintains the Ice Age Trail in this county has divided it into five connecting segments, each of which can be hiked in a day. The south end of the southernmost segment is on County Highway C about 7¾ miles east of Knowlton. The north end of the northernmost segment is at the Eau Claire Dells County Park, 13 miles east of Wausau on County Z, then a mile north on County Y.
Length: 35 miles.
U.S.G.S. Quads: Dewey Marsh, 7.5 minutes; Wausau, 15 minutes; Hatley, 15 minutes; Hogarty, 7.5 minutes.
Description: The trail is marked with yellow blazes. It passes through more or less flat glacial outwash plains on county forestlands in the Leathercamp, Kronenwetter, and Ringle Marsh sections. It climbs into hilly country on a moraine through the Plover River and Eau Claire Dells segments. Camping is theoretically allowed anywhere in a county forest, but you may have difficulty finding a suitably large high and dry spot in the three southernmost sections. There is a developed campground at Eau Claire Dells County Park.

Here are brief descriptions, including access points, of the five sections. Maps and a detailed brochure are available from the Plover River Chapter of the Ice Age Trail Council, c/o Stanley Presley, 322½ North 5th Avenue, Wausau, Wisconsin 54401.

Leathercamp Segment (7½ miles). Southernmost access is at a parking area on County C about 7¾ miles east of Knowlton. Northernmost access is on Wisconsin 153 about 9.5 miles east of U.S. 51. The trail in this section crosses a beaver dam, a recently logged area growing up in shrubs and young aspens, and several larger stands of aspen and white birch trees. It passes through hardwood forests along the edges of tag alder and tamarack swamps, and into a stand of large hemlocks on the east bank of the Little Eau Claire River.

Kronenwetter Segment (7¾ miles). Southernmost access is on Wisconsin 153, 9½ miles east of U.S. 51. A midway access is on Martin Brothers Road a mile west of County J (about 4 miles south of Wisconsin 29), and the northernmost access is on West Town Line Road a half mile east of Highway J (about 3 miles south of Wisconsin 29). The trail continues through flat country on county forestlands in this section; parts of it, in fact, are underwater in spring. Hikers are encouraged to avoid it until midsummer; autumn is even better. The forest is mainly aspen and birch in this section, with tag alder in the wet areas. The trail follows logging roads for part of the distance. There are usually bridges across the creeks and in some of the swampy areas. There are toilet facilities at the parking area on Martin Brothers Road.

Ringle Marsh Segment (7½ miles). To reach the south end of this section, take County J south 3 miles from Wisconsin 29, then a half mile east on West Town Line Road to a parking area. The north end is off a road called Second Avenue, just north of that road's intersection with

Marathon County—south section

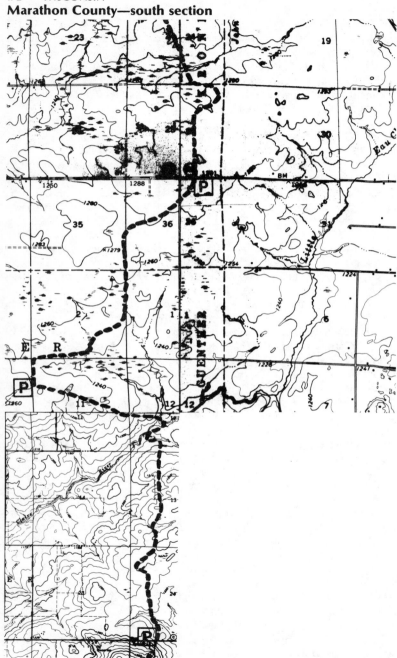

Marathon County—west-central section

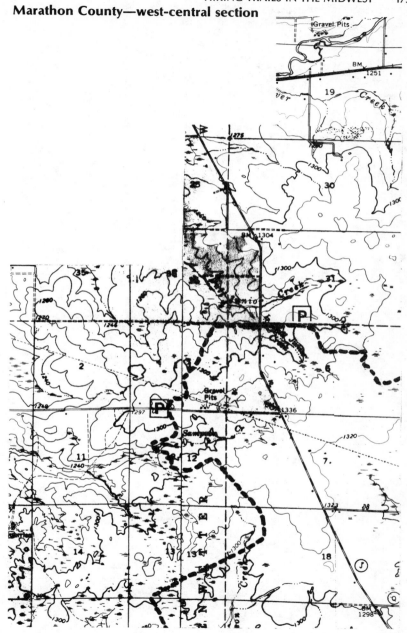

Marathon County—east-central section

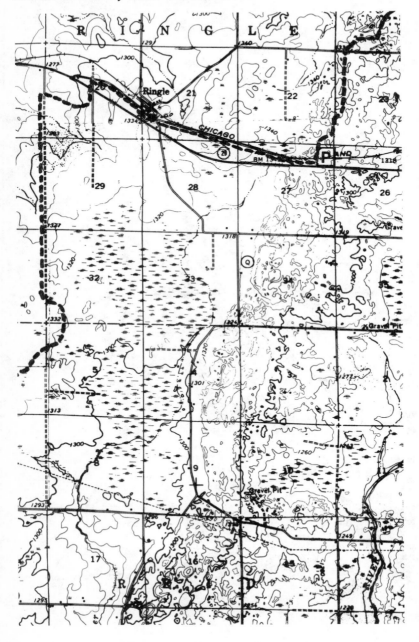

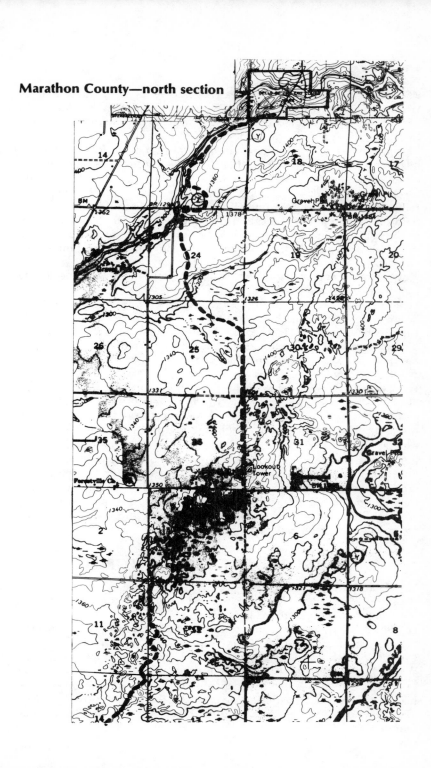

Wisconsin 29 about 1½ miles east of Ringle or 10½ miles east of Wausau. The yellow paint blazes in this section follow logging roads part of the time and also cut cross-country through mature hardwood forest stands and a few hummocky wet forest areas containing balsam fir and birches. The trail crosses an open meadow and follows the east edge of a large open marsh. Then it passes through a small stand of pines, and by some abandoned farm buildings, a cutover area, and several sections of young aspen and birch woods. Large stumps are reminders of the giant white pine forests that occupied the region before heavy lumbering at the turn of the century. The trail also passes through the town of Ringle; this may be the only section of the Ice Age Trail anywhere in the state in which you can buy hot sandwiches and pizza at trailside.

Plover River Segment (6 miles). Southernmost access is at the Ringle trail head on Second Avenue. Northern access is on Marathon County N at its junction with Helf Road. The trail in this section threads hardwood clad glacial ridges, mainly on land owned by the Wausau Paper Mills Company. Tree cover includes basswood and sugar maple, birches and aspens, white spruce and red pine. There are also open meadows and a few recently logged areas. Long stretches of this segment follow logging roads.

Eau Claire Dells Segment (5¾ miles). Southernmost access is on County N. Northern end of the trail is at Eau Claire Dells County Park, 13 miles east of Wausau on County Z, then a mile north on County Y. Topography on this section is rolling hills, mostly forested in hardwoods and especially attractive in autumn. There also are scattered stands of hemlock and clumps of alder bushes where the trail skirts wet areas. The trail follows the banks of the Eau Claire River for a brief period, then climbs north and east across a meadow. The trail connects with a trail system in Eau Claire Dells County Park at a stone shelter. The yellow blazes end at this point, and hikers have the choice of several routes leading to the park campground.

TRAILS IN BLACK RIVER STATE FOREST

SKI TRAIL LOOP

Location: Four miles east of Millston on County O, then left (north) a mile on Smrekor Road to a parking area.

Length: 8-mile loop with cutoff trails that make a network of 14 miles.

U.S.G.S. Quad: Millston, 15 minutes.

Description: This trail system was designed primarily for cross-country skiers, but because it is on high ground the single lane trail does effective double duty (and is maintained as such) as a warm-weather hiking trail. No motor vehicles are allowed; the terrain is steep enough and the curves sharp enough that trail bikers are not likely even to be tempted.

Black River State Forest (west trail is Snowmobile Loop, east trail is Ski Trail Loop)

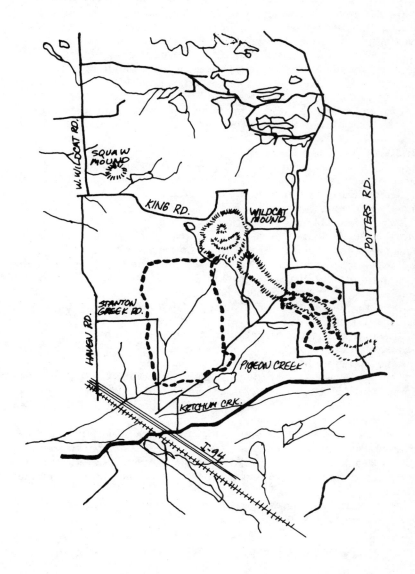

The forest consists mainly of oaks and jack pines. There are views of the surrounding countryside from several open areas on ridge tops. There is a shelter and a pump at roughly the halfway point on the 8-mile outer loop. (Shorter trails cut across the loop at two points.)

Camping is allowed at the shelter or anywhere along the trail. Cross-country hiking off-trail is also permitted.

Hikers are asked to used only downed wood for campfires and to refrain from building fires during periods of especially dry weather.

The trail is marked with square wooden signs featuring a stylized drawing of a skier.

For maps and more information, write Black River State Forest, Route 4, Box 5, Black River Falls, Wisconsin 54615.

SNOWMOBILE TRAIL LOOP

Location: The trail begins at the Pigeon Creek Campground in Black River State Forest. Take U.S. 12 northeast from Millston to North Settlement Road. Turn right to the campground.

Length: A 12-mile loop.

U.S.G.S. Quad: Millston, 15 minutes.

Description: Although there are more than 40 miles of snowmobile trails in this forest, this is the only one considered suitable for hiking as well. The main reason is that, unlike the others, this is on high ground—mostly on flat sandy ground covered with oak and jack pine. It also follows a trail rather than roads.

The path crosses several small streams, but all water should be boiled before drinking.

The loop is shaped roughly like a rectangle, with Pigeon Creek Campground at its southeast corner and a small lake called Wildcat Flowage at the northeast corner.

From the flowage, it heads west and then south, crossing Stanton Creek Road twice (once on a bridge over Glen Creek) on its way back to North Settlement Road, which it follows for about a quarter mile east to the campground.

The trail is marked with orange diamond-shaped signs and, at road crossings, with the silhouette of a snowmobile. (Remember to take the left fork and head west from Wildcat Flowage, however. Another snowmobile trail, with the same marker, continues north from the flowage.)

For maps and brochures, write Black River State Forest, Route 4, Box 5, Black River Falls, Wisconsin 54615.

TRAILS IN NORTHERN HIGHLAND STATE FOREST

This state forest, which covers a big part of Vilas, Oneida, and Iron counties in northern Wisconsin, contains more wild public land (182,000 acres—most of the parcels contiguous) than several of the national

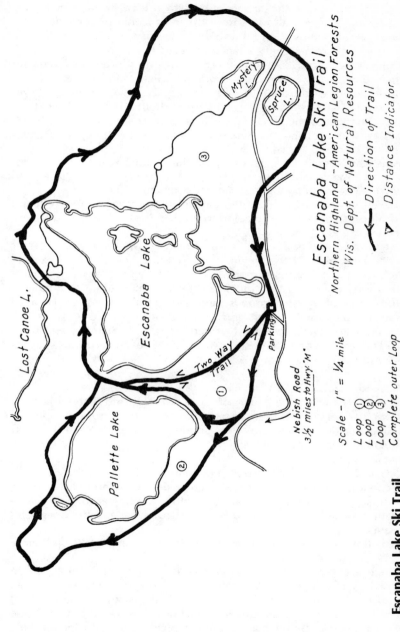

Escanaba Lake Ski Trail
Northern Highland - American Legion Forests
Wis. Dept. of Natural Resources

Direction of Trail
Distance Indicator

Scale - 1" = ¼ mile

Loop ①
Loop ②
Loop ③
Complete outer Loop

Nebish Road
3½ miles to Hwy. "M"

Mystery L.
Spruce L.
Escanaba Lake
Lost Canoe L.
Pallette Lake
Two Way Trail
parking

Escanaba Lake Ski Trail

forests in our region. The land—dotted with at least 200 birch-bordered clear natural lakes—is also in one of the most scenic areas of the North Woods. It was known and loved by fishermen long before hikers, canoeists, and cross-country skiers discovered it.

The northern and southern units of the forest were two separate forests until a few years ago. Northern Highland State Forest was established in Vilas County in 1911 to protect the watersheds of two rivers—the Flambeau and the Wisconsin—both of which have their headwaters within the forest boundaries. Now the northern and by far the biggest unit of the combined state forest, it contains 140,000 acres of public land and 150 lakes.

American Legion State Forest, now the southern unit of Northern Highland, was established in 1929 from cutover land the state had gradually been purchasing from timber companies since 1907.

Aspen and paper birch are the most common trees. White, red, and jack pines, sugar and red maple, northern red oak, black spruce, and tamarack are also typical.

We have chosen to describe a few of the trails we think work best for backpacking trips. There are many more snowmobile trails (many of them on roads), several more interconnecting networks of cross-country ski trails (most of them less than 5 miles long), self-guiding nature trails near campgrounds, and, of course, fire lanes. Detailed maps and brochures (which also describe canoe and other primitive campsites) are available from Northern Highlands State Forest, Trout Lake Forestry Headquarters, Route 1, Box 45, Boulder Junction, Wisconsin 54512.

ESCANABA LAKE SKI TRAIL

Location: In the northern unit of Northern Highland State Forest. To reach a parking area at the trail head, proceed south from the town of Boulder Junction about 3 miles on County M to Nebish Road. Turn left and continue east about 3½ miles.

Length: 7½ miles.

U.S.G.S. Quad: Boulder Junction, 15 minutes.

Description: Designed for cross-country skiers of intermediate ability, this trail passes through rolling hill country, winding around two large and three small lakes and through forests of sugar maple, aspen, and balsam.

A cutoff trail passes between Pallette and Escanaba lakes for those hikers who prefer shorter trips.

There are picnic tables and beaches at several canoe campsites on the shores of Pallette and Escanaba lakes. Canoeists may have reserved these in advance. It's worth checking with the forest headquarters at Trout Lake before you start to find out if you can camp at one. These are incredibly beautiful places, even if picnic tables do look a little strange on a backpacking trip.

McNaughton Lake Ski Trail

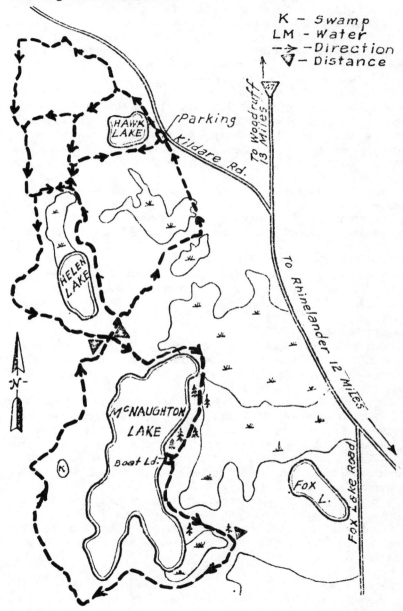

K – Swamp
LM - Water
–→ –Direction
▽– Distance

MCNAUGHTON LAKE SKI TRAIL

Location: In the southern unit of Northern Highland State Forest. The trail head is at a parking area on Kildare Road west of Wisconsin Route 47, 12 miles north of Rhinelander (13 miles south of Woodruff).

Length: The network for skiers totals more than 7 miles, but that includes several short cutoff trails. The two outer loops that form the frame for the network total about 6 miles.

U.S.G.S. Quads: Minocqua, Heafford Junction; both 15 minutes.

Description: Most of this trail follows old logging roads, but the scenery is nonetheless attractive enough to make it a worthwhile weekend trip. The path winds through a variety of timber types and around three lakes. Lake Helen, in the middle, is accessible only on foot. McNaughton Lake, biggest of the three, has a boat landing on its east shore.

The only tricky part of the trail for summer travelers is a boggy section west of McNaughton Lake. Ask for advice (and information about recent weather) from the ranger station in Woodruff or the Department of Natural Resources district headquarters in Rhinelander.

NORTHERN HIGHLAND TRAIL

Location: In the northern unit of Northern Highland State Forest. Trail heads with parking are on County M just south of Boulder Junction, on County N, and on Wisconsin 70 about a mile east of Little Arbor Vitae Lake.

Length: 40 miles.

U.S.G.S. Quad: Minocqua, 15 minutes.

Description: This is basically a snowmobile trail, and much of it follows roads; we encountered a *truck* near the southern end in an area being logged in the summer of 1979.

The most attractive stretch for backpackers begins at a parking area on County N just north of Lake Little John Jr. and heads south to a road crossing just south of Benedict Lake. The distance is about 12 miles.

This segment passes by seven small lakes and includes a side trail east to Fallison Lake. The forest of old sugar maples and basswoods is especially attractive when the leaves start to change color in late September.

A loop of about 25 miles (including the segment described above) can be made of the southern portion of this snowmobile trail.

A map with a rough outline of the trail is available from the Trout Lake office of the Northern Highland Forest, Route 1, Box 45, Boulder Junction, Wisconsin 54512.

LAKELAND TRAIL

Location: Southern unit of Northern Highland State Forest. An access point with parking lot is 4.5 miles south of Woodruff at the junction of Wisconsin Highway 47 and Fish Hatchery Road.

Northern Highland Trail

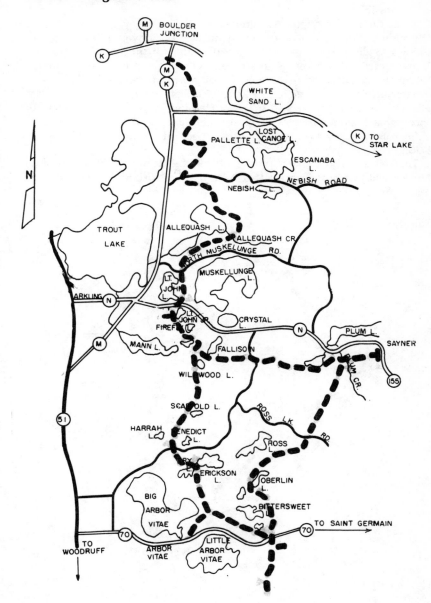

Length: 18.2 miles with a cutoff trail, making a shorter loop of 14.5 miles possible.

U.S.G.S. Quad: Minocqua, 15 minutes.

Description: Because it is designed mainly for snowmobiles, this trail follows logging roads and old railroad grades for much of its distance. Least attractive for hikers is an area of recent logging from just south of the main entrance and parking lot to just north of Three Little Lakes.

Most attractive is a section of about 6 miles that heads east from Fish Hatchery Road on the north shore of Hemlock Lake (through a mature forest that includes hemlocks), past Clear Lake, then south on the east shore of Sweeney Lake to an access road off County E by Sureshot Lake.

There is a heron rookery not far off the trail at one point. Great blue herons will not nest in areas that have been disturbed (or even visited

Lakeland Trail

too often by overeager birders). If you stumble on this rookery by accident, *leave it alone.*

The trail passes through a boggy area south of Hasbrook Lake. It is passable—with slight rerouting—in summer, but if the weather has been unusually wet just before your trip, consult with the district ranger office in Woodruff or at Trout Lake near Boulder Junction.

ST. CROIX RIVER TRAIL

Location: In St. Croix River State Forest, adjacent to the St. Croix National Scenic Riverway in Burnett and Polk counties. To reach the north end of the trail, take Wisconsin 70 west from Grantsburg to the trail head on the east side of the St. Croix River. The south end, inaccessible by car, is at an old ferry crossing where the Sunrise River empties into the St. Croix from the Minnesota side.

Length: 22 miles.

U.S.G.S. Quads: Rush City, Pine City; both 15 minutes.

Description: This trail follows the east bank of the St. Croix River. The entire stretch is forested, although the view across the river in Minnesota is often of farmlands. The south section of the trail is on flat ground, partly along a rocky beach, although it moves inland to skirt a few marshy areas.

Just south of a mid-point access on County O the path climbs to bluffs above the river. Between County O and Highway 70 the trail follows roads for short distances. It also passes by an old Indian cemetery.

A short piece of the trail where Wood River flows into the St. Croix was not completed in the fall of 1979; hikers detoured briefly by road. An extension was also planned to continue north of Highway 70.

For up-to-date information, write St. Croix River State Forest, Box 367, Grantsburg, Wisconsin 54840.

ROCK ISLAND STATE PARK

Location: Rock Island State Park is a 900-acre wooded island at the northernmost tip of the Door County peninsula that makes up the eastern shore of Lake Michigan's Green Bay.

The peninsula is accessible by two state highways, 57 from Green Bay and 42 from Manitowoc. The park, which allows no motorized vehicles, is accessible by two pedestrian ferries, operated privately with contracts from the state. One ferry leaves twice daily (at 10 A.M. and 2 P.M.) during the summer from the mainland port of Gills Rock. The other leaves hourly between 9 A.M. and 4 P.M. during July and August from Washington Island's Jackson Harbor (see map). In spring and fall (June 1 to July 1 and September 4 to October 15) the ferry from Washington Island to Rock Island leaves at 10 A.M., noon, 2 P.M., and 4 P.M.

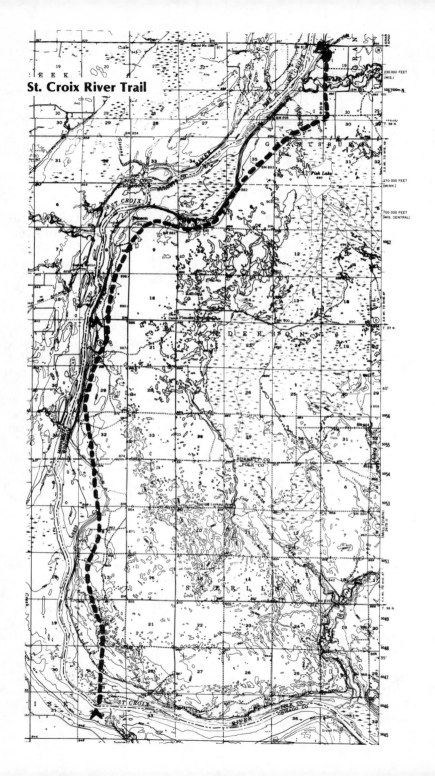

St. Croix River Trail

Rock Island State Park

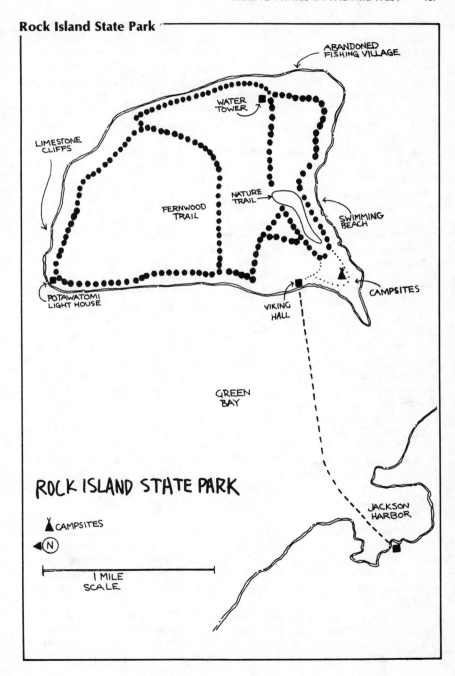

Washington Island lies between the mainland and Rock Island and is definitely worth a visit by itself (see following description). If you go that route, however, you must take an extra ferry. A fleet of three car ferries runs frequently in July and August between Gills Rock and Washington Island (every half hour when traffic is heavy). In spring and fall the gaps in service can sometimes be up to two hours, and from December through March the boats run only twice daily. But if you want to visit Rock Island in the winter, you have to rent a snowmobile or trudge across the ice.

Length: Approximately 8 miles of interconnecting trails.

U.S.G.S. Quad: Washington Island, 15 minutes.

Description: The trails in this state park are ideal for beginners or for hikers shaking down new equipment. The terrain is varied, but there is no steep climbing. Trail surfaces are well maintained (no jagged rocks or potholes), and we have never encountered more than a dozen mosquitoes even in the wettest springs and summers. There is only one campground, from which all the trails are easily accessible, so day hikes are in order and there is no need to carry more than a picnic lunch unless you are testing a new backpack.

The campground is located on the southwest side of the island; there are 40 sites, most of them on the shore but some inland as well. All are far enough apart to ensure privacy. Pit toilets, picnic tables, fireplaces, and firewood are available. Drinking water is available at a faucet near the dock. There is an electric generator on the island, so there is no need to pump the water up by hand. Fees for camping are $2.25 a night per site, and check-out time is 3 P.M. A state park ranger lives permanently on the island and is available at all times for information, advice or aid.

The main trail, which takes about 3 hours to hike at a leisurely pace, skirts the edge of the island all the way around it. Two more trails cut across the interior from east to west. To understand some of the things you will see on these trails, it help to know a little of the island's history.

It was settled first by Potawatomie Indians and later visited by French explorers, trappers, and traders—among them Marquette, Joliet, Nicolet, and LaSalle.

Archeologists from Lawrence College in Appleton have developed several excavation sites adjacent to the trail on the southern shore of the island which reveal the location of one Indian village dating from the 16th century. They also have found remains of some storage buildings and defense ramparts thought to have been erected by LaSalle's men.

In 1836 the first lighthouse in the state of Wisconsin was built on Rock Island and named for the original Potawatomie settlers. Its interior is closed today to visitors, but the exterior is still in excellent condition. The beautifully landscaped grounds behind it and the panoramic view make it a perfect resting point on your trek around the island's periphery.

A brother of Daniel Boone, his two sons, and David Kennison, the last surviving member of the Boston Tea Party and a veteran of Bunker Hill, were among English residents of the early and mid-19th century.

A few Irish fishermen founded a village on the east coast in 1840, and the crumbling foundations of their cottages can be seen near the trail. Three cemeteries on the island, two with marked graves, date from this period.

It was 1870, however, before any sizable number of white settlers came to the area. In that year, a Dane named W. F. Wickman induced thousands of Icelanders to come to the United States. The majority came to Washington and Rock Islands, and to this day many of the names on the mailboxes of Washington Island indicate Icelandic ancestry.

In 1910, an Icelandic electric equipment inventor named Chester Thordarson bought the entire island for $5,735. He built a house and a gigantic assembly hall from native stone. The hall is open to visitors. It contains a fireplace engraved with Icelandic runes, a hearth suitable for mead drinking, and furniture designed and built by Thordarson himself from local trees. A collection of dried indigenous flora is usually on display in the hall as well.

The inventor cleared some 30 acres for settlement on the southwest side of the island, but the remaining 745 acres remained undisturbed during his 55 years of ownership. In 1965 he sold it to the state for a park.

There are quite large specimens of maple, birch, cottonwood, and other hardwoods on the island, as well as groves of red cedar and pine.

Meadows on the south and east sides adjacent to the circular trail abound in berries and wildflowers; the interior trails have more deep woods foliage, including a large collection of waist-high ferns. The island is a haven for herring gulls and swallows.

You are sure to want to stay at least a week once you are there, but if you do, you will have to make supply trips back over to Washington Island. Owners of the Karfi ferry charge $1.60 round trip for commuters, $2 for folks carrying camping gear.

Any hiking you do on Washington Island will have to be on public roads; there are no trails. A number of people live year-round on this 36-square-mile island, so if you get lonesome for civilization this is the nearest source of it. There are grocery stores, bars, a community center, post office, and a number of cottages and motels. There is also one public campground on the north shore at Schoolhouse Beach. Several festivals are scheduled on the island during the summer. We can heartily recommend the fish boils; two are held annually in July.

For up-to-date information, you can contact the Washington Island Tourist Bureau, Washington Island, Wisconsin 54246.

6

ONTARIO

THE BRUCE TRAIL

The Bruce Trail is a 430-mile footpath running along the Niagara Escarpment from the northern tip of the Bruce Peninsula—which divides the main body of Lake Huron from Georgian Bay—to Niagara Falls. The escarpment is one of the most persistent geological features in the world. It is formed of dolomite, an erosion-resistant limestone rich in magnesium, laid down during the Silurian Period more than 400 million years ago.

Niagaran dolomite forms some of the bedrock under Chicago, and from Milwaukee northward the escarpment begins to be obvious in the landscape. The Door County peninsula that divides Lake Michigan and Green Bay is part of the Niagara Escarpment. From there, the escarpment continues in a great arc around the northern end of Lake Michigan, through the islands of northern Lake Huron, and from there south through the Bruce Peninsula and across Ontario to Niagara Falls.

Along the route of the Bruce Trail, the escarpment is almost always a prominent feature of the landscape. It often forms steep cliffs and sometimes high promontories that rise several hundred feet above the surrounding country. Waterfalls are common.

The rugged terrain of the escarpment makes it a little island of wildness in even the most heavily populated areas, so the Bruce Trail can go right through the city of Hamilton on a woodland path.

However, the nature of the country around the trail changes consid-

The Bruce Trail

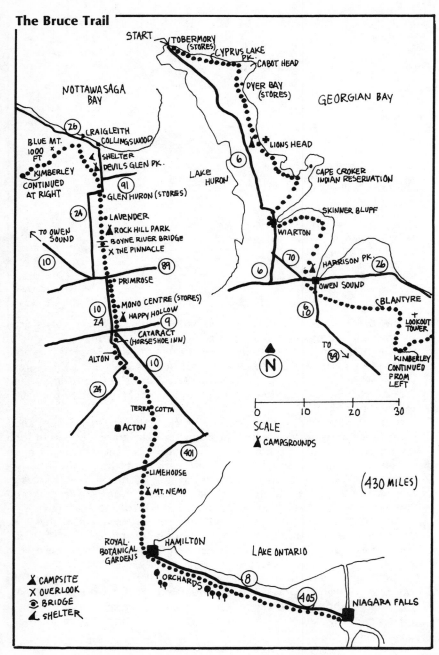

START
TOBERMORY (STORES)
CYPRUS LAKE PK.
CABOT HEAD
DYER BAY (STORES)
GEORGIAN BAY
NOTTAWASAGA BAY
26
CRAIGLEITH
COLLINGSWOOD
BLUE MT. 1000 FT
SHELTER
DEVILS GLEN PK.
LIONS HEAD
6
LAKE HURON
CAPE CROKER INDIAN RESERVATION
KIMBERLEY
CONTINUED AT RIGHT
91
GLEN HURON (STORES)
SKINNER BLUFF
2A
LAVENDER
ROCK HILL PARK
BOYNE RIVER BRIDGE
THE PINNACLE
WIARTON
TO OWEN SOUND
10
89
PRIMROSE
70
HARRISON PK.
26
OWEN SOUND
6
MONO CENTRE (STORES)
10
2A
HAPPY HOLLOW
9
6
10
BLANTYRE
LOOKOUT TOWER
CATARACT (HORSESHOE INN)
ALTON
10
TO
89
N
KIMBERLEY CONTINUED FROM LEFT
24
TERRA COTTA
ACTON
0   10   20   30
SCALE
CAMPGROUNDS
401
LIMEHOUSE
MT. NEMO
(430 MILES)
ROYAL BOTANICAL GARDENS
HAMILTON
LAKE ONTARIO
ORCHARDS
8
CAMPSITE
OVERLOOK
BRIDGE
SHELTER
405
NIAGARA FALLS

erably between Tobermory and Niagara. The northern sections of the trail—through the Bruce Peninsula—are often in wilderness or semi-wilderness areas. South of there you will usually look out from the high ground of the escarpment onto a rural landscape of plowed fields and pastures. At the southern end your view may be of Toronto.

Most of the trail is routed over private land whose owners have granted easements. Obviously hikers should take care to do nothing that might jeopardize the continuation of these easements. The trail has frequent recourse to back roads, and the withdrawal of an easement usually means more such routing.

The Bruce Trail was created by hiking enthusiasts formed into an organization called the Bruce Trail Association. The association is a federation of local clubs that do the actual work of routing, clearing, and marking trails; building shelters; and developing campsites. The association publishes a guidebook to the trail that includes a very detailed text and 31 foldout topographic maps on a scale of 1:56,000. The maps show the trail and all the campgrounds, shelters, springs and other facilities along the way.

You can buy a guidebook from the association at P. O. Box 857, Hamilton, Ontario, Canada L8N 3N9 for $7. If you wish to join the association, student memberships are $3 a year, and adult or family memberships are $6. Guidebooks are $5 for members. Membership in the association brings with it—if you wish it to—membership in one of the 11 local clubs that take actual responsibility for working on the trail. Each club is responsible for working on a specific section of the trail. We will list the names and addresses of the local clubs at the head of our description of the appropriate trail section.

A trail as long as the Bruce that is routed over so much private land is bound to undergo frequent route changes. The guidebook is bound in such a way that new pages can be inserted, and, from time to time, a whole new guide is issued. Current plans call for issuing such a new edition in the spring of 1980. We strongly recommend that you buy the guide before you hike the trail. Contacting the local club in charge of the section you want to hike would also be a good idea.

The Bruce Trail is marked by white paint blazes on trees, rocks, fence posts, or stiles. Two blazes—one just above the other—mean that a change of direction is imminent. Blue blazes mark side trails that may lead to water, a campsite, or a point of interest.

TOBERMORY TO DYER BAY (32 miles)
Peninsula Bruce Trail Club
P. O. Box 145
Tobermory, Ontario, Canada N0H 2R0

The trail begins at a rock cairn overlooking Tobermory Harbor. From there it follows city streets out of town on the way to the escarpment, which here forms high steep cliffs overlooking Georgian Bay. This northern section is the wildest and most rugged portion of the trail.

DYER BAY TO HOPE BAY (30 miles)
Lions Head Bruce Trail Club
Box 302
Waterloo, Ontario, Canada N2J 4A4
   This section of the trail follows dirt roads and rock shorelines. It passes chutes where logs were skidded off the cliffs into the bay, caves formed in the limestone bedrock, and one of the few sand beaches on this side of the Bruce Peninsula. Supplies are available at villages along the route.

HOPE BAY TO WIARTON (28 miles)
Lower Bruce Bruce Trail Club
Box 491
Wiarton, Ontario, Canada N0H 2T0
   Through birch woods and along cliff tops offering spectacular views of the bay, this section of the trail goes through Cape Croker Indian Reservation and then into the town of Wiarton.

WIARTON TO BLANTYRE (62 miles)
Sydenham Bruce Trail Club
Box 431
Owen Sound, Ontario, Canada N4K 5P7
   You'll pass more caves and a marshy lake dolorously named the Slough of Despond. Farmers' fields alternate with woodland, and the spectacular views from the top of the escarpment begin to include farms and towns.

BLANTYRE TO CRAIGLEITH (48 miles)
Beaver Valley Bruce Trail Club
Box 1327
Meaford, Ontario, Canada N0H 1Y0
   The trail follows the rim of the Beaver Valley, going south around its head and then back north. Cliffs are common along the valley, and one—called Kimberley Rock—is 300 feet high. The views are mostly of small farms, and at no point does the trail run for more than 3 miles without crossing a road.

CRAIGLEITH TO LAVENDER (33 miles)
Blue Mountains Bruce Trail Club
Box 306
Barrie, Ontario, Canada L4M 4T5
   High bluffs cut by deep wide valleys characterize this section. The

Blue Mountains are the highest ground along the trail, 1,771 feet above sea level at one point. The best views are north toward Lake Huron.

LAVENDER TO MONO CENTRE (24 miles)
Dufferin Hi-Land Bruce Trail Club
Box 354
Shelburne, Ontario, Canada L0N 1S0
  Pleasant woodland walks plus good views from the high ground over farmland typical of central Ontario are provided. And you'll get a taste of what is to come. City dwellers from the south are beginning to buy property here for weekend cottages.

MONO CENTRE TO TERRA COTTA (43 miles)
Caledon Hills Bruce Trail Club
Box 302
Waterloo, Ontario, Canada N2J 4A4
  Moraines left by the glaciers replace the escarpment as the dominant features in the landscape in this section. Road crossings of busy highways become more common.

TERRA COTTA TO KELSO (20 miles)
Toronto Bruce Trail Club
Box 44
Station "M"
Toronto, Ontario, Canada M6S 4T2
  A bit of wild country, swamps, beaver dams, and a limestone canyon are all close to the big city. A loop trail off the main path visits Hilton Falls.

KELSO TO GRIMSBY (66 miles)
Iroquoia Bruce Trail Club
Box 183
Hamilton, Ontario, Canada L8N 3A2
  This trail generally follows the ancient shore of Lake Iroquois, the immediate postglacial ancestor of Lake Ontario. It goes right through Hamilton but is almost always surrounded by a band of woods. Some spectacular waterfalls, plus a preview of what is to come in the trail's last section are found here.

GRIMSBY TO QUEENSTON (47 miles)
Niagara Bruce Trail Club
Box 1
St. Catharines, Ontario, Canada L2R 6R4
  Still surprisingly bucolic, this section ends at the Niagara River.

RIDEAU TRAIL

Location: The Rideau Trail follows the route of the historic Rideau Canal from Kingston, where Lake Ontario empties into the St. Lawrence Seaway, north and east to Ottawa.

Easy access points for short hikes are in the villages of Sydenham, Perth Road Village, Chaffeys Locks, Jones Falls, Westport, Perth, Smiths Falls, and Merrickville.

Length: 200 miles.

Description: The Rideau Trail is relatively new (1971), so it is not yet as crowded as the Bruce Trail. For the most part the terrain is also gentler, although some sections on the Canadian shield are quite rugged.

The idea for this trail evolved in the spring of 1971 when some Kingston residents were discussing the lack of hiking trails in their area of Ontario. The Bruce Trail Association's experience had shown them what volunteer commitment could do, so they soon set out to find individuals in Ottawa and the towns between the two cities who might be interested in developing a footpath. In May of 1971 the Rideau Trail Association was formed, and in October the entire 200 miles was completed. Much of the labor was performed by 30 students on a federal Opportunities for Youth grant.

The main trail is marked by orange triangles; side trails and loops are marked by blue triangles. No motorized vehicle of any type is allowed on the path except where it follows roads.

Permission to cross private land was granted on the guarantee of the trail association that hikers would be extremely careful. Fires are not permitted except in designated campgrounds, and litter is absolutely forbidden. If there was room for a full container in your backpack, there is room for an empty one.

Camping is permitted outside designated areas with the permission of the individual landowners. We have not had a chance to hike this trail ourselves. All our information comes from the Rideau Trail Association and particularly from one of its members, Stan Segel of Kingston, who has hiked much of the trail himself. If you decide to explore the Rideau Trail, you will want to contact the association yourself (P. O. Box 15, Kingston, Ontario, Canada K7L 4V6) and get a copy of its detailed brochure and excellent topographical maps.

Here is a rough sketch to give you an idea of where the trail goes and what you will see along the way.

It begins in Ottawa at Richmond Landing near the Chaudiere Falls and for the first 5½ miles it follows a city bicycle path along the banks of the Ottawa River.

Scenic attractions include Brebeuf Park, where you can see part of the old portage use by voyageurs to bypass the Chaudiere Falls; and

Rideau Trail

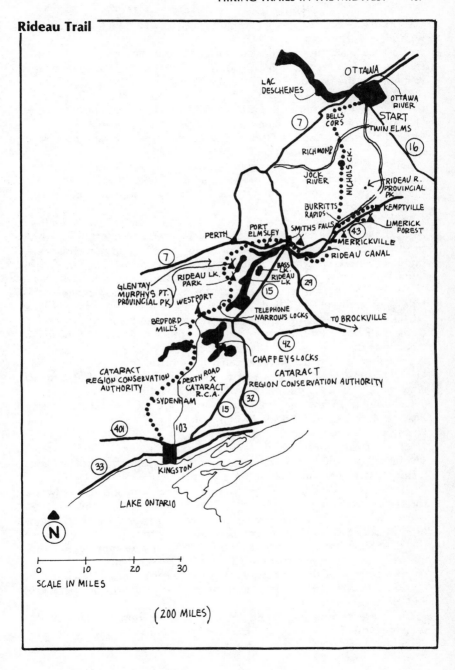

OTTAWA

LAC
DESCHENES

OTTAWA
RIVER

7   BELLS
     CORS

START
TWIN ELMS

16

RICHMOND

JOCK
RIVER

NICHOLS CK.

RIDEAU R.
PROVINCIAL
PK

BURRITTS
RAPIDS

KEMPTVILLE

LIMERICK
FOREST

PERTH

PORT
ELMSLEY

SMITHS FALLS

43

MERRICKVILLE

7

RIDEAU CANAL

RIDEAU LK.
PARK

BASS
LK.
RIDEAU
LK.

15

29

GLEN TAY
MURPHYS PT.
PROVINCIAL PK.

WESTPORT

TELEPHONE
NARROWS LOCKS

TO BROCKVILLE

BEDFORD
MILLS

42

CHAFFEYS LOCKS

CATARACT
REGION CONSERVATION
AUTHORITY

PERTH ROAD
X
CATARACT
R.C.A.

CATARACT
REGION CONSERVATION AUTHORITY

SYDENHAM

32

401

103

15

33

KINGSTON

LAKE ONTARIO

N

0   10   20   30

SCALE IN MILES

(200 MILES)

the homesite of the area's first settler, a man named Ira Honeywell, who built a cabin there in 1811.

The trail leaves the bicycle path at a 350-foot-long boardwalk over a swamp in the Ottawa/Carleton Conservation Centre. A beaver dam is visible from the boardwalk.

Toilets, drinking water, and parking are available at this point. A network of short nature trails maintained by the Ontario Department of Natural Resources crisscrosses the trail near the conservation centre. One of them is called the Stony Swamp Hiking Trail, about 4 miles long with a picnic site halfway along it.

South of the conservation centre and past a Boy Scout Association Camp, the trail heads east along a small creek, then turns south along the Jock River to the community of Twin Elma (about 16½ miles from the trail's beginning).

The Rideau Trail guidebook notes that "in walking this stretch of river, the hiker will pass near a cairn which commemorates the death of the Duke of Richmond. He died of rabies near this spot, having been bitten by a pet fox while inspecting the proposed route of the Rideau Canal in his capacity as Governor-in-Chief of Canada."

Another point of interest to watch for as you proceed includes a 6-mile spur trail (marked with blue blazes), which leads through the Nichols Creek wetland, an area of tamarack and spruce bogs with displays of bog laurel, bog rosemary, and other unusual wildflowers in midsummer.

Your first look at the Rideau Canal for which the trail is named will be at milepost 48 in the town of Burritts Rapids, named after a family who came to Canada during the American Revolution.

Continuing south, the trail passes through the Howard Ferguson Provincial Forest, the Rideau River Provincial Park, Limerick Provincial Forest, and Murphy's Point Provincial Park.

It uses roads intermittently with brushed trails, and passes through several villages along the way. The Rideau Trail guidebook offers local history information on each of these villages.

The terrain varies from ridge tops to rolling farmland to hardwood forests on flatland to sections that border wetlands. At mile 110 (20 miles south of Perth), the trail passes by a private developed campground called Rideau Lakes Park. South of the campground it heads for the canal and follows it for a mile or so before turning inland to a marked side trail where there are a series of beaver dams.

The path passes the Narrows Locks on the canal, to Spy Rock (a cliff above the town of Westport), along the southeast shores of Buck Lake, and on to Chaffeys Locks.

There are several loop trails leading to small remote lakes in this section. One of the wildest sections of the trail is through Frontenac Park. Stan Segel told us that three or four hiking parties a year are lost or stranded there and have to be rescued, although the trail is marked better today than when our first edition was published.

The trail follows the north shore of Gould Lake and then passes through hilly country on the Cataraqui Region Conservation Authority land before coming into civilized farm country again. On the last 20-mile section, between Sydenham and Kingston, fields and woodlots replace the forests.

GANARASKA TRAIL

Location: The newest of Ontario's hiking trails, the Ganaraska is planned eventually to provide a walking route from Port Hope on Lake

Ganaraska Trail

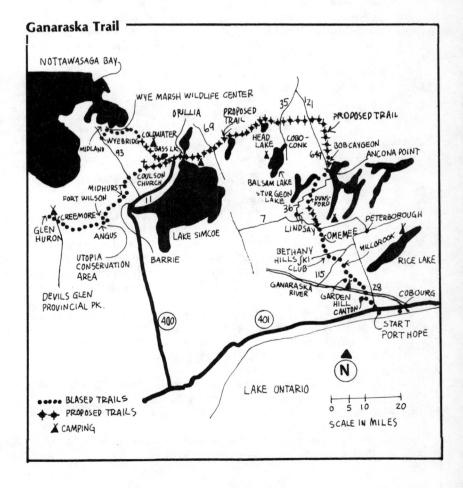

Ontario through the Kawartha Lakes and the southern Muskoka resort area, linking up with the Bruce Trail at Glen Huron, near Collingwood. *Length:* The only sections currently completed are:

1. a stretch of some 40 miles between Glen Huron and Orillia on Lake Simcoe;
2. a day hike of 8 miles or so from Bobcaygeon along the shores of a part of the Kawartha Lakes chain to Dunsford; and
3. a winding trail of about 20 miles from Port Hope to Highway 7A west of Cavan.

Description: These finished parts offer some rough terrain, impressive vistas, and a broad spectrum of geological formations and native plant life. This part of the province has been the home of Huron Indians, French fur traders, and Anglo-Saxon settlers.

Access points from towns and highways are identified by an arrow-head symbol, painted in brown on a white square. At intervals along the trail signs are posted listing the courtesy rules all hikers are asked to follow—stow your trash, put fires out, don't pick wildflowers, etc.

Provincial parks on or near the trail route include Devil's Glen at Glen Huron, Springwater near Barrie, and Bass Lake and Mara near Orillia.

For detailed information on further facilities and on progress of the trail, you may contact the Ganaraska Trail Association, Box 1136, Barrie, Ontario, Canada L4M 5E2.

QUINTE-HASTINGS RECREATIONAL TRAIL

Location: The trail begins near Wellington Bay on Lake Ontario— specifically on County Road 18 near the entrance to Outlet Provincial Park in Prince Edward County. It heads north and slightly west to Lake St. Peter Provincial Park about 20 miles south of the entrance on Highway 60 to the vast Algonquin Provincial Park wilderness.

The trail is seldom more than a couple of miles from main roads and sources of supply; for most of the distance it closely parallels Provincial Highway 62.

Easiest access points are at the places where the trail actually crosses this highway: at Crookston, near the village of St. Ola, about 9 miles south of Bancroft, and in the town of Maynooth at a point some 7 miles south of the trail's northern end at Lake St. Peter.

Length: 235 miles.

Public Transportation Access: Voyageur Colonial Limited bus lines (265 Catherine Street, Ottawa) follows Highway 62 within a few miles of the trail for its entire length on a route that begins in Toronto and runs to Pembroke.

Description: This is another fairly new trail. Construction began in January, 1972, through a federally funded Winter Works project. Main-

Quinte-Hastings Recreational Trail

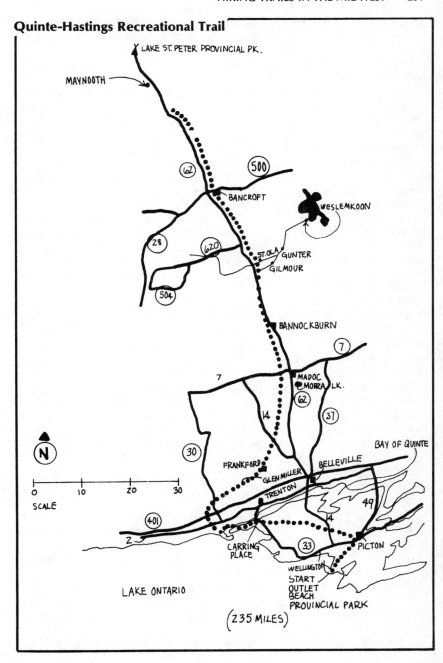

tanance and improvements are carried on by a series of trail clubs that form the Quinte–Hastings Recreational Trail Association. You can become a member and supporter by sending $5 to the association's offices at 14 Bridge Street West, Belleville, Ontario. Maps and a guidebook are also available from this office.

The trail is marked by rectangular orange or red painted aluminum strips 2 inches by 7 inches, or by blazes of the same colors on rocks or trees. On stretches of the trail where there is little risk of losing the route, the blazes tend to be infrequent. The trail group plans to install more as soon as funds are available.

Abrupt changes in direction or forks in the trail are marked by two blazes or aluminum rectangles, one above the other. Place names, points of special interest, and direction to roads and highways are indicated by a variety of signs along the trail route.

The terrain is much like that on other long trails in that part of Ontario south and east of Lake Superior. Small farms and cleared fields are the norm; second growth forests and marshes fill the spaces in between. There are frequent lakes and streams. No large cities can be found along the entire length of this particular trail, but villages and small towns abound.

Camping is allowed where not specifically prohibited.

From there the trail heads north and then east to the Moira River Conservation Authority's O'Hara Mill Conservation Site. The trail makes a wide circle around Moira Lake, crossing Moira River at the far eastern edge of the lake, and comes into the town of Madoc from the east. Food and lodging are available in Madoc.

The next 20 miles or so, between Madoc and the Jordan Lake area, consists of more rolling hills. The trail parallels Highway 62 for a few miles north of Bannockburn, so this is another easy place to locate the trail from the highway and perhaps begin a day hike.

The trail actually comes only within 2½ miles of Jordan Lake, but signs will direct you to the lake if you want to make a short detour.

For the next 6 to 8 miles, the trail passes through marsh country. Streams and rivers cross the trail at several points. Watch for herons and beaver dams.

The Ontario Department of Natural Resources publishes an excellent book called *The Beaver in Ontario*, which we recommend to anyone planning to hike in that province.

Your chances of observing these creatures, or at least their habitats, are nearly 100 percent. According to the Natural Resources people, the industrious rodents are in a dangerous state of overpopulation at the moment. A helicopter survey crew found 425 active colonies on one 184-square-mile area in 1969, and their numbers have decreased very little since then.

At the village of St. Ola on the southern end of St. Ola Lake, the trail turns west and continues more or less in that direction to the town of Coe Hill, a distance of some 18 or 20 miles.

It turns east and then north from Coe Hill, and after about 8 miles it joins a paved road, which it follows to a point about a mile west of Bear Shanty Lake (2½ miles west of Highway 62).

North of this you will come into a lovely section of little lakes and hills. At one point it passes within two miles of the town of Bancroft, where supplies and lodging are available. Signs will direct you.

From Bancroft the route continues almost directly north, past the town of Hybla and Hybla Lake to the town of Maynooth, at the junction of Highways 62 and 127.

From there it travels across country some seven miles to the entrance of Lake St. Peter Provincial Park and the trail's end.

TRAILS IN ALGONQUIN PROVINCIAL PARK

HIGHLAND HIKING TRAIL

Location: Algonquin Provincial Park, the largest of eastern Ontario's parklands. It is situated on the dome of hills between Georgian Bay and the Ottawa River. Plans are to expand the Highland Trail into a network of trails for exploring the 2,910 square miles of park interior.

Length: 22 miles.

Description: This trail is truly in wilderness country. There is little access by road to any part of the Algonquin Park. The terrain includes forests, lakes, and the headwaters of several rivers.

These tributaries carried pioneer lumbermen into Algonquin's vast old stands of pine timber beginning in about 1835. Tom Thomson, the well-known Canadian Group of Seven artist, painted in the area during his last creative years and died in the park in 1917.

Bears are found in the park; so are many smaller wildlife specimens, including ravens, loons, and other northern birds.

Around the park, several perimeter access points lead by water routes as well as foot trails into the interior. From Highway 60, serviced campgrounds, picnic areas, canoe information centers, parking areas, beaches, stores, and restaurants are available.

For more detailed information write Ministry of Natural Resources, Box 219, Whitney, Ontario, Canada K0J 2M0.

WESTERN UPLANDS HIKING TRAIL

This trail includes three loops with round trips of 20, 34, and 43 miles respectively. The trail begins at the Oxtongue River Picnic Grounds at Kilometer 3 (Mile 2) on Highway 60. It has been designed for backpackers who wish to explore on foot the rugged hills of Algonquin's westernmost portion. Experienced hikers will have little difficulty covering each loop in about three days.

Highland Hiking Trail

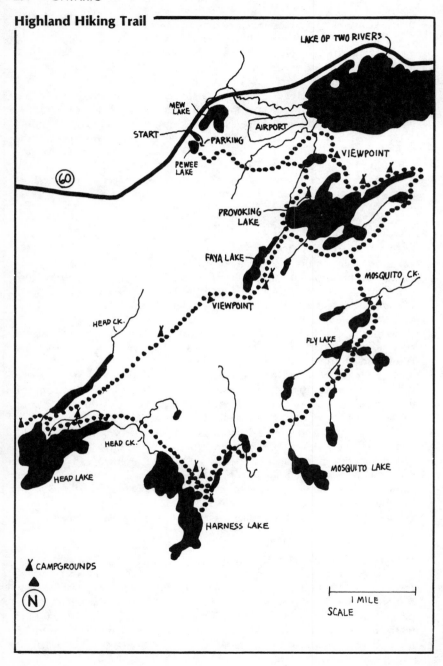

LAKE OF TWO RIVERS

MEW LAKE

START

PARKING

AIRPORT

VIEWPOINT

PEWEE LAKE

60

PROVOKING LAKE

FAYA LAKE

MOSQUITO CK.

VIEWPOINT

HEAD CK.

FLY LAKE

MOSQUITO LAKE

HEAD CK.

HEAD LAKE

HARNESS LAKE

X CAMPGROUNDS

N

1 MILE
SCALE

Further information is available from the Ministry of Natural Resources, Box 219, Whitney, Ontario, Canada K0J 2M0.

An excellent brochure, *Algonquin Provincial Park Hiking Trails*, is also available from the above address for 50 cents.

VOYAGEUR TRAIL

Part of this trail is built and part is still in the planning stage. One day it will stretch across the central part of northern Ontario from South Baymouth on Manitoulin Island (with ferry connection to Tobermory and the Bruce Trail) to Gros Cap on Lake Superior, west of Sault Ste. Marie, and eventually around the rugged Lake Superior north shore to Thunder Bay.

A section called the Rainbow Trail, approximately 10 miles long through the LaCloche Mountains near Espanola, has been completed.

Under construction when we went to press was another 100 miles from Gros Cap to north of Thessalon, incorporating sections labeled Saultteaux, Echo Ridges, Desbarats, and Thessalon.

More information is available from the Voyageur Trail Association, Box 6, Sault Ste. Marie, Ontario, Canada P6A 5L2.

7

IOWA

Trails in State Forests
  Backpack Trail, Yellow River State Forest
  Backpack Trail network, Stephens State Forest

IOWA—AN INTRODUCTION

Because Iowa was blessed by nature with a great deal of prime agricultural land, it has been blessed with very few pieces of landscape that lend themselves to wilderness recreation.

There are, however, backpacking trails of above average quality in two state forests. One is situated on bluffs along the Mississippi River and is accessible on a weekend from the major urban areas of Chicago and Milwaukee.

The other is south of Des Moines in rolling hills that formed when the Nebraskan and Kansan glaciers left deposits of glacial till over the exposed sedimentary rock. Later, westerly winds blew even more soil—ground fine by the Wiconsinan glacier and called loess—to cover up the first layers. In some sections of southern Iowa this rich loess soil is 100 feet thick.

The streams in eastern Iowa that flow from the limestone bluffs into the Mississippi are fast flowing and clear with gravel bottoms. Those in the southcentral portion of the state tend to move slowly, dry up completely at times, and have mud banks.

Vegetation on public lands tends to be the oaks and hickories that once dominated prairie groves; cottonwoods, elms, ash, and walnuts along creek banks; or open prairie grass and wildflower meadows.

Although we have chosen to describe only the state's two backpacking trails, there are many shorter day-hike trails in various state parks.

For more information, write to the Iowa Conservation Commission, Wallace State Office Building, Des Moines, Iowa 50319.

TRAILS IN STATE FORESTS

BACKPACK TRAIL, YELLOW RIVER STATE FOREST

Location: In the Paint Creek Unit of the 5,800-acre Yellow River State Forest. Access is off Iowa Highway 76 about 12 miles north of McGregor (the Iowa town directly across the Mississippi River from Prairie du Chien, Wisconsin).

Length: 20-mile loop.

U.S.G.S. Quads: Prairie du Chien, Wisconsin–Iowa, 15 minutes; Waterville, Iowa, 7.5 minutes.

Description: This forest is situated on limestone bluffs above the Mississippi River in rugged terrain that is unusual for Iowa. It is drained by Big and Little Paint creeks, both of which are swift, clear, and stocked regularly with trout.

The trail begins at the information area adjacent to the forest headquarters and is marked by brown signs containing the yellow letters *BP* (for backpack). Nicky Sains of the Chicago chapter of American Youth Hostels says the signs could be confusing because a bridle path that crosses this one (and joins it for a brief stretch) is also marked *BP*.

The route passes by seven car campsites; there are also three backcountry trail campsites.

As you proceed south and then west from the forest headquarters, the initial segment of the trail goes through a forest that features tree species in all stages of succession—including a kind of outdoor museum of larch and pine plantings from worldwide seed sources. The trail descends from the forested ridge to enter a valley at the county access road by the Paint Creek Bridge at the Waterville Access Road. It turns east then along the bed of a former railroad adjacent to the creek. Two car campgrounds are adjacent to the trail in this section. The path curves sharply northwest through one of these campgrounds and proceeds north along the route of the Bluff Hiking Trail to the top of two developed overlook areas on sheer limestone bluffs. Camping is permitted at the overlooks.

The trail follows a road for a short distance north of the bluffs into a small stand of hardwoods, passes a cleared area with a wildlife pond, and then follows a fire lane through rows of red pine, white pine, jack pine, and spruce planted in 1948 on abandoned farm fields. The trail crosses an access road into an area that was clear-cut in 1974 to salvage what was left of oak trees damaged by infection. It continues downhill on a road again to a narrow valley with ferns and shade-tolerant trees into the car campground at Little Paint Recreation Area.

The trail follows the access road to a horseback trail campsite, past two rebuilt log structures, and then along a spring-fed stream (a tributary of the Little Paint) to another wildlife clearing. It follows

Backpack Trail, Yellow River State Forest

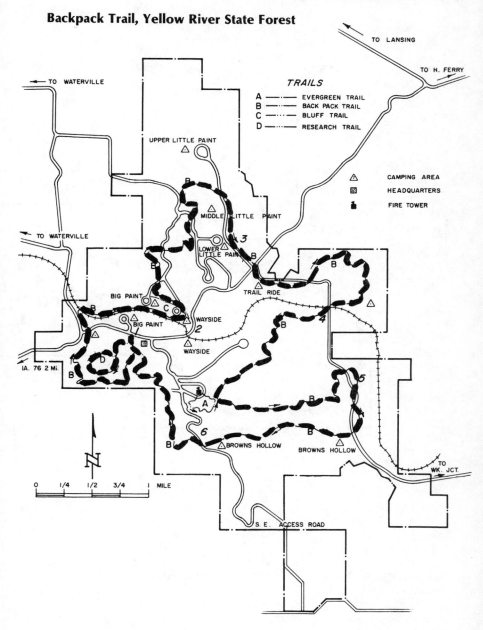

TO LANSING

TO H. FERRY

TO WATERVILLE

TRAILS

A ———— EVERGREEN TRAIL
B ———— BACK PACK TRAIL
C ———— BLUFF TRAIL
D ———— RESEARCH TRAIL

UPPER LITTLE PAINT

CAMPING AREA
HEADQUARTERS
FIRE TOWER

MIDDLE LITTLE PAINT

TO WATERVILLE

3

LOWER
LITTLE PAINT

BIG PAINT

TRAIL RIDE

B

4

C

WAYSIDE

BIG PAINT

2

B

IA. 76 2 Mi.

D

WAYSIDE

5

B

A

B

6

B

B

BROWNS HOLLOW

BROWNS HOLLOW

TO
WK. JCT.

N

0   1/4   1/2   3/4   1   MILE

S. E. ACCESS ROAD

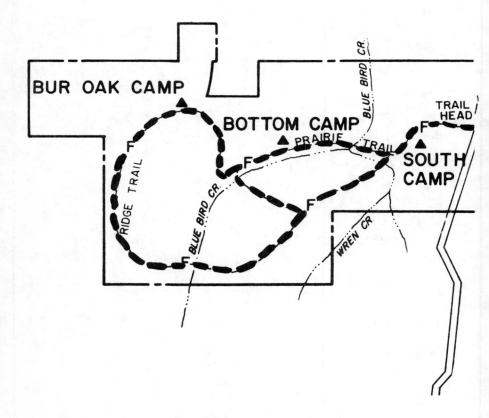

Backpack Trail Network, Stephens State Forest

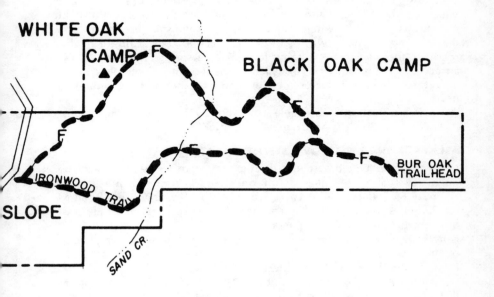

WHITE OAK

CAMP

BLACK OAK CAMP

IRONWOOD TRAIL

SLOPE

SAND CR.

BUR OAK
TRAILHEAD

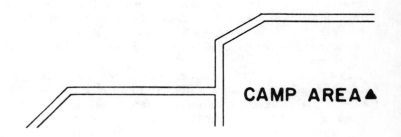

CAMP AREA▲

another access trail to an overnight car camp area and on to the banks of Big Paint Creek. The path coincides with the Bridle Path for a mile or two past wildlife ponds and other clearings, then into a walnut and butternut grove.

A side trail heads right to a fire tower. The main trail continues east along the ridge through an open area, then downhill to the Paint Creek Valley on the Waukon Junction road. It follows the road to the right into Brown's Hollow where there is a trail campsite (no water) in a dense stand of young walnut trees. The second trail campsite near a road has the advantage of being located by a spring. The trail follows an access road to an S curve, which winds left into a recently cutover area, through a small cleared meadow and back into a forest to the trail head.

More information is available from Yellow River State Forest, c/o Area Forester, Box 115, McGregor, Iowa 52157.

BACKPACK TRAIL NETWORK, STEPHENS STATE FOREST

Location: The Whitebreast unit of Stephens State Forest. To reach the trail, travel about 4 miles south on U.S. 65 from the junction of Highway 65 and U.S. 34 at Lucas. Turn west on Lucas County Road M for 3½ miles, then a half mile south and three quarters of a mile west on a gravel lane to a parking area.

Length: A network of smaller trails can be combined into a single loop of about 12 miles.

U.S.G.S. Quad: LeRoy, 7.5 minutes.

Description: As you leave the Bur Oak trail head, the trail passes through crop fields of corn and hay planted by local farmers who receive a share of the crop in return for providing winter food and cover for wildlife. The first forest you enter is a young one, grown up from old fields in the last 15 or 20 years. After passing a fence corner at the boundary of the forest, you will arrive at the first of five backcountry campsites, called Black Oak Camp for the predominant species of tree there.

Continuing, the trail descends into a rich bottomland forest of walnut, cottonwood, and ash trees and crosses Sand Creek. The trail ascends the ridge opposite through forest and open fields, reaches White Oak Campsite, and then crosses a graveled road to the head of Prairie Trail.

Prairie Trail follows the ridge for some distance to the South Slope Campsite before descending to Bluebird Creek. After crossing the creek, the trail passes through a series of bottomland fields containing such prairie grasses as big bluestem, little bluestem, switchgrass, Indian grass, and cordgrass. There is another trail campsite in these fields by Bluebird Creek.

Ascending the ridge again, the trail reaches its westernmost point at the Bur Oak Backcountry Campsite.

The Ridge Trail leads south from Bur Oak Camp through open fields to the south boundary of the forest, then cuts east to cross Bluebird Creek again and ascend to the ridge opposite. The trail follows this ridge to junction with the Prairie Trail. Retrace your steps along that trail, across the gravel road again, to the junction of the Bur Oak Trail (the northern route already described as the first leg of the loop) and Ironwood Trail.

Ironwood Trail leads through open fields and then into an oak-hickory forest. You will see the ironwood trees for which the trail was named when you descend into another bottomland forest along Sand Creek. The trail follows the creek briefly and then rejoins Bur Oak Trail near the trail head where you started.

For more information, write Stephens State Forest, c/o Area Forester, Route 3, Chariton, Iowa 50049.

8

ILLINOIS

ILLINOIS—AN INTRODUCTION

The course of human history in this state has had a profound and highly visible effect on the type of outdoor recreation space now available in Illinois.

Since John Deere's steel plow made the rich prairie soil accessible to farmers, almost every acre of it has been turned over, smoothed out, and planted in long rows of corn and soybeans. Illinois even exports soybeans to the Orient.

The few patches of public land that exist tend to cluster in the unglaciated southern portion of the state, in marshy areas, or spread out along stream and canal banks. Parks also tend to be located on the rare sites where limestone or sandstone rock outcroppings break up the terrain.

Another source of public recreation land is former strip-mined sites. Illinois is still the fourth largest coal producer in the country; it is the third largest producer of strip-mined coal. Strip mining as a feasible commercial operation had its origin in what is now Kickapoo State Park near Champaign.

Typically, the mining company exhausts the mineral possibilities of a particular location, then donates the property or sells it for the cost of tax payments. The buyer, usually the state, converts the former mine pits to lakes, stocks them with fish, and decks out the shores with picnic areas and campsites. Presto! A new state park.

The most undomesticated portion of the state is at the far southern end, where the Shawnee National Forest and a group of state parks and wildlife areas occupy land in what is essentially an extension of the Ozark Plateau. Hikers in this part of the state can expect dense oak-hickory forests, clear streams with gravel rather than mud bottoms, and more craggy bluffs than they can count.

The bucolic farm scenery available to hikers on the Illinois–Michigan and Hennepin Canal trails, however, has its own charm, as do old fields and prairie remnants that alternate with prairie oak groves in many state parks.

There are also surprisingly large blocks of forested land on the fringes of Chicago. Forest preserve districts in the five-county metropolitan area offer a wide choice of day hikes to city residents and visitors with a day to spare from more urban-oriented businesses and pleasures.

The Department of Conservation coordinates trail information for the state. Write Trails Specialist, Illinois Department of Conservation, 605 William G. Stratton Building, 400 South Spring Street, Springfield, Illinois 62706.

TRAILS IN SHAWNEE NATIONAL FOREST

This forest is a patchwork of about 257,000 acres that lies within an area bound by the Ohio River on the east and south, the Mississippi River on the west, and Illinois Highway 13 on the north. The forest and the limestone and sandstone beneath it are considered extensions of the Ozark Plateau, except that the soil here in the Shawnee is deeper and richer. Although the glaciers that once covered most of Illinois never reached here, layers of the fine-grained glacial soil called loess were blown this far south.

For hikers in the Shawnee today, that means that timbered ridges and woodland streams are going to alternate along almost any trail with patches of relatively civilized farmland. The Shawnee is not a forest primeval, but bucolic scenery, too, has its charms.

Rangers in the Shawnee have been slow to focus attention on trail-building, partly because there are so few areas large enough to contain trails that don't require easements across private property.

Many trails marked on the official forest maps actually follow primitive (or sometimes not so primitive) roads. With the help of forester and recreation specialist Art Zdzieblowski, we have selected a few areas to recommend, including a combination of cross-country navigation and trail hiking in two proposed wilderness areas.

RIVER TO RIVER TRAIL

Location: This ambitious project is scheduled eventually to run along a continuous path from the Ohio River at a point just east of Camp Cadiz, a forest service campground, to Fountain Bluff on the Mississippi River, almost a hundred miles. Currently complete are about 50 miles between Camp Cadiz (3 miles east of Illinois Route 1 on the Cadiz Road in the Elizabethtown Ranger District) and a radio tower on U.S. 45 about 7 miles north of Vienna in the Vienna Ranger District.

Length: Approximately 50 miles.

U.S.G.S. Quads: Saline Mines, Karbers Ridge, Herod, Eddyville, Glendale, Stonefort, Creal Springs; all 7.5 minutes.

Description: The trail uses old jeep roads and occasionally major forest or county roads along at least half of the route. It is marked with blue paint blazes in the shape of the small letter *i*, a vertical line with a circle above it. Spur trails are usually marked with white plastic diamonds.

The trail follows an unsurfaced road for the first half mile or so west of Camp Cadiz; it then becomes a single-lane trail for about a mile. Then it is transformed briefly into a gravel road, then cross-country again. At the point where the trail crosses a paved road, a spur trail heads north (as the main trail continues west) on an unsurfaced roadway to Pounds Hollow Recreation Area and then east and south to Camp Cadiz—a loop of about 12 miles.

The section of the River to River Trail between the High Knob picnic area and Garden of the Gods Recreation Area Campground (about 4½ miles) follows a road that is severely eroded and gets a lot of off-road vehicle use.

The 3- or 4-mile stretch through Garden of the Gods Wilderness is a single-lane trail along a ridge line.

The trail then turns south on a gravel road to the hamlet of Herod. There is officially a half-mile gap in the trail where it leaves a paved road just south of Herod and crosses Hart Creek on private property. It

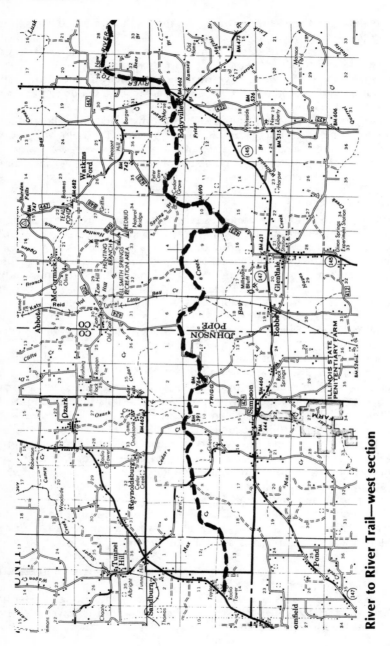

River to River Trail—west section

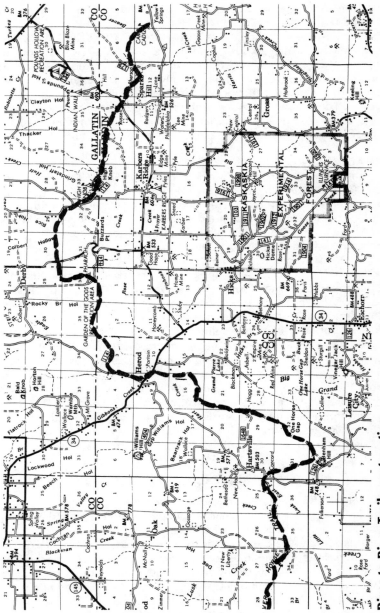

River to River Trail—east section

enters forest service land again and is carved out as a single-lane woodland trail about 2 miles to One Horse Gap.

The next 6-mile stretch, according to Forester Art Zdzieblowski, who has hiked the entire existing and proposed route, is one of the prettiest. It crosses the watersheds of Lusk and Little Lusk creeks through the Indian Kitchen area, mostly on a single-lane trail, then follows a road again south about 3 miles to Eddyville.

West of Eddyville it alternates from one-lane trail to unsurfaced road, crosses under a railroad trestle, and follows old roads for most of the last dozen miles to the radio tower on U.S. 45 south of Tunnel Hill.

HERITAGE HIKING TRAIL

Location: From Bell Smith Springs Recreation Area Campground on Forest Road 848 north to Murray Bluff on the Saline River (at an unnamed and unnumbered gravel road about 4 miles east of Oldtown).
Length: About 12 miles. A planned extension will eventually head east from Murray Bluff and then south to join the River to River Trail south of Hart Creek for a loop of about 40 miles.
U.S.G.S. Quad: Stonefort, 7.5 minutes.
Description: The trail passes through two proposed but not currently recommended wilderness areas—Burden Falls and Murray Bluff. It is, in spite of whatever reservations the authorities had, one of the loveliest and wildest areas of the forest. The streams are clear, with gravel rather than mud bottoms. Bluffs are sometimes 50 feet high, and the forest is mature oak and hickory with little undergrowth. A dilapidated and long-abandoned log cabin along the route bears witness to pioneer settlement.

From the campground at Hunting Branch the trail heads north along Hunting Branch Creek and then east, briefly on a road, to Teal Pond Campground, then north to Burden Falls, east and then north again to the Saline River. The trail follows the slopes above this stream for the last 3 or 4 miles to Murray Bluff.

AREAS TO EXPLORE CROSS-COUNTRY

GARDEN OF THE GODS WILDERNESS (proposed)

Location: Access is from the Pharoh Campground in the Garden of the Gods Recreation Area on Forest Road 114.
Length: No formal trails except for the River to River Trail that skirts its south edge. Hikers sometimes follow Rocky Branch Creek from where it crosses a road west of Derby south about 3 miles to its headwaters just west of the campground. Map and compass are recommended.
U.S.G.S. Quads: Rudemont, Equality; both 7.5 minutes.
Description: This 4,373-acre tract was recommended for inclusion in the U.S. Wilderness system by the Carter administration in 1979. The

Heritage Hiking Trail

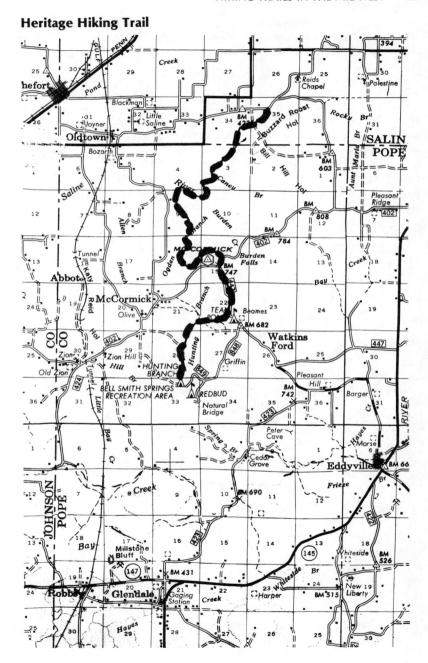

topography varies from nearly level, broad ridge tops to precipitous cliffs and steep narrow ravines. Elevation ranges from 410 to 860 feet above sea level. Sandstone outcrops along bluffs form grotesque shapes.

Rose Creek, Little Eagle Creek, and Rocky Branch flow through the wilderness. They are small but unusually pure; their watersheds contain no domestic cattle grazing areas. Oak-hickory forests form the main vegetative cover on ridge tops. There are occasional pine plantations and a few old fields being invaded by red cedar, winged elm, sassafras, and persimmon trees. The trees on lower slopes are mainly red and white oaks, sugar maple, beech, tulip poplar, and some hickory.

Various mosses, lichens, and ferns are typical occupants of north-exposure cliffs. Southern exposures are less heavily vegetated but typically support red cedar, farkleberry, and prickly pear cactus.

Garden of the Gods Wilderness (proposed)

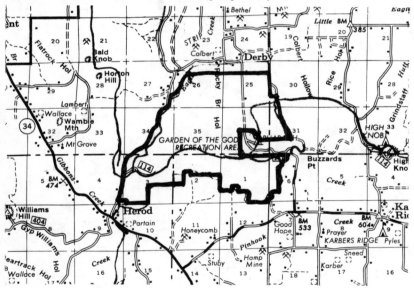

CLEAR SPRINGS WILDERNESS (proposed)

Location: Access points are at Clear Springs Campground on Forest Road 382 southeast of Howardton, Forest Road 236 just north of Winters Pond Campground, and Forest Road 279 along the southern boundary.

Length: No formal trails, but an old jeep road crosses the center of the property from west to east from Forest Road 236 just south of Winters Pond Campground. Spur trails that were also former roads head both south and north from this main de facto trail. The spur trail to the

Clear Springs Wilderness (proposed)

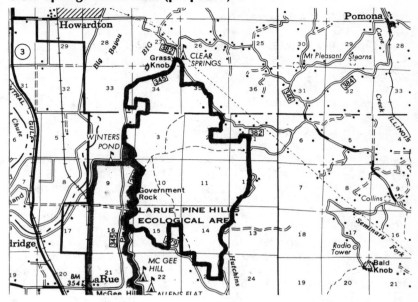

south eventually narrows to a single-lane trail and then turns east to connect with an old gravel road that continues east across the adjacent Bald Knob Wilderness to a forest road just north of Bald Knob Mountain.

U.S.G.S. Quad: Wolf Lake, 7.5 minutes.

Description (we quote forester Art Zdzíeblowski): "Ridge tops are narrow and sharp in this wilderness. Slopes are steep and creek bottoms narrow. Elevations range from 400 to 980 feet:

"Hutchins Creek and its tributaries drain both this and the adjacent Bald Knob Wilderness.

"Most of the ridge tops have never been cleared for agriculture. In the occasional exceptions, one finds old fields growing up in sassafras, persimmon, and winged elm. White oak dominates the upper slopes in association with black oak, pignut hickory, and shagbark hickory. On lower slopes and in ravines there are red oak, black gum, beech, tulip poplar, and sugar maple. Understory trees include redbud, dogwood, and red maple.

"Proximity to a former course of the Mississippi River rather than wind-blown glacial soil accounts for the accumulation of loess on the ridges in this area.

"Wild turkeys have become well established in this section of the Shawnee; the pileated woodpecker is found in comparative abundance in the older hardwood forests."

STATE PARK TRAILS

ILLINOIS-MICHIGAN CANAL STATE TRAIL

Location: The towpath parallels the former Illinois-Michigan ship canal from Channahon on U.S. 6 just west of I-55 to Seneca, also on U.S. 6, 25 miles west. A separate 5-mile stretch of the path is also maintained for recreation from LaSalle (on U.S. 6 a mile east of U.S. 51) east to Utica.

Length: 25 miles from Channahon to Seneca; 5 miles from LaSalle to Utica. Eventually 61 miles of continuous towpath will link Joliet and LaSalle.

U.S.G.S. Quads: Channahon, Minooka, Lisbon, Morris, Seneca, Marseilles, Ottawa, Starved Rock, and Lasalle; all 7.5 minutes.

Description: Construction on the canal began in 1836 and was completed in 1848. It made the long overland Chicago Portage obsolete and was an important step in opening up a route for large-scale commercial traffic from the Mississippi River to the Great Lakes.

The Illinois Department of Conservation acquired the property in 1974 to develop hiking and bicycle trails and a canoe route. The segments from Channahon to Morris (15 miles) and from Utica to LaSalle (5 miles) are surfaced with crushed limestone and suitable for bicycling. The section from Morris to Seneca is brushed and cleared only and therefore usable only by hikers.

The canal passes through the towns of Channahon and Morris. It passes through a long stretch of woods and below the 100-foot-high Kankakee Bluffs where the Kankakee River flows into the DesPlaines River. It passes along the north side of Goose Lake Prairie State Park and along the south edge of Gebhard Woods State Park. The largest tree in the state is a mile west of Gebhard Woods on the south side of the canal. The tree is an eastern cottonwood 120 feet tall. Otherwise the scenery is of Illinois farm country, except for a thin band of trees bordering the canal.

Water, toilets, and picnic tables are available at McKinley Woods Forest Preserve in Will County about 2½ miles southwest of Channahon and at Gebhard Woods State Park 15 miles from Channahon.

Toilets, picnic tables, and a shelter, but no water, are available at Lock 8 (8 miles southwest of Channahon) where Aux Sable Creek crosses the canal.

Camping is available at Channahon State Park and Gebhard Woods State Park. Site superintendent David Carr said small trail campsites will eventually be in place, possibly in 1980 or 1981, at 3- to 5-mile intervals throughout the whole length of the trail.

Camping permits for these sites will be available at Gebhard Woods, Morris, Illinois, which serves as headquarters for the trail.

On the 5-mile stretch of towpath between LaSalle and Utica, camping is available at Starved Rock State Park, 3 miles south of the canal by road from Utica. When the trail is extended, facilities at Buffalo Rock State Park and at Illini State Park will also be made available to canal hikers.

Private hunting clubs abut the canal at several points, so hikers are advised to wear bright clothing if they hike the trail in autumn.

HENNEPIN CANAL STATE TRAIL

Location: This towpath, which parallels an abandoned ship canal, is part of an unusual state park, the Hennepin Canal Parkway. It is 104.5 miles long and from 380 feet to a mile wide. It spans Rock Island, Bureau, Henry, Lee, and Whiteside counties.

The portion of the towpath that is continuous and maintained for recreation totals no more than about 40 miles at present, however. The eastern terminus is where Illinois Highway 29 crosses the canal at the town of Bureau Junction on the Illinois River.

A visitor center and headquarters for the park is near Sheffield, off Illinois Highway 88 about a mile south of I-80 and a quarter mile north of U.S. 6 and 34.

To reach the western terminus of usable towpath, take Cleveland Road northeast from the town of Green Rock about 2½ miles to Wolf Road. Turn right (east) on Wolf Road, then right again (south) at the second township road. Travel about 2 miles to a parking area at the towpath.

Length: About 40 miles continuous plus intermittent stretches over the entire 104.5-mile route, which includes the 29.3-mile feeder canal.

U.S.G.S. Quads (east to west): DePue, 7.5 minutes; Princeton South, 7.5 minutes; Buda, 15 minutes; Annawan, 15 minutes; Atkinson, 7.5 minutes; Geneseo, 7.5 minutes; Green Rock, 7.5 minutes.

Description: The Hennepin Canal was used for navigation between the Illinois and Mississippi rivers between 1907 and 1951. When the idea for it was conceived in 1834, it was expected that boats would use it to cross the divide between the Mississippi and the Illinois rivers and enter the Illinois and Michigan Canal which empties into Lake Michigan at Chicago. Traffic would then proceed eastward across the Great Lakes to the Erie Canal and on to New York.

Because construction was delayed, the canal was almost obsolete before it went into operation. Commercial use was always disappointing; the Army Corps of Engineers finally closed it to commercial traffic in 1951 but left it open for recreational use. The state of Illinois acquired the property for a park in 1970.

The water for the canal is drawn from the Rock River, and Lake Sinnissippi at the north end of the feeder canal is its actual reservoir. The water from the feeder canal flows into the mainline 28 miles west of the Illinois River at the highest elevation point.

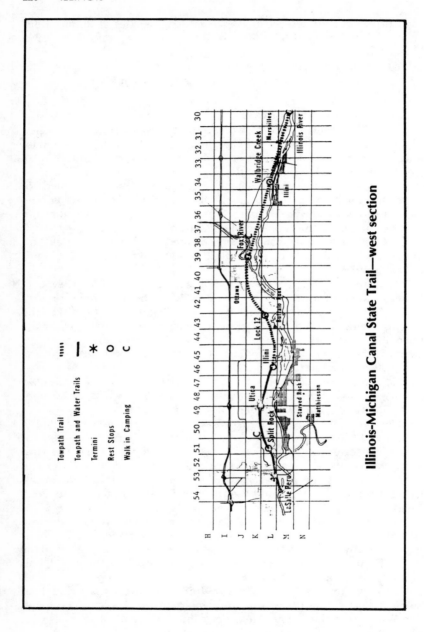

Illinois-Michigan Canal State Trail—west section

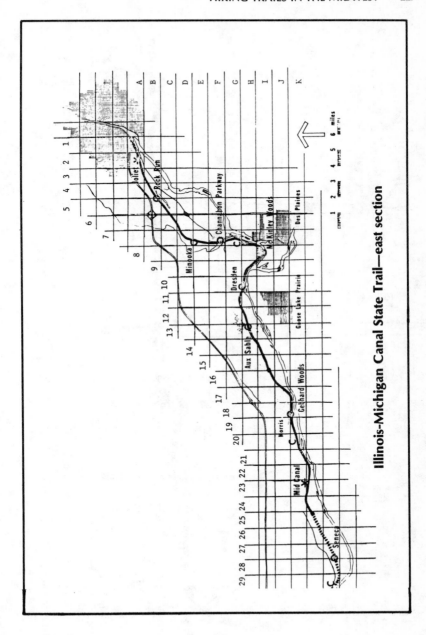

Illinois-Michigan Canal State Trail—east section

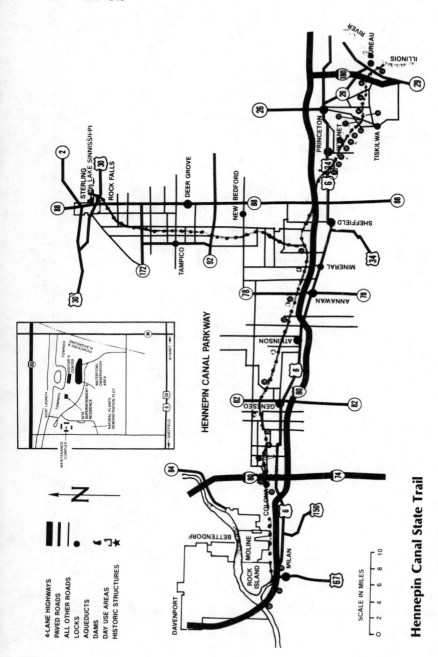

Hennepin Canal State Trail

There were originally 32 locks on the canal. Lock 1 has been under the Illinois River for more than 50 years; the other 31 are still visible. Four have been restored to working condition. The old gates and machinery were removed from the other 27; most of them now function as spillways with waterfalls on the upstream end.

The eastern section of the canal flows through wooded, moderately hilly country. The canal drops 196 feet in 18 miles from the junction with the feeder canal east to the Illinois River.

West, the land flattens out and the views—beyond the thin line of trees bordering the canal—are mainly of farmland. The canal descends only 93 feet in 46 miles from the feeder canal junction west to the Mississippi River.

The only designated tent campsite on the towpath is at Lock 21, although there is also a private campground near the path just east of the feeder canal. The site superintendent is currently trying to get a ruling from the state Department of Conservation on whether camping at nondesignated sites can be permitted. The canal comes within a mile of one town, Wyanet, where overnight lodging is available. It comes within 3 miles of several other towns (see map).

Drinking water is available at Locks 6, 11, 21, 22, and 23; at Bridge 15; and at the Visitor Center area.

There are toilets at Locks 6, 11, 17, 21, 22, 23, and 24; at Bridges 14 and 15; and at the Visitor Center.

Five miles of the towpath immediately east of the Visitor Center are gravel surfaced for bicycle use. The towpath is used in winter by snowmobilers, and there is a 4-mile network of trails for cross-country skiing at the Visitor Center near Sheffield.

For more information, write Hennepin Canal Parkway Visitor Center, RR 1, Sheffield, Illinois 61361.

RED CEDAR TRAIL—GIANT CITY STATE PARK
Location: Giant City State Park near Makanda, 12 miles south of Carbondale off U.S. 51.
Length: 16-mile loop.
U.S.G.S. Quad: Makanda, 7.5 minutes.
Description: The park lies within the Shawnee Hills, for which the adjacent Shawnee National Forest was also named. They lie south of the glaciated portion of the state and range in elevation from 500 to 1,060 feet. The park's name, Giant City, refers to a particularly striking group of huge sandstone formations.

The trail was just opened in the fall of 1979 and makes a loop that, for the most part, lies just inside the park boundaries all the way around. It passes mainly through oak-hickory forests, although there is one stand of shortleaf pine, plus several old fields and one small prairie

Red Cedar Trail—Giant City State Park

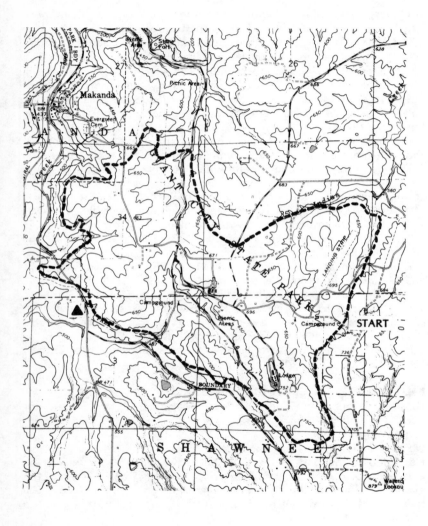

remnant. A few stretches of the trail follow the edge of high bluffs, and one borders an apple orchard.

The trail fords several small streams, a few with modest waterfalls. The streams in the eastern half of the park are part of the Indian Creek drainage. Those in the west end flow into Drury Creek.

The only designated campsite, called the Red Cedar Camp, is situated roughly at the halfway point of the loop. It is the former home of a farmer who grew daffodils commercially, and many of the flowers still grow wild there. There are picnic tables and toilets but no water. Hikers are advised to carry their own. Water from the creeks should be boiled thoroughly. Cows graze upstream. The former access road to the Red Cedar Camp has been closed and gated, so entry is by foot only.

The trail was originally marked with bands of white paint on trees, a double band signaling change of direction. When it was discovered that the white paint closely resembled a local tree fungus, red spray paint dots were superimposed on the blazes.

Hikers are requested to secure a permit in advance to hike the trail and to display it on their car windshield. For the permit and other information on the park, write Interpretive Center, Giant City State Park, Makanda, Illinois 62958.

Plans were also being discussed in the fall of 1979 to build a new long-distance trail that would link Giant City State Park with the nearby Crab Orchard and Devil's Kitchen wildlife areas.

PYRAMID BACKPACK TRAILS—PYRAMID STATE PARK

Location: Pyramid State Park on Illinois Highway 127 about 6 miles south of Pinckneyville in Perry County.

Length: 10-mile loop with smaller loops inside it totaling about 6 miles.

U.S.G.S. Quad: Pinckneyville, 15 minutes.

Description: Pyramid State Park is a 2,524-acre reclaimed strip mine area; the former pits are now filled with water and stocked with largemouth bass and bluegill, their shores made into backcountry campsites. The park was named for the coal company that formerly operated in the area.

The park contains about 20 acres of mature white oak and hickory forest near its western boundary in an area that was never mined. The rest of the park's woodland consists of pine plantations, cottonwood, box elder, and sycamore, plus oak and hickory saplings.

The topography is rough, carved out with multiple ridges and cuts during the landscape's mining days.

The 10-mile loop trail is not currently very well marked or maintained. A group of local Boy Scouts was planning to work on it in the spring of 1980. It begins at the campground west of Heron Lake, heads north along the west shore of Boulder Lake and the south shore of

Pyramid Backpack Trails
—Pyramid State Park

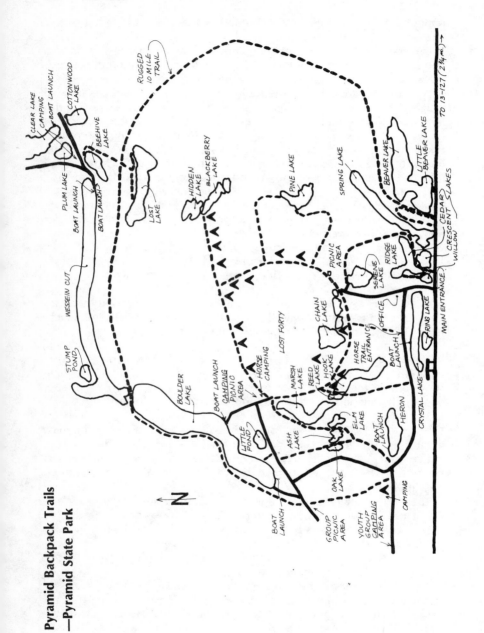

Wessein Cut, and makes a circle that encloses (but does not pass within sight of) all but a handful of small lakes at the north entrance and Beaver Lake near the south entrance.

A separate loop trip of approximately 6 miles can be made by combining several other trails inside the big 10-mile loop (see map). There are 25 walk-in campsites along these smaller trails, but no formal campsites on the big 10-mile loop. Most of the trails are two lanes wide and mowed with a tractor.

For more information, write Pyramid State Park, RR 1, Box 115-A, Pinckneyville, Illinois 62274.

BACKPACK TRAIL—SILOAM SPRINGS STATE PARK
Location: 28 miles east of Quincy in far western Illinois. Take Illinois Highway 104 east from Quincy about 13 miles. When the highway curves right sharply, continue east instead on the Kellerville Road. Turn south just west of Kellerville 3 miles to the park. There are signs directing visitors to the park on Highway 104 and on U.S. 24.
Length: 6-mile loop.
U.S.G.S. Quad: Mt. Sterling, 15 minutes.
Description: The springs for which this 3,183-acre park was named were the center of a health spa in the 1880s. They are no longer accessible to the public. There is, however, a 58-acre manmade lake stocked with largemouth bass, bluegill, channel catfish, and rainbow trout. The terrain is gently rolling hills covered mainly in oak and hickory trees. Springs Creek is the largest of several small creeks that cross the property.

The trail begins at a picnic and parking area near the site of the former springs, heads southeast across an old steel bridge, crosses a creek that is dry part of the year but can be uncomfortably high in spring, goes up a hill and follows a ridge, then comes out near a gravel road that divides the park in half. It heads back to the springs area, crossing several streams and a few old fields along the way. There is one designated backcountry campsite outfitted with two pit toilets and a barrel that is kept filled with water to put out campers' fires. A road into the campsite is gated except for use by maintenance vehicles.

Mailing address is Siloam Springs State Park, RR1, Clayton, Illinois 62324.

PROPOSED TRAILS
LAKE SHELBYVILLE RECREATION AREA
An 18-mile trail had been flagged but not constructed in late fall, 1979. It will proceed north from the Dam West Recreation Area to Possum Creek, on to Coon Creek and Lone Point, then to Eagle Creek State Park—all on the west edge of Lake Shelbyville.

At the north end of Eagle Creek Park, a mile-long auto bridge crosses

Backpack Trail—Siloam Springs State Park

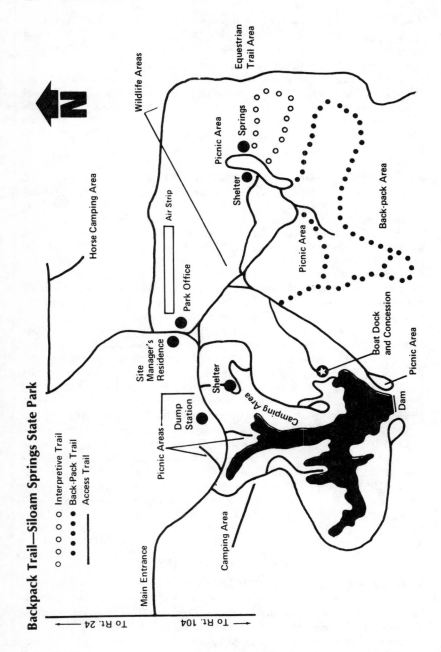

o o o o o Interpretive Trail
● ● ● ● ● Back-Pack Trail
——————— Access Trail

the lake. The trail will commence again across that bridge on Lake Shelbyville's eastern shore. From Wolf Creek State Park, it will head south to Lithia Springs Campground and end near the Visitor Center in the Dam East Recreation Area.

For information on the progress of this trail, write the Lake Shelbyville Management Office, U.S. Army Corps of Engineers, Route 16 East, P. O. Drawer 126, Shelbyville, Illinois 62565. A set of 22 topographic maps with contour intervals of 5 feet is available from the above address for $1.50.

PERE MARQUETTE STATE PARK

A route has been chosen for a 6-mile backpack trail through this park, but in fall of 1979 construction had not yet begun. The 8,000-acre park is situated on bluffs overlooking the Illinois River 5 miles west of Grafton on Illinois Highway 100.

The trail is to begin at the ferry landing on the Illinois River and proceed north and west through the main spine of the park—past the picnic area, south of the group camp, and north along a ridge to an equestrian campground near the park's northern boundary.

The mailing address of Pere Marquette State Park is Box 325, Grafton, Illinois 62037.

URBAN WILDS

COOK COUNTY FOREST PRESERVE DISTRICT

Cook County, which contains Chicago and the sprawling suburbs that surround it, also contains 64,500 acres of wild forestland crisscrossed with a 175-mile network of hiking and ski trails. Group camping only is allowed in designated sites.

Timber hasn't been cut on this land since 1915, when the Cook County Forest Preserve District was chartered. Golf courses, picnic groves, swimming pools, and ball diamonds are scattered here and there in the district's 10 separate divisons, but 85 percent of the property is maintained in a natural state. Most wildlife species typical of the Midwest are found there. Beaver and wild turkey were also reintroduced several years ago and are thriving.

The largest and most interesting forest preserve division for hikers is the 10,000-acre Palo Division. Hills and pothole lakes, relics of the Ice Age, offer a variety of terrain that is unusual for Chicago. This region, southwest of the city, was once the shoreline for glacial Lake Chicago.

To reach Palos from Chicago, travel west on the Stevenson Expressway (I-55) to U.S. 45. Head south on U.S. 45 to 87th Street. The division extends from 87th Street to 143rd Street and west to Illinois 83. Most of the trails are between 87th and 123rd streets.

Maps for all the forest preserve divisions are available from Cook County Forest Preserve Headquarters, 536 North Harlem Avenue, River Forest, Illinois 60305.

DU PAGE COUNTY FOREST PRESERVE DISTRICT

Adjacent to Cook County on the west, the DuPage County Forest Preserve District contains 12,000 acres of land maintained in a natural state. For hikers, the jewel of the system is Waterfall Glen, a 3,000-acre doughnut of a preserve surrounding the Argonne National Accelerator Laboratory. Trails through the glen explore plantation groves of red, white, and jack pine; oak-hickory woodlands; meadows and prairie remnants; and marshes. There are ravines and canyons, and part of the trail system follows a bluff above the Des Plaines River. There are no camping facilities in this preserve, but naturalists there have begun experimenting with occasional ranger-led overnight backpack outings.

Other good hiking areas in the DuPage district include the Roy C. Blackwell Preserve, with horseback and foot trails through sugar maple and oak groves.

West DuPage Park includes upland and riverbank forests, marshes, prairie remnants and old fields, and a steep-sided valley with hillside springs that empty into the West Branch of the DuPage River.

The Illinois Prairie Path (see separate listing) passes through the Pratt-Wayne Woods in DuPage County. There are also trails of varying length up to 5 miles in the Herrick Lake, Fullersburg Woods, Maple Grove, and Greene Valley units.

Maps are available from the DuPage County Forest Preserve Headquarters, 881 West St. Charles Road, Lombard, Illinois 60148.

MCHENRY COUNTY CONSERVATION DISTRICT

Equivalent to the Cook and DuPage county forest preserves, this district in the rolling farm country north of Chicago contains 2,600 acres in 11 separate parcels. Six of the parcels (averaging about 150 acres each) have nature trails up to 3 miles in length; several of them are equipped with walk-in campsites. Maps are available from the McHenry County Conservation District, 6512 Harts Road, Ringwood, Illinois 60072.

KANE COUNTY FOREST PRESERVE DISTRICT

These preserves, southwest of Chicago, contain about 3,000 acres in 20 separate divisions. The district is currently developing a hiking/bicycle trail in conjunction with DeKalb County, which adjoins Kane County on the west. About 14 miles along an abandoned railroad grade had been finished by the fall of 1979. The trail is eventually scheduled to be 30 miles long. The eastern edge will be at LeRoy Oakes Forest Preserve in St. Charles. The portion already finished begins off Illinois Route 64 in Virgil and heads west into DeKalb County.

Camping is allowed in Bliss Woods west of Aurora. Other divisions that contain trails include Hampshire, Burnidge, Tyler Creek, and Compton. Maps are available from Kane County Forest Preserve District, 719 Batavia Avenue, Geneva. Illinois 60134.

LAKE COUNTY FOREST PRESERVE DISTRICT

The county woodlands in this district total 11,344 acres and contain 11 separate recreation areas, all but three of them with trails. The terrain is gently rolling forest, interspersed with small lakes, meadows, and wetlands. Weathered stone foundations along several of the trails are the remnants of long-vanished farmsteads. Lilac bushes and jonquils bloom in the former yards of these homesteads in spring.

Maps are available from the Lake County Forest Preserve District, 2000 North Milwaukee, Libertyville, Illinois 60048.

ILLINOIS PRAIRIE PATH

This trail, conceived and coaxed into existence by a local naturalist, the late May Thielgaard Watts, follows an abandoned railroad bed 40 miles through western Chicago suburbs. The high wooded banks that once protected residents from the noise of the train now shield hikers from scenes of backyard barbecues and swimming pools and offer an illusion of country hiking. Sections of the prairie path also pass through farm country, marshes, and wooded forest preserve lands.

Most of it is surfaced with fine gravel for bicycle use. There are picnic tables at intervals along the route.

The prairie path is maintained by local hiking clubs and conservation groups who coordinate work through an association called the Illinois Prairie Path Association, Inc., P. O. Box 1086, Wheaton, Illinois 60187. The association distributes maps of the trail on request.

GREEN BAY TRAIL

This foot and bicycle path follows the right-of-way of the abandoned Chicago, North Shore, and Milwaukee Railroad and runs from Winnetka Avenue in the village of Winnetka (a suburb north of Chicago) to Lincoln Avenue in Highland Park, a distance of about 6 miles. The trail is just east of and parallel to Green Bay Road for its entire length, so automobile access at any point is convenient.

The trail, traversing middle and upper middle class residential areas, is used more by local residents than by tourists. Early in the morning you can see men out jogging before they go to work; in the afternoon you will see children riding up and down it on their bicycles. Through Winnetka the trail is paved with a rough asphalt emulsion.

ILLINOIS BEACH STATE PARK

This 1,651-acre park on Lake Michigan in the far north Chicago suburb of Zion is also easily accessible by urban dwellers for day hikes. Special features include the dunes with their unique plant and animal life, small prairie remnants, and a forest of Austrian and Scotch pine, planted in 1860. The park is a major stopover for migrating waterfowl and shorebirds in spring and fall. There are a campground, lodge, and about 4 miles of trails in addition to beach hiking. Maps and brochures are available from Illinois Beach State Park, Zion, Illinois 60099.

9

INDIANA

INDIANA—AN INTRODUCTION

Most of the hiking trails in Indiana are clustered in the hillier southern half of the state south of Indianapolis. The hills, actually a series of plateaus with rivers cutting steep-sided valleys through them, are part of what geologists know as the Crawford and Norman uplands.

Rock outcroppings and formations are usually sandstone, although a strip of bedrock that runs south through western Brown County and along the eastern edge of Hoosier National Forest is limestone. There are a number of interesting caves—some of them wild and some commercial—along this strip of limestone. At least two are along trail routes.

The forests that grow on the rich soil of slopes and valleys in southern Indiana are beech and maple, spectacular for their gold and red colors in autumn. Hilltops and drier ridges tend to be covered with various species of oaks and hickories. The native pine is shortleaf, but white pine, jack pine, Virginia pine, and red pine have also been planted in both the national and state forests over the last 40 years.

In this state, as in others, we have described only those trails that are

239

suitable for backpacking—those that (a) are long enough for an overnight trip, and (b) allow trailside camping away from roads. There are many more attractive day hikes that we did not mention in Yellowwood, Morgan-Monroe, and Brown County state forests, as well as in Hoosier National Forest and several state parks. Write the state Department of Natural Resources, 612 State Office Building, Indianapolis, Indiana 46204 for details on those.

TRAILS IN HOOSIER NATIONAL FOREST

Hoosier National Forest is located in hill country known as the Crawford and Norman uplands of southern Indiana. The forest contains 180,000 acres of public land in patches within a 645,042-acre area. Basically, there are two units of this forest—a northern one near Bloomington and a southern one that stretches from west of Bedford, the forest headquarters, south to the Ohio River.

Geologically speaking, the hills, like those in the Ozarks, are not actually hills but severely eroded plains. Until the streams cut valleys into the sandstone and limestone, the area was a relatively flat plateau.

The majority of the forest is shale and sandstone, but a strip of limestone that runs through it from north to south creates a phenomenon known as "karst" topography (named after similar terrain in an area of Yugoslavia). The porous nature of rock in karst areas causes streams to disappear underground at random intervals and also creates caves. Wyandotte Cave, one of the most scenic and best known among such commercial attractions in the Midwest, is a few miles east of the forest on the Ohio River.

The forest cover is mainly what foresters call "upland central hardwoods." That means a variety of oaks and hickories, black walnut, beech, tulip poplar, ash, sugar maple, and sassafras. There is some native shortleaf pine, as well as plantations of both shortleaf and white pine. A 77-acre virgin forest worth seeing as a reminder of what this region looked like before settlement is preserved as the Pioneer Mothers Memorial Forest and is southwest of a V-shaped intersection of Indiana Route 37 and U.S. 150 near the town of Paoli. A state highway wayside borders the forest on Highway 37.

HICKORY RIDGE HIKING TRAIL

Location: In the northernmost section of Hoosier National Forest near Bloomington. Access is from the Hickory Ridge Lookout Tower. To get there take Indiana Highway 446 south from the east side of Bloomington, across the Lake Monroe Bridge, and turn left (east) on Tower Road. (It's a half mile south of the turnoff from 446 to the Hardin Ridge Recreation Area.) If you're on the right road, you'll pass the Blackwell

Pond Picnic Area in about half a mile. Continue east about 6 miles to the fire tower.
Length: 20-mile loop.
U.S.G.S. Quad: Elkinsville, 7.5 minutes.
Description: This trail traverses the 6,380-acre Grubb Ridge area, recommended for official United States Wilderness status by the Carter Administration in 1979. The terraine is hilly, but the hiking is never difficult. Elevation varies from 600 to 898 feet above sea level, but most of the trail is at an elevation of 650 to 700 feet. A brief caution: Keep your eye on the diamond-shaped paint blazes. There are a lot of other trails and old fire lanes around to confuse hikers.

The forest is mainly oak and hickory, with beech and maple groves in the hollows and some pine plantations along the slopes. There are also scattered wildlife ponds and a few old fields. One of the best times to hike here is in early spring, when most of the trees are still bare but redbud and shadbush are blooming and early wildflowers like hepatica, bloodroot, and Dutchman's breeches are breaking through old leaves on the forest floor. Indiana hiking can be a beastly hot business in midsummer.

The trail crosses several streams and follows the banks of several more. Some are intermittent. Axsom Branch, on the other hand, can be high enough to be troublesome when water backs up in it from the Monroe Reservoir. There are views of this reservoir from high points on the trail.

One long section circles the wooded edges of the flat-topped Terril Ridge. West of Axsom Branch it follows John Grubb Ridge for about 5 miles. It returns to the lookout tower along Frank Grubb Ridge.

A special feature is Patton Cave, accessible from a short spur trail at the westernmost point of the loop above the Saddle Creek arm of the lake. Patton Cave is a small cavern on a western spur of John Grubb Ridge. It is an anomaly, a small pocket of limestone in an area that is more typically underlain with sandstone. The Mt. Carmel Fault, which runs from north to south across this section of the state, is said to have had something to do with this geological oddity.

TWO LAKES HIKING TRAIL
Location: Perry County in the southern section of Hoosier National Forest. Access is from a road leading west from the campground on Lake Celina west of Indiana Highway 37.
Length: 12.2-mile loop.
U.S.G.S. Quads: Branchville and Bristow, both 7.5 minutes.
Description: The trail encircles two lakes created in 1966 and 1968 by dams on the Middle Fork of the Anderson River. There are two car campgrounds on the northeast side of Lake Celina, but Indian Lake is

Hickory Ridge Hiking Trail

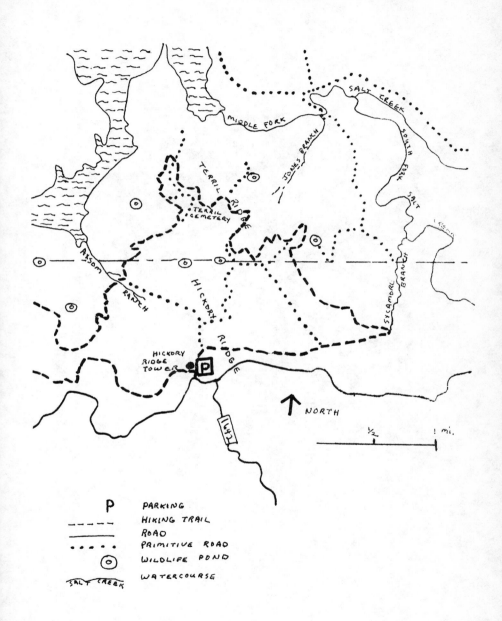

P PARKING
      HIKING TRAIL
      ROAD
•••• PRIMITIVE ROAD
  ◉ WILDLIFE POND
       WATERCOURSE
SALT CREEK

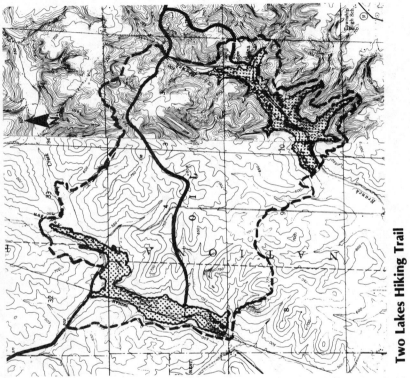

Two Lakes Hiking Trail

undeveloped except for a single boat landing on the east side (the trail passes along the west side).

There is a lot of up-and-down walking on this trail, but none of the climbs is very steep. Elevation varies from 600 to 775 feet, but there are few abrupt changes from one extreme to the other.

Water is scarce except for the lakes themselves and a few intermittent streams. Backpackers should plan to carry their own in the stretches between the lakes.

Although the lakes themselves expect to get heavy recreational use in the future, the sections of forest between them are—at least at the moment—among the most remote and isolated in the forest. The only roads that cross the trail are two at the Lake Celina end that provide lake access.

The forest is a rich and, in sections, fairly mature one with northern red oak, scarlet oak, and chestnut and chinquapin oak on the ridge tops; sugar maple, ash, beech, and walnuts on the slopes and in sheltered coves; sassafras and yellow poplar pioneering in old fields. Persimmon and pawpaw trees provide ripe fruit in late fall.

Pick your own campsite.

MOGAN RIDGE HIKING TRAIL

Location: Perry County in the southernmost unit of Hoosier National Forest. Access is from a parking area on Forest Road 1011, east of Indiana Highway 37 about 5 miles south of Bandon.

Length: 21-mile loop.

U.S.G.S. Quad: Derby, 7.5 minutes.

Description: This trail gets our vote for the best one in this forest. It lies within one of the largest blocks of solid national forest ownership, approximately 6,000 acres. It offers isolation; the few roads that enter the area were closed and gated in 1963, when a wild turkey flock was introduced. It has variety in terrain and scenery. The trail follows ridge tops and slopes but also dips down to follow streams occasionally, and at one point it offers a spectacular view of the Ohio River in the distance (trees obstruct the view somewhat in summer). The trail crosses numerous streams; there is no shortage of water. It should all be boiled for at least 10 minutes before drinking, however. Some of the creeks flow from farmlands outside the forest.

Vegetation is mainly central upland hardwoods. The gold and red mixtures of beech and maple trees are almost blinding in intensity in autumn. There are occasional patches of white and shortleaf pine.

Mogan Ridge Hiking Trail

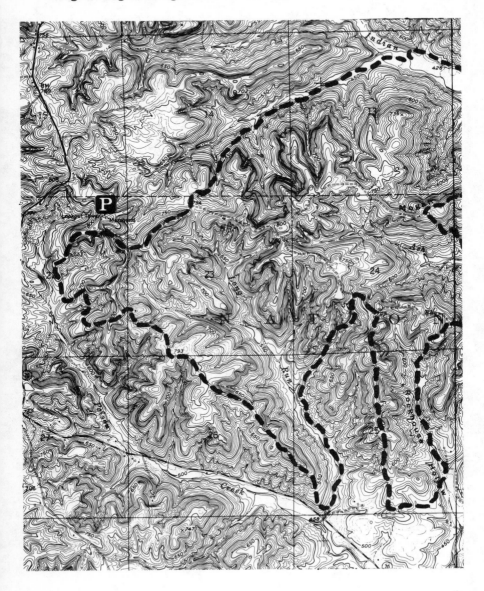

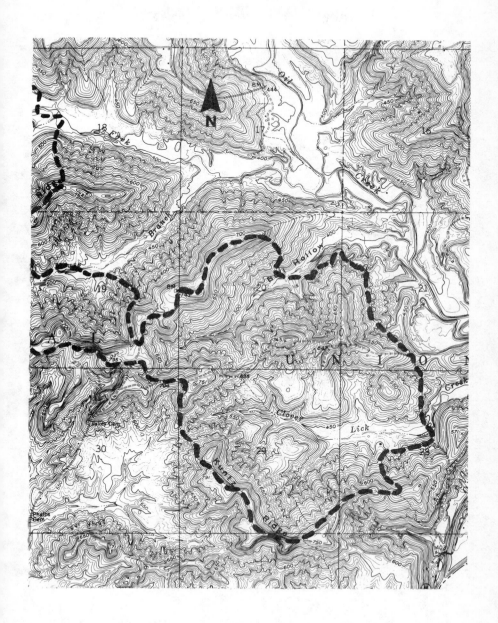

AREA TO EXPLORE CROSS-COUNTRY

COPE HOLLOW
Location: The northern unit of Hoosier National Forest, on the south side of Monroe Reservoir near Bloomington. Tower Road, east of Indiana Highway 446 to Hickory Ridge Lookout Tower, forms the north

Cope Hollow

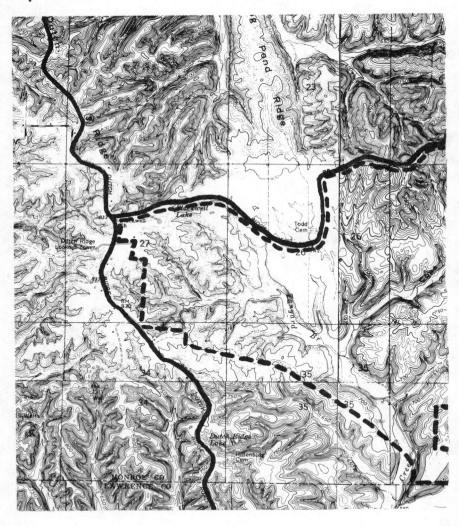

boundary of this roadless area.

Length: No formal trails but an abundance of old fire trails, creeks, and ridge lines to follow with the aid of map and compass.

U.S.G.S. Quads: Allens Creek, Elkinsville, Bartlettsville, Norman; all 7.5 minutes.

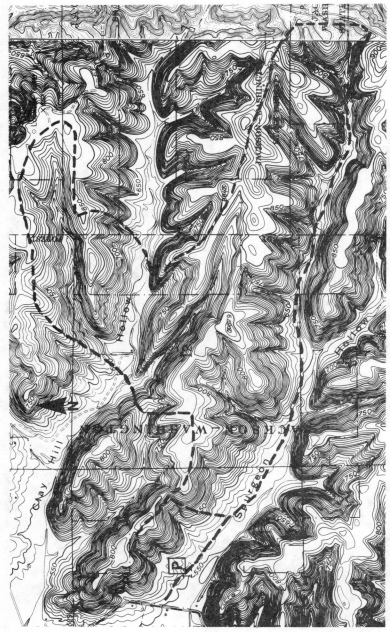

Knobstone Ridge Trail, Jackson-Washington State Forest

Description: This 3,529-acre area was recommended by the Carter Administration in 1979 for inclusion in the United States Wilderness system. It is separated only by a forest service road on its north boundary from the proposed Grubb's Ridge Wilderness (see Hickory Ridge Trail description).

TRAILS IN STATE FORESTS

KNOBSTONE RIDGE TRAIL, JACKSON-WASHINGTON STATE FOREST.

Location: Jackson-Washington State Forest. Access to the trail is off' Indiana Highway 135 about 15 miles south of Brownstown or 10 miles north of Salem. From Salem, proceed north 4 miles on Highway 135, then turn right on a county road. It heads east about 2 miles, then makes a 90-degree left turn and continues about 3½ miles north to Spurgeon Hollow. A road turns right one eighth of a mile to a parking lot by a small lake.

Length: 8-mile loop. (This is also a good area for cross-country exploration.)

U.S.G.S. Quad: Kossuth, 7.5 minutes.

Description: A 2,544-acre area that encompasses this trail has been designated a "backcountry area," to be used only for "passive recreation" (meaning backpacking) and for one-tree-at-a-time timber harvesting of mature and damaged trees.

The trail is marked with a yellow maple leaf on black posts.

The terrain is much more rugged than most people imagine exists in Indiana. The slopes of the hills are quite steep, but the wide meadows and rich bottomland forests in the hollows between the ridges make ideal campsites.

Three scenic overlooks at scattered points along the route provide views of the surrounding forest. There are several intermittent streams, but they cannot be depended on as year-round water sources. Backpackers are advised to carry their own.

Maps and information are available from Jackson-Washington State Forest, Route 2, Brownstown, Indiana 47220.

BACKCOUNTRY AREA, CLARK STATE FOREST

Location: Clark State Forest. Access is from a parking area on Taylor Road at the east end of this 2,000-acre tract. To reach it, head west from the town of Underwood (4 miles north of the forest headquarters at Henryville on U.S. 65) on Salem Road about 6 miles to Taylor Road. Turn north (right) on Taylor Road about 1¾ miles to the parking area.

Length: No formal trails. Hikers are free to explore and camp wherever they like. There are old fire lanes and also wide bottomlands along several creek banks. A map and compass are essential. Hikers should check with the forest office in Henryville before they set out, so that someone knows where they are and how long they plan to be in the backcountry.

U.S.G.S. Quads: Henryville, Scottsburg, Little York, and South Boston; all 7.5 minutes.

Description: This 2,000-acre area is the state's equivalent of a wilderness area. No motor vehicles are allowed except when the foresters engage in sporadic and very limited logging operations. The terrain is quite rugged, with an elevation range of 640 to 980 feet. The forest is the upland central hardwood type typical of the lower Midwest. The principal trees are oaks and hickories on ridge tops; ash, walnut, tulip poplar, and sassafras on lower slopes and in bottomlands. Seventy-five small wildlife ponds are scattered through the area.

Plans are currently underway to build a 50- to 75-mile trail that will link Clark and Jackson-Washington state forests. It may be complete by the summer of 1980 and will extend from near Deam Lake at the

Backcountry Area, Clark State Forest

southern end of the Clark Forest to the north end of Jackson-Washington State Forest. It will pass through the backcountry areas of both forests. Some 1,200 acres of land between the two forests has been purchased for a right-of-way.

Detailed maps and information on the backcountry are available from Clark State Forest, Box 119, Henryville, Indiana 47126.

ADVENTURE TRAIL, HARRISON-CRAWFORD STATE FOREST

Location: Harrison-Crawford State Forest. To reach the main entrance, head 8 miles west of Corydon on Indiana Highway 62, then north on Indiana Route 462 about 3 miles. There are several access points to the trail, but numbered posts begin at the River Picnic Area on the Ohio River south of the Wyandotte Woods Campground.

Length: 30 miles.

U.S.G.S. Quads: Leavenworth and Corydon West, both 7.5 minutes.

Description: If this very attractive trail has any faults, it is that it is too well marked. There are numbered posts (that accompany an interpretive brochure) every 100 feet. Major junctions are indicated with directional arrows. There are several cutoff trails within the main loop for those hikers who prefer a shorter journey.

The scenery is spectacular—especially on the stretch of about 5 miles east of the River Picnic Area where the path follows bluffs above the Ohio River. The limestone bedrock beneath the forest has created numerous caverns, sinkholes, and rock outcroppings.

There are several three-sided overnight shelters along the route. They are built of red cedar with hand-split wooden shingles. Each shelter is 4 by 8 feet. There is also easy access from the trail to the Stage Stop and Wyandotte Woods car campgrounds.

Wyandotte Cave, a commercial cavern with guided tours, is a three quarters of a mile walk from the trail on Wyandotte Road.

The trail crosses several creeks, but they are not necessarily safe to drink from. Drinking water is available, however, at the River Picnic Area, at Wyandotte Cave, at the Stage Stop Campground and Wyandotte Woods Campground, and also at the park office on Highway 462 half a mile west of where the trail crosses 462 at the archery range.

The interpretive brochure and accompanying map are available from Harrison-Crawford State Forest, Route 2, Corydon, Indiana 47112.

TEN O'CLOCK LINE TRAIL, YELLOWWOOD STATE FOREST

Location: Yellowwood State Forest. Take Indiana Route 46 southwest from Nashville to Duncan Road. Turn right (north) on Duncan Road past Somerset Lake to the Yellowwood Lake Road. Head east and north on Yellowwood Lake Road past the Yellowwood State Forest office to the group camping area and trail head.

Length: 16 miles.

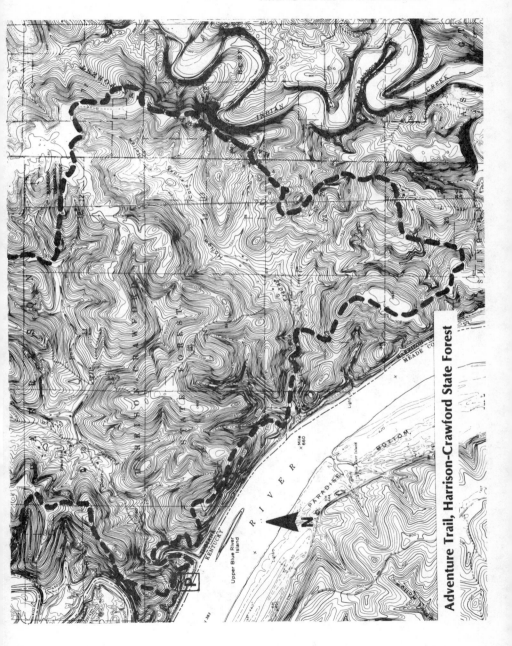

Adventure Trail, Harrison-Crawford State Forest

U.S.G.S. Quads: Belmont, Nashville; both 7.5 minutes.
Description: The trail runs generally in an east-west direction between Yellowwood Lake and the fire tower on Weed Patch Hill in Brown County State Park. Access to the fire tower is by a road that heads south from Indiana Highway 46 about 2 miles west of Nashville. The road crosses the North Fork of Salt Creek on a covered bridge.

Two by six inch white rectangular blazes mark the trail route.

Ten O'Clock Line Trail—west section

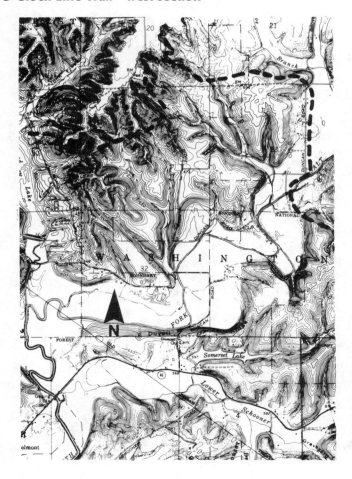

Changes in direction are indicated either by double white blazes or by orange triangles. Wooden signs with arrows indicating the preferred direction to take mark the trail at road intersections.

The trail derives its name from the northern boundary line of a 3-million-acre purchase of Indian land ratified at the Treaty of Fort Wayne in 1809. Governor William Henry Harrison negotiated the sale

Ten O'Clock Line Trail—central section

for $10,000 with chiefs of the Miami, Wea, and Delaware tribes. The property stretched from the Wabash to the White River, and the northern boundary was determined by the shadow cast by the sun at 10 A.M. on September 30, the day the treaty was signed.

The path crosses ridges and valleys, following old stagecoach roads, Indian trails, and occasionally forest roads, as well as cutting cross-country on single-lane trails.

Camping is not allowed on the trail itself at present; it still crosses patches of private land. Camping is available at either end of the trail, however. Contact Yellowwood State Forest, Route 1, Nashville, Indiana 47448.

Ten O'Clock Line Trail—east section

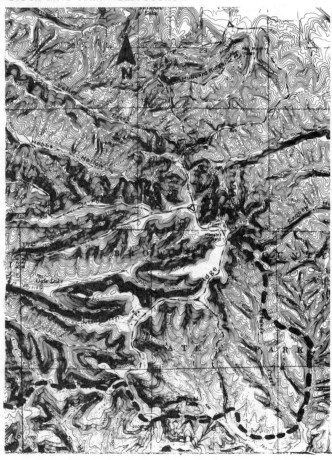

URBAN TRAILS
INDIANA DUNES NATIONAL LAKESHORE
Location: This national park consists of scattered patches of land that stretch for 13 miles along the south shore of Lake Michigan between Gary and Michigan City. Access is off U.S. 12. The park's west unit, centered around a big beachhouse complex, is immediately adjacent to the Gary community of Miller.

Length: A network of about 27 miles of trails is currently being developed in the west unit, and shuttle buses—expected to be in operation for the summer of 1980—will transport visitors from that unit to the eastern units where there are about 30 more miles of trails. The park also contains a 12.5-mile bicycle trail along a utility right-of-way adjacent to the Chicago, South Shore, and South Bend electric railway.

U.S.G.S. Quads: Gary, Portage, Chesterton, Dune Acres, Michigan City West; all 7.5 minutes.

Description: Trails in the west unit will explore the beach and dune areas, interdunal ponds that lie behind the dunes, oak forests that were bare dunes some 8,000 years ago, prairie remnants, and the shores of Long Lake, a narrow marshy body of water that was a lagoon of prehistoric Lake Chicago, ancestor to Lake Michigan.

Trails already in place in eastern units of the park include:

The Bailly Homestead Trail (3 miles). This path explores two pioneer homes—one owned by an early French fur trader and the other by a Swedish farmer—a beech-maple climax forest, and old fields returning to a natural state.

The Ly-Co-Ki-We Trail (3½ miles). A loop trail that follows the oldest glacial beach ridge in the area through a mature hardwood forest.

The Cowles Bog Trail (4 miles). A trail that traverses wooded dunes and marshes, and offers a glimpse of a northern bog that is rare this far south in the Midwest.

The Little Calumet River Trail (4 miles). A loop trail which follows along that stream and through woods.

The Calumet Bicycle Trail (12 miles). On a utility right-of-way north of U.S. 12 and adjacent to the Chicago, South Shore, and South Bend Railroad.

More trails were to be constructed in 1980 and 1981.

There are no campgrounds in the national lakeshore, but several former homes along the trail routes were in the process of being converted to hostels when we went to press.

There is a car campground nearby at Indiana Dunes State Park.

Public transportation access to the national lakeshore and state park is via the Chicago, South Shore, and South Bend Railroad.

Maps and other information are available from Indiana Dunes National Lakeshore, 1100 North Mineral Springs Road, Porter, Indiana 46304.

INDIANA DUNES STATE PARK
Location: Take Indiana Route 49 north from Interstate 94, 3 miles to the road's end at the park entrance.
Length: 16½ miles of interconnecting trails.
U.S.G.S. Quad: Dune Acres, 7.5 minutes.
Description: This park lies within the overall boundaries of Indiana Dunes National Lakeshore although it is administered separately by the state. We include it in our listing of urban trails because it is easily accessible to residents of Gary and the Chicago metropolitan area—by Chicago, South Shore, and South Bend Railroad. The proposed national lakeshore shuttle bus will also transport visitors from the west unit of that park to eastern portions of the national lakeshore that are adjacent to the state park.

Detailed descriptions of trails are available from Indiana Dunes State Park, Box 322, Chesterton, Indiana 46304.

FURTHER SOURCES

Streams and Trails Coordinator
Division of Outdoor Recreation
Department of Natural Resources
612 State Office Building
Indianapolis, Indiana 46204

Hoosier National Forest
1615 J Street
Bedford, Indiana 47421

Indianapolis Hiking Club
c/o Harrison Feldman
4622 Evanston Avenue
Indianapolis, Indiana 46205

Sassafras Audubon Society
6620 East State Road 45
Bloomington, Indiana 47401

Hoosier Chapter
Sierra Club
Joseph L. Colbourn
3216 Cherry Tree Lane
Elkhart, Indiana 46514

RECOMMENDED READING

Glenda Daniel, *Dune Country, a Guide to Indiana Dunes for Hikers and Naturalists*, $4.95, Swallow Press, 811 West Junior Terrace, Chicago, Illinois 60613.

Student Committee, Sassafras Audubon Society. *A Hiker's Guide to Nebo Ridge* (in the Grubb Ridge, Hickory Ridge, Cope Hollow Area of Hoosier National Forest), $1.60, Room 48-M, Indiana Memorial Union, Bloomington, Indiana 47401.

G. Neal Overbey, Streams and Trails Coordinator for the Indiana Department of Natural Resources, informs us that his office is also currently writing a state hiking guide. Write him, c/o Department of Natural Resources, 612 State Office Building, Indianapolis, Indiana 46204.

10

OHIO

OHIO—AN INTRODUCTION

Settlement in this state of fertile valleys, rich woodlands, and streams began in the 1700s and was well under way at the turn of the 19th century. Major urban centers developed along Lake Erie and on the rivers that fed into it—the Maumee, the Sandusky, the Huron, and the Cuyahoga.

For hikers, the most interesting terrain—and the area with the most public land—is in the hilly southern portion of the state. Coal mining, iron mining, and timber harvest have been the major sources of that region's income until recent years. Now recreation is beginning to play a bigger role. There are only two backpack trails in state forests right now, but the state's Department of Natural Resources predicts that more state park and state forest trails will be modified for overnight use in the future. A prime possibility for such conversion is the 26-mile Logan Trail, currently designated for day use only (with no backcountry campsites), in Tar Hollow State Forest.

There are currently three trails, two of them contiguous, for back-packers in Wayne National Forest; but cross-country navigation with map and compass is allowed anywhere on the federally owned land.

For more information, contact the Ohio Department of Natural

Resources, Division of Forestry, Fountain Square, Columbus, Ohio 43224.

Headquarters for Wayne National Forest are shared with those for Indiana's Hoosier National Forest: at 1615 J Street, Bedford, Indiana 47421.

TRAILS IN WAYNE NATIONAL FOREST

VESUVIUS TRAIL

Location: In the Wayne National Forest, a mile east of Ohio Route 93, 8 miles north of Ironton.

Length: 15 miles.

U.S.G.S. Quads: Sherrits, Kitts Hill; both 7.5 minutes.

Description: The U.S. Forest Service has created the Lake Vesuvius Recreation Area around an artificial lake created by damming Storms Creek. The trail is a loop that winds through the hilly wooded country starting and ending near the Vesuvius Iron Furnace. The furnace was built in 1833 and used to smelt iron until 1906.

The recreation area has two campgrounds with 69 sites, five picnic grounds, a boat dock with 40 rowboats for rent, a space for private rowboat mooring, and a bathing beach. Powerboats are not allowed.

Camping is allowed anywhere along the main trail. No camping is allowed on an 8-mile loop that follows the shores of Lake Vesuvius inside the main loop.

The main trail is marked with orange blazes, the inside loop trail with white blazes.

A trail map and brochure are available from the District Ranger, Wayne National Forest, Ironton, Ohio 45638.

BLUEGRASS TRAIL

Location: In the Vesuvius Recreation Area of Wayne National Forest east of Portsmouth. Access is from the Kimble Lookout Tower, which is also the easternmost point of the Vesuvius Backpack Trail loop.

Length: 10 miles. Combining this with the Vesuvius Backpack Trail, one can devise a backpack trip of 26 miles.

U.S.G.S. Quads: Sherrits, Kitts Hill; both 7.5 minutes.

Description: The trail is named for Blue Grass Ridge, located at the easternmost point and along the south side of the loop. The trail follows this and other ridges in a circle around Dean Hollow; it also dips twice into the bottomland forests along Elkins Creek. The path follows a gravel road for about a quarter mile east along Elkins Creek. Otherwise it follows a forest service single-lane trail through oak-hickory forests and scattered pine plantations.

Camping is allowed anywhere; there are no designated sites.

For more information, write the District Ranger, Ironton Ranger District, U.S. Forest Service, Ironton, Ohio 45638.

WILDCAT HOLLOW TRAIL

Location: Wayne National Forest adjacent to Burr Oak State Park. From Athens take U.S. 33 north to Ohio Route 13. Turn right on 13 and continue north past the Burr Oak Campground. Signs will direct you to the trail head on Forest Road 298.

Length: 13-mile loop.

U.S.G.S. Quads: Corning, Deavertown; both 7.5 minutes.

Description: From the parking area the trail heads northeast through meadows and a bottomland forest of ash, walnut, and elm trees along the banks of Eels Run Creek. It heads gently uphill past an old one-room schoolhouse, an oil well site, and an abandoned farmhouse, then continues north on ridge tops and slopes forested with oaks and hickories.

It follows old roads for brief stretches on this eastern half of the loop, then turns east, crosses old State Road 16, passes a former oil drilling site, and heads south, mostly along forest roads 297, 113, and 112, now closed to motor vehicles and reserved for foot traffic only.

At the point where the trail reaches the creek called Cedar Run, another old forest road (No. 114) heads west up Wildcat Hollow. Side trips up that road or, alternately, up Cedar Run Creek, make for nice detours with several good natural campsites.

There are no designated campsites on the whole trail. Backpackers may camp wherever they like on national forestland.

For more information, write Athens District Ranger, Wayne National Forest, Athens, Ohio 45701.

TRAILS IN STATE FORESTS

SHAWNEE BACKPACK TRAIL

Location: In the Shawnee State Forest along the Ohio River west of Portsmouth. The trail is a loop that begins at a parking area on Ohio 125 across from the Shawnee State Park Lodge on Turkey Creek Lake. (The boundaries of the state park lie within and adjacent to those for Shawnee State Forest.)

Length: 57.9 miles including side trails. Main trail loop is 42.8 miles.

U.S.G.S. Quads: Otway, West Portsmouth, Buena Vista, Pond Run, Friendship; all 7.5 minutes.

Description: The countryside here is hilly and covered with hardwood forest. Elevations along the trail range from above 1,200 feet on the hilltops to less than 700 feet in the hollows. The trail crosses a number of hollows, so there is a good deal of up-and-down walking.

The trail heads east from the start, crossing Forest Road 1 after about 3 miles and Forest Road 14 after another 3. Along the way it crosses six separate hollows. These are dry most of the time, but they may have running water in wet seasons. Just beyond Forest Road 14 there is

Vesuvius Trail

Welcome to the Wayne National Forest and to the Lake Vesuvius hiking trail system.

These trails wind through some of the most striking natural beauty in Ohio. With your help in preventing fires, littering and vegetation destruction, the area will remain beautiful for generations to come.

The trails will lead you through a variety of plant types and near many types of wildlife. You will see open fields, brushland, mature forest and new forest. Along the way you will recognize man's influence and management techniques.

With proper planning, quiet and careful travel, and keen observation, your hike can become an experience you will long remember.

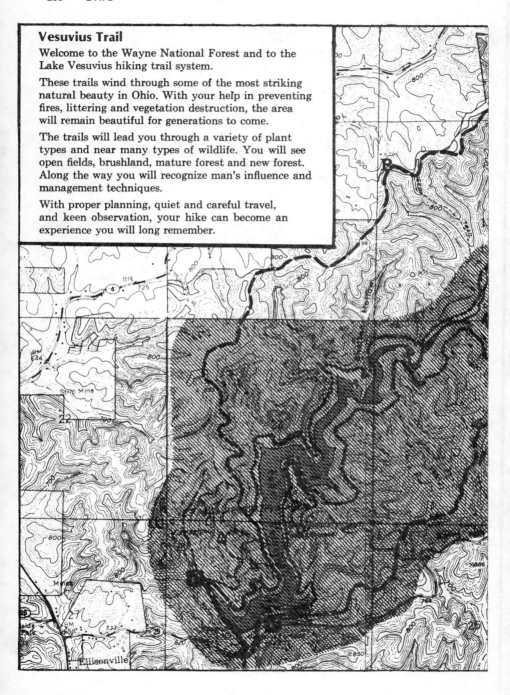

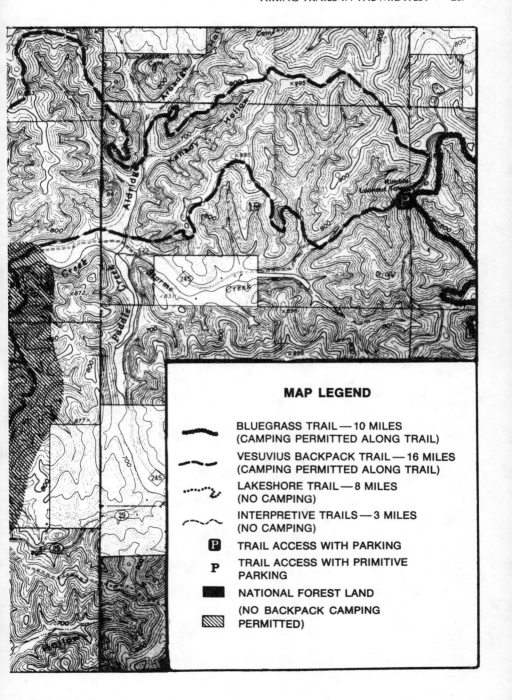

MAP LEGEND

BLUEGRASS TRAIL — 10 MILES
(CAMPING PERMITTED ALONG TRAIL)

VESUVIUS BACKPACK TRAIL — 16 MILES
(CAMPING PERMITTED ALONG TRAIL)

LAKESHORE TRAIL — 8 MILES
(NO CAMPING)

INTERPRETIVE TRAILS — 3 MILES
(NO CAMPING)

P TRAIL ACCESS WITH PARKING

P TRAIL ACCESS WITH PRIMITIVE
PARKING

NATIONAL FOREST LAND

(NO BACKPACK CAMPING
PERMITTED)

Bluegrass Trail

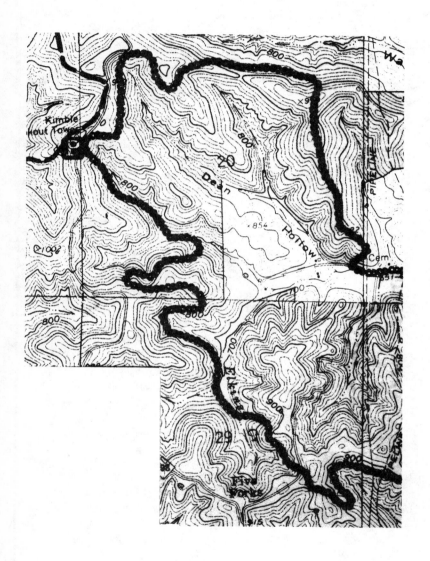

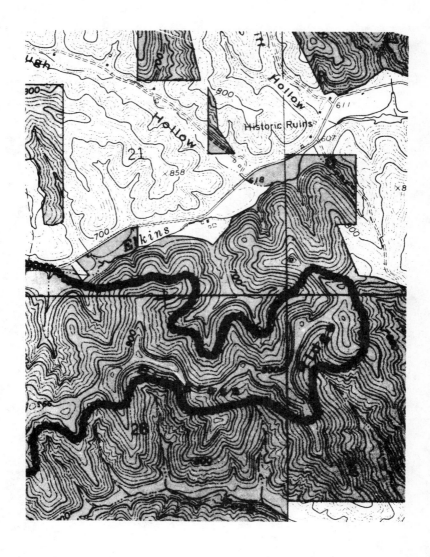

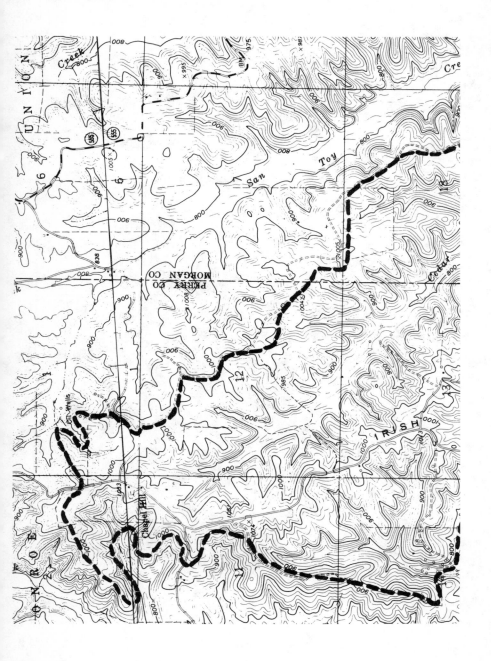

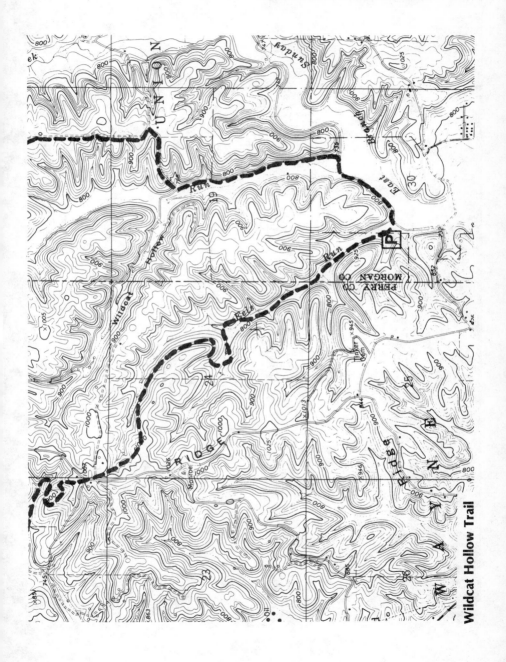

Wildcat Hollow Trail

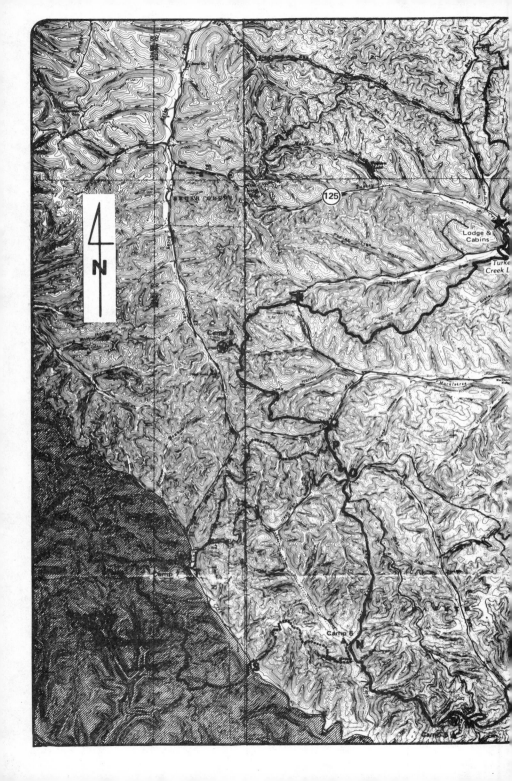

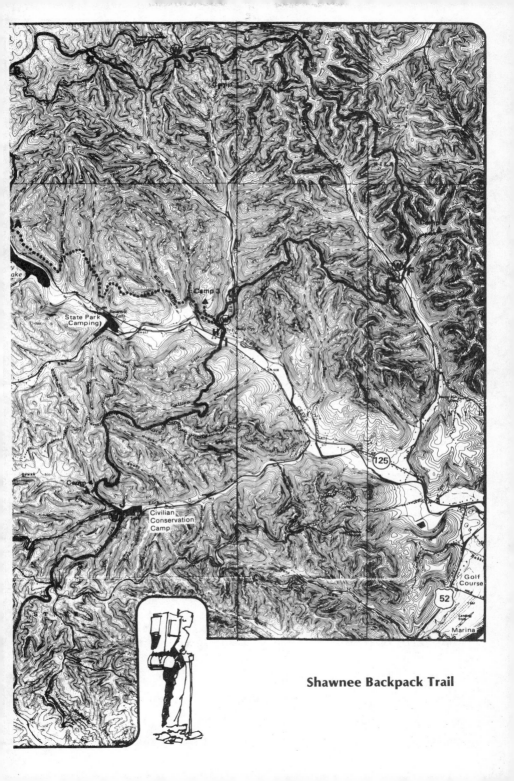

Shawnee Backpack Trail

drinking water and a primitive campsite on the hillside above Zarne Hollow.

The trail heads northwest from here, roughly parallel to 14. It crosses Forest Road 1, and then goes straight west for about 5 miles. There is another campsite at the head of Rock Lick Hollow, and drinking water is available where the trail touches Forest Road 6 near Copperhead Lookout Tower. The trail crosses Route 6 twice along this stretch before heading south for about 3 miles back to the starting point.

The main trail is marked with orange blazes, and side trails to campsites are marked with white. Camping is permitted only in the prepared campsites, and fires are allowed only in fire rings at these sites. There are rattlesnakes and copperheads in this area, and a snake bite kit should be brought along.

Registration forms are provided at the starting point, and all hikers are required to fill them out before starting on a hike.

Since our first edition of this book was published, the state forest has extended the trail with a 29.2-mile loop south of Ohio Route 125 and yet another loop extension of about 10½ miles that explores a remote roadless area designated as a state wilderness. All of the main trail, including the northern loop, is now marked with orange blazes. Side trails are blazed with white.

The original loop trail was 20 miles; the current one is almost 60 miles and passes through much more rugged and remote country. This part of the state is referred to by Ohioans as the "Little Smokies."

The south loop follows ridge tops and slopes wherever possible, thus avoiding roads (except for occasional crossings). The roads tend to follow the bottomlands along creeks.

There are four designated campsites on the new southern part of the main trail. One of those, on the site of an old Civilian Conservation Corps Camp, is also accessible by car. Water, stored in cisterns, is available at three scattered sites near roads. The cisterns cannot be counted on to contain water when you arrive, although they usually do. State forest personnel refill them at regular intervals.

The 10½-mile side loop into the Shawnee Wilderness Area has two designated campsites, one of them at the easternmost junction with the main trail. It has one cistern water source by a road the trail crosses at the wilderness boundary.

Further information: Planometric maps of the Shawnee State Forest and topographic maps of the trail itself are available from the Ohio Department of Natural Resources, Division of Forests and Preserves, Fountain Square, Columbus, Ohio 43224.

ZALESKI BACKPACK TRAIL

Location: Zaleski State Forest in Vinton and Athens counties, about 20 miles west of the town of Athens. The trail head, at which there is a box for self-registration, is on Ohio Route 278 at the north end of Lake Hope.

Length: 21.7 miles.

U.S.G.S. Quads: Mineral, Union Furnace; both 7.5 minutes.

Description: The land this trail traverses hasn't been what anybody would call wilderness for a very long time. Indians of a mound-building culture called the Adena had villages in the area (one along the trail route) between 800 B.C. and 700 A.D. Iron mining was a source of local income at the time of the Civil War. The region was more heavily populated in the 1870s, however, than it is today. Still, the ghost towns, abandoned farm sites, and other scenes of former human activity combine with forest scenery to make a pleasant country hike.

The terrain is moderately hilly with elevations in the 800- to 1,000-foot range. Because the trail follows a combination of old township roads, forest roads, and abandoned railroad beds, it can usually be depended on to follow the paths of least resistance. There are no really strenuous climbs.

Water is theoretically provided in cisterns placed at strategic intervals along the trail. The cisterns have been known to leak, and they are not always refilled as soon as they empty. It is hard for the forest service to gauge how many people will use the trail—or how much water they will drink—on a particular weekend.

The main trail is marked with orange blazes, side trails with white blazes. From the trail head at Lake Hope the path leads east along a ridge about 2 miles to the first designated campsite. From the campground, it heads south on a road that was, until 1870, the main route from Marietta to Chillicothe.

The trail turns sharply north, then to the head of Bass Hollow and follows it downhill to a creek called Hewett Fork. The point where the trail reaches a railroad track was the site of an iron mining town called Ingham Station a hundred years ago. An old cellar hole by the trail is one of few existing remnants of civilization. The entrance to the old Ingham Mine is farther up the trail and to the left.

The path heads north uphill and turns northwest to the site of a ceremonial ring used by mound-building Indians of the Adena group active in southern Ohio between 800 B.C. and 700 A.D. You are again following the old Marietta to Chillicothe Road at this point. The chips of black flint in the road surface are said to have been "the third most important flint" to the Indians of Ohio in prehistoric times.

After the trail crosses King Hollow Road it turns west again to intersect a shortcut trail leading west along the north slope of a hill above Harbargar Hollow back to the trail's beginning point at Lake Hope.

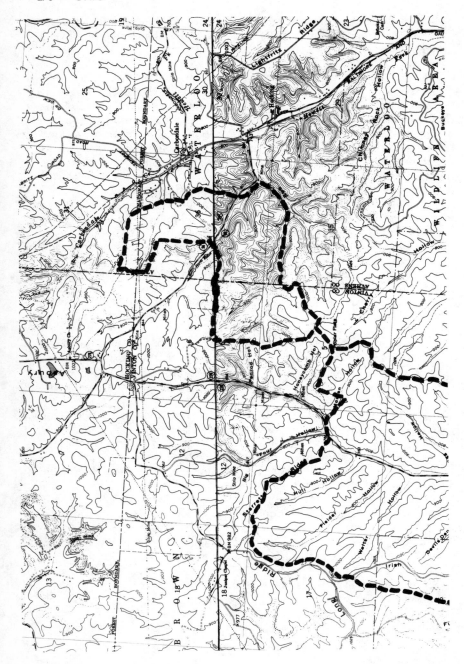

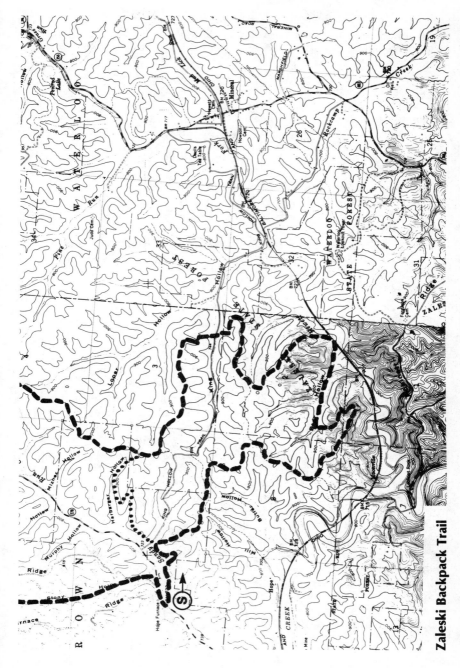

Zaleski Backpack Trail

The main trail continues north through a management area where wild turkey was introduced several years ago. The trail also passes by an Adena Indian burial ground on a high ridge on this stretch. About half a mile past the burial mound, hikers have the choice of continuing north and east for a 5.7-mile loop hike that will come back to this point or of taking the left fork and continuing west and then south about 5 miles to Lake Hope.

Points of interest on the smaller northern loop include a 60-acre unmanaged pine plantation that dates from 1906. A total of 197 species of vascular plants were collected, identified, and deposited in the Bartley Herbarium of Ohio University during a 1964–65 ecological study of the forest.

The route back follows an old township road past the site of a former "drift mine." The vein of coal, exposed by natural drainage, was extracted by hand and cart. The vein was mined wherever it drifted; thus its name.

Foundation stones, fencerows in disrepair, and ornamental shade and fruit trees are reminders of former farms along this last stretch of trail.

For more information on the trail and the forest, write Zaleski State Forest, Division of Forestry, Zaleski, Ohio 45698.

BRIEFLY NOTED TRAIL

THE BUCKEYE TRAIL

Because this 900-mile trail mainly follows county and township roads through the state, we have not described it in this book, which is meant mainly for backpackers. Sections of it make pleasant day hikes or bicycle trips, however, especially in the hilly southern part of the state where it passes through a number of state park and state forestlands. In Tar Hollow State Forest (Route 1, Londonderry, Ohio 45647), it has been rerouted in the last year (1978 and 1979) to run parallel to but off roads for a 16-mile segment. We chose not to describe that segment in detail only because no backcountry camping is allowed along it. That policy, too, may change in the next few years.

The Buckeye Trail begins at the Ohio River in Cincinnati. One branch extends northward through Dayton toward Toledo. The other branch heads east, passing south of Chillicothe, Lancaster, and Zanesville. It then turns north, passing east of Cambridge and through Massillon. Just north of Massillon, it splits into two parts. One part skirts the western edge of Akron and the eastern edge of Cleveland through the metroparks system (see Urban Trails). The other branch goes around Akron to the east and then heads north toward Lake Erie. The two branches meet just south of the lake, and the trail ends on the lakefront near a spot called Fairport Harbor.

The Buckeye Trail Association—a group of volunteers who develop, extend, and maintain the trail—is headquartered at 913 Ohio Departments Building, 65 South Front Street, Columbus, Ohio 43215. They sell maps of the trail for 25 cents apiece. (Each map covers roughly a single county.) Memberships are $3 for individuals, $5 for families, and $10 for organizations. Membership entitles you to a quarterly newsletter which, among other things, lists organization outings. The trail is marked throughout its length with 2 by 6 inch blue blazes.

URBAN WILDS

CLEVELAND METROPARKS
The Cleveland Metroparks system is a greenbelt of 18,500 acres maintained, for the most part, in a natural state along Cleveland area watercourses—the Cuyahoga, Rocky, and Chagrin rivers; and Tinkers Creek. A 100-mile network of trails, including a segment of the statewide Buckeye Trail, winds through the park's 12 separate units. No camping is allowed, but the trails make pleasant day hikes.

The woodlands, according to chief naturalist Robert F. Furlong, include beech and maple groves on moist hillsides; oaks and hickories on the well-drained ridges; cottonwoods, sycamores, and willows in the floodplains.

Special attractions include Tinker's Creek Gorge, where that stream flows between cliffs nearly 200 feet high, and the Lake Isaac Wildlife Sanctuary in the Big Creek division.

Special events, including guided tours with park naturalists, are listed in a free monthly newsletter called the Emerald Necklace.

Maps and detailed information on each park in the system are available from Cleveland Metroparks, 55 Public Square, Cleveland, Ohio 44113.

CUYAHOGA VALLEY NATIONAL RECREATION AREA
One of the newest of a series of "urban parks" established in recent years by the National Park Service, Cuyahoga was created in 1974 along the river between Cleveland and Akron. There are no developed trails yet, but this is an area for hikers to watch in the next few years.

The address is Cuyahoga Valley National Recreation Area, P. O. Box 158, Peninsula, Ohio 44264.

11

MISSOURI

Trails in the Mark Twain National Forest
  Hercules Glade Wilderness—Ava District
  Ridge Runner Trail—Willow Springs District
  John J. Audubon Trail—Fredericktown District
  Berryman Trail—Potosi District
  Moses Austin Trail—Potosi District
  Victory Trail—Poplar Bluff District
  Trace Creek Trail—Fredericktown District
  Big Piney Trail—Houston District
  Whites Creek Trail—VanBuren District
  Devil's Backbone Trail—Cedar Creek Purchase Unit
Areas to Explore Cross-Country
  Rockpile Mountain Wilderness (proposed)
  Bell Mountain Wilderness (proposed)
  Devil's Backbone Wilderness (proposed)
  Piney Creek Wilderness (proposed)
National Park Service
  Big Spring Ozark Trail—Big Spring National Park/Ozark
    National Scenic Riverways
Trails in State Parks
  Lake Wappapello Backpack Trail—Lake Wappapello State
    Park
  Whispering Pine Trail—Hawn State Park
  Mudlick Mountain Trail—Sam A. Baker State Park
  Peewah Trail—Trail of Tears State Park
  Rocky Wood Trail—Washington State Park
Taum Sauk Trail
Moniteau Wilderness Trail, Rudolph-Bennett State Wildlife
  Area
Ozark Trail
Urban Wilds

THE OZARKS—AN INTRODUCTION

GEOLOGY
Strictly speaking, the Ozark Mountains are not mountains at all but a

series of broad plateaus deeply dissected by rivers. In Missouri there are three of these plateaus: the Springfield Plateau in the west, the Salem Plateau in the southcentral part of the state, and the St. Francois Mountains in the east. Of the three, the St. Francois range has the highest elevations and the oldest exposed rocks; the Salem Plateau has the broadest ridge tops and tableland.

The geologic history of the region began with a spate of volcanic activity that occurred between 1.2 and 1.5 billion years ago. Several different outbursts produced masses of rhyolite, granite, and basalt.

The sea began to rise over this landscape some 525 million years ago. Algal reefs grew around the submerged areas, and sand settled on the edges. In time the algal reefs became limestone; the sand, sandstone. Lead and zinc ore were created during this period. So was chert, a dense quartzlike mineral that is everywhere. The Indians used it to make scraping tools and arrowheads. You will probably encounter it the first time you try spreading a sleeping bag on a rocky Ozark hillside.

Through much of the Paleozoic Era, the Ozarks lay under the sea. As the seas receded, the area was subjected to uplift several times, the most significant about 380 million years ago.

The land that rose above that ancient sea was at first flat, a thick accumulation of sediments from the sea bottom. The rivers went to work then, creating the present landscape.

They cut the narrow, meandering, steep-sided valleys. They sculpted the spectacular bluffs that wall in the valleys. In places, they cut through the sedimentary rock down to the basalt and granite and rhyolite that underlay the plateau.

The waters working in porous limestone created the caves that honeycomb the Ozarks. The porous nature of this typical rock also tends to remove water from the surface very rapidly. Valleys big enough to support a substantial stream elsewhere are often dry in the Ozarks except after a heavy rain.

With so much water underground, springs—some producing an enormous amount of water—are common. Creeks and rivers sometimes simply disappear into the porous rock, only to reappear downstream. "Lost Creek" is a typical name for streams throughout the region.

Many of the ridge tops are still broad enough to sustain farms, a fact that is important to hikers. Streams running through wild lands often contain water unsafe for drinking because cows graze in the fields above.

FLORA AND FAUNA

Ozark flora and fauna are diverse, because the region is at the edge of the eastern deciduous forests where they meet the Great Plains.

Oak-hickory and oak-pine forests are the most common associations.

Typical understory trees include sassafras and flowering dogwood, redbud, shadbush, witch hazel, pawpaw, deciduous holly, southern buckthorn, wild plum and crabapple, locust, and silver bell. Red cedar predominates on barren limestone or granite "glades," largely open patches of ground covered with prairie grasses and wildflowers.

Many mammals that were once abundant have been extirpated by hunting and habitat destruction. The elk, bison, and puma are gone. Bears and beaver disappeared for a while, but they have been successfully reintroduced in several areas.

Birds are generally those of the eastern woodlands, with some invasion by western species such as the road runner and the scissor-tailed flycatcher. Turkey vultures, locally known as Ozark eagles, seem slightly less common than robins. Wild turkey and ruffed grouse have been reintroduced in recent years and are apparently thriving.

The plants and animals that pose problems for backpackers include poison ivy, chiggers, ticks, mosquitoes, and several species of venomous reptiles.

TRAILS IN THE MARK TWAIN NATIONAL FOREST

HERCULES GLADES WILDERNESS

Location: Ava Ranger District of the Mark Twain National Forest. To reach the trail head and official wilderness entry point at the Hercules Fire Tower, drive east from Branson 18 miles on U.S. 160, then left (north) on Missouri Highway 125 for 7½ miles.

Length: 25-mile network (approximately).

U.S.G.S. Quad: Hilda, 7.5 minutes.

Description: The cedar glade is a particularly Ozark phenomenon. It occurs on southern and southwest slopes, on limestone or granite bedrock with very little topsoil, and is characterized by a great deal of open ground where prairie grasses and flowers grow. Hercules Glades, a 12,315-acre area, was officially designated a United States Wilderness in 1976 to preserve an unusually fine example of this habitat.

A majority of the scattered trees are red cedar; some are the similar-looking Ashe juniper. The American smoketree, which grows only in a tiny portion of the Appalachians, in this small section of the Ozarks, and in another small area in Texas, is also something special to watch for.

The prairie plants include shooting star, prairie coreopsis, Missouri primrose, various species of larkspur (delphinium), big and little blue-stem, sideoats grama, and switch grass.

Animals atypical of most of the Ozarks that frequent this special environment include the road runner (a bird more common farther west), stingertailed scorpion, and collard lizard.

While glades are interesting and beautiful to see, they are not

Hercules Glades Wilderness—west section

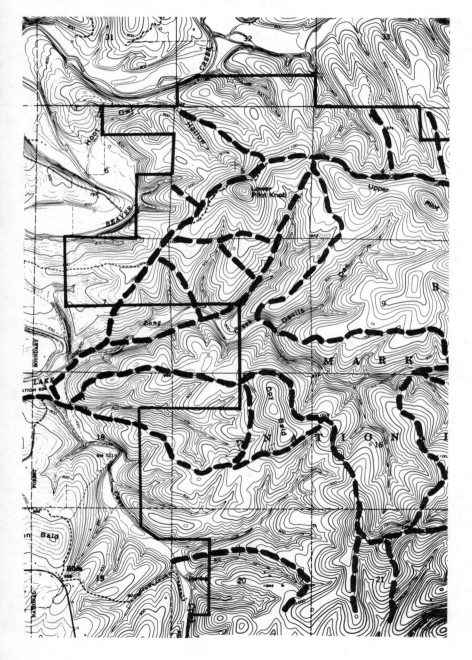

Hercules Glades Wilderness—east section

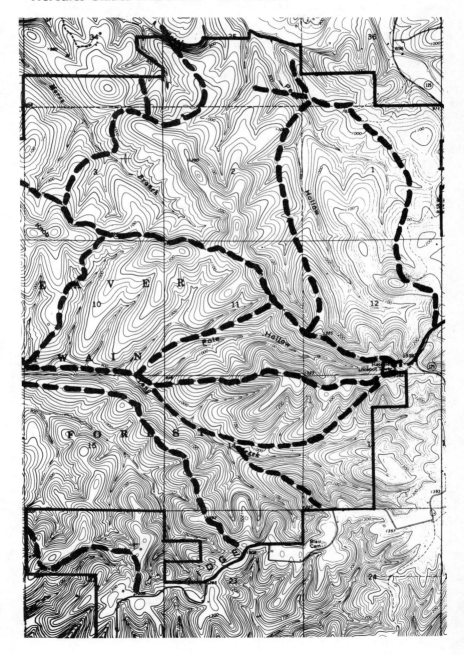

especially hospitable to overnight camping, as you will already have deduced. The acreage contained in the wilderness, however, also includes more typical Ozark oak-hickory forests, as well as some breathtakingly beautiful meadows and rich bottomland forests along the banks of three streams—Brushy Creek, Long Creek, and Cane Creek.

The wilderness also encompasses the upper reaches of the Beaver Creek Arm of Bull Shoals Lake.

Long Creek is especially noted for a series of waterfalls—including one 6 feet high and another 10 feet high, the latter cascading through a dolomite cleft.

The trail network is basically a loop of about 15 miles with smaller loops inside it. Most of the trails have grown there naturally over long years of use by local hunters, fishermen, and hikers. Several of them are extensions of old fire trails and logging roads. They follow ridge lines, slopes, and creeks, and offer side trips to various "balds"— mountaintops with vegetation consisting solely of grass, shrubs, and wildflowers. The views are numerous and spectacular.

The slopes just below the Hercules Tower are rife with flowering dogwood in spring.

Elevation varies from the high point of 1,382 feet at the tower to 700 feet on Long Creek at the western boundary.

RIDGE RUNNER TRAIL
Location: Willow Springs Ranger District in the Mark Twain National Forest. The north end of the trail is at Noblett Lake Recreation Area, and the southern end is at North Fork Recreation Area adjacent to the proposed Devil's Backbone Wilderness.

To reach Noblett Lake head west on Missouri Highway 76 from Willow Springs about 7 miles to Missouri Highway 181. Turn left (south) on 181, 1½ miles to County Highway AP. Turn left on AP about a half mile to the Noblett Lake entrance road. There are signs.

To reach the North Fork Recreation Area on the North Fork River, drive west from the town of West Plains on County Highway CC about 17 miles.
Length: 21 miles. Two additional loops are planned but were not built as of 1979.
U.S.G.S. Quads: Dora, Siloam Springs, Dyestone Mountain; all 7.5 minutes.
Description: This trail, built early in 1979, has been nominated for special designation as a National Recreation Trail and was laid out to provide as much variety in Ozark scenery as possible.

It is a standard 4-foot-wide forest service trail, does not use any existing roads, and is marked with white or orange plastic diamonds.

There are cedar glades with uncommon prairie plants on south-facing

Ridge Runner Trail—north section

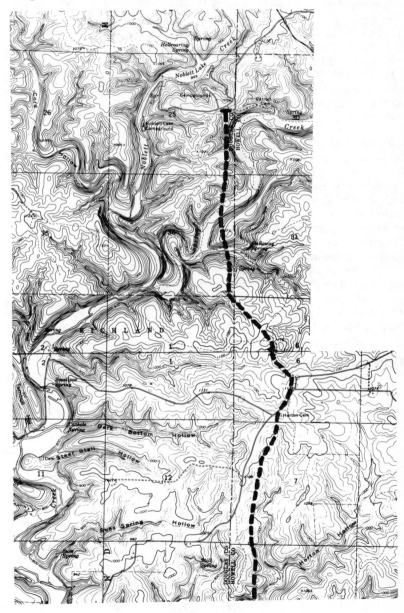

slopes, shortleaf pine and oak-hickory on north slopes. There are views of the North Fork River from atop limestone bluffs, and in the hollows the forest is rich with walnut, sassafras, and dogwood trees. Redbud shrubs bloom in March (late February in some years), dogwoods in early April. There are also periodic wildlife openings, planted in clover and winter wheat.

North Fork River, which parallels the trail for several miles at the trail's south end, and Spring Creek near the northern end, flow year-round. Taber and Dry creeks are intermittent. Hikers should carry their own water to make sure of a supply.

JOHN J. AUDUBON TRAIL
Location: In the Fredericktown District of the Mark Twain National Forest, about 50 miles south of St. Louis, 20 miles southwest of Ste. Genevieve. From Ste. Genevieve on I-55, take County Highway B south and west to County Highway W. Go east (left) on W to Clearwater. From the Clearwater post office, proceed 1.5 miles, then turn right on an unmarked gravel road. Follow it for 0.5 mile, then turn right again on another gravel road for 0.4 mile. Turn left on Forest Road 2199, for 6.5 miles to the trail head, where the road fords Bidwell Creek.

If you're approaching from Fredericktown, head north on County Highway OO to Highway T, turn right (east) on T to Forest Road 2199 a mile east of Womack, then left (north) on Forest Road 2199, 4.6 miles to the Bidwell Creek Ford.
Length: 12-mile loop.
U.S.G.S. Quad: Womack, 7.5 minutes.

Ridge Runner Trail—southeast section

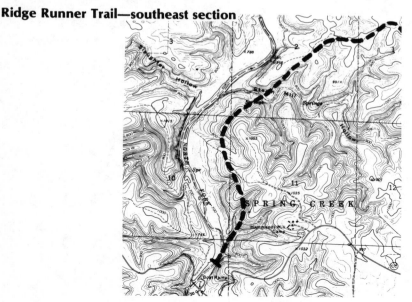

Ridge Runner Trail—central section

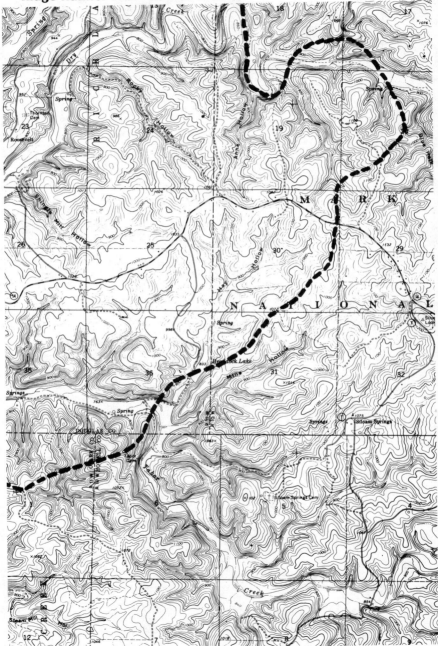

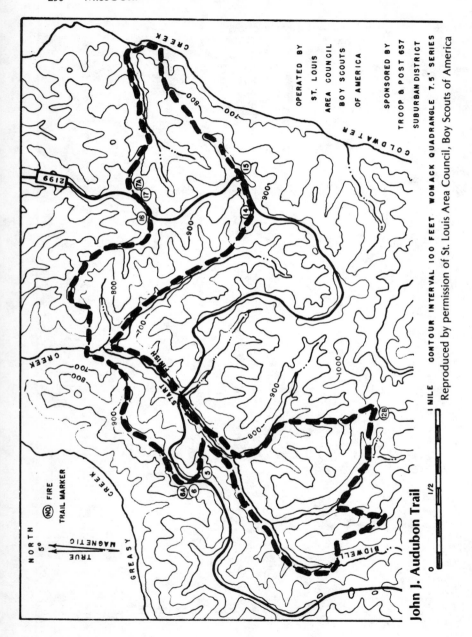

John J. Audubon Trail

Description: John J. Audubon, the 19th-century naturalist and bird artist, lived and worked in nearby Ste. Genevieve between 1810 and 1840, and his trips to the woods often brought him to this area. The St. Louis Area Council of the Boy Scouts of America built and maintains this trail, and they offer a trail patch featuring a scarlet tanager, one of the birds Audubon painted from specimens obtained near here. (If you are in the area on an Audubon pilgrimage, you may want to visit the Ste. Genevieve City Museum, which contains an exhibit featuring birds mounted by Audubon.)

The trail markings—rectangular 2 by 6 inch white paint blazes—assume travel in a counterclockwise direction. Terrain is rugged. According to a brochure available from the Scouts, "the hiker will encounter about 3,000 vertical feet of ups and downs on the 12-mile route." Elevation ranges from 700 to 1,000 feet.

The trail alternates between following the banks of perennial streams and following the slopes of ridges. Open glades along the streambeds offer trail camping possibilities during much of the year. Spring hikers should be alert for flash floods.

Vantage points from the tops of two knobs and several ridges along the trail offer views of the surrounding countryside.

The path crosses Forest Road 2199 four times and at one point follows the road for about a quarter mile.

Willows, sycamores, and cane line the creek banks. The forest on higher slopes is mainly oak and hickory, with sassafras and dogwood on richer sites.

The Scouting organization asks hikers not to smoke or hunt along the trail. For more information on this and other Missouri trails managed by Scouts, write St. Louis Area Council, Boy Scouts of America (see list of sources at end of chapter).

BERRYMAN TRAIL

Location: Potosi Ranger District of the Mark Twain National Forest. To reach the trail head at the Berryman Campground, drive west from Potosi 17 miles on Missouri Highway 8, then north (right) a mile on Forest Road 2266.

Length: 24 miles.

U.S.G.S. Quads: Berryman, 15 minutes; Anthonies Mill, 7.5 minutes.

Description: The trail winds through forests of oak, pine, and bottom-land hardwoods, climbing switchback fashion from narrow valleys to high cherty ridges. Old fields and open cedar glades alternate with the wooded tracts.

There are four campsites with picnic tables, fireplaces, and toilets but no drinking water along the route. (The artesian wells are for stock watering only. This trail was constructed originally for equestrians.) Hikers may also choose their own backcountry tent sites. Brazil Creek

Berryman Trail

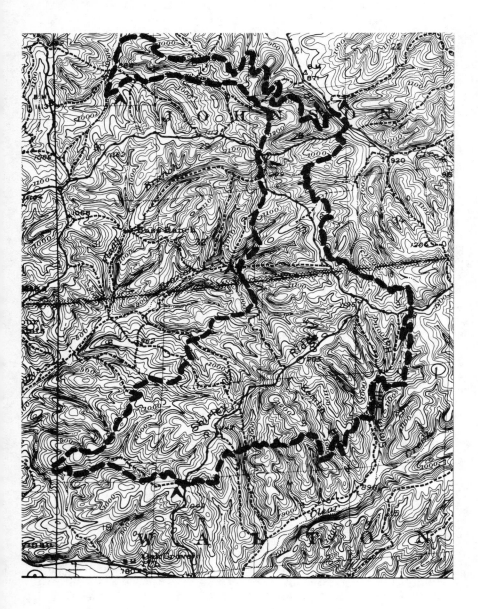

contains water year-round; the other streams are intermittent.

A gravel road which intersects the trail just south of the Brazil Creek Campground leads uphill 3 miles to the Floyd Lookout Tower on Little Pilot Knob Mountain (elevation 1,412 feet). A ½-mile trail from the tower links up with the Moses Austin Trail. The Forest Service plans soon to connect the Trace Creek Trail with the other two for a 120-mile loop.

MOSES AUSTIN TRAIL

Location: Washington County in the Potosi Ranger District of the Mark Twain National Forest. From the junction of state highways 8 and 21 in Potosi, drive west on Missouri Highway 8 for 11 miles, then north (right) on County Road AA for 3.3 miles, then left (west) on an unmarked gravel road for 1.5 miles to the junction with a fire trail. Turn right or left and park in the open areas off the fire trail.

Length: 14.5-mile loop plus a 1.2-mile side trail to the summit of Little Pilot Knob.

U.S.G.S. Quad: Shirley, 7.5 minutes.

Description: Moses Austin founded the settlement of nearby Potosi with a land grant from the Spanish governor in 1798. He mined lead and manufactured lead shot and sheet metal in the area, then founded a St. Louis bank with his profits.

When the bank failed in the Panic of 1819, he moved to Texas with his family and there developed plans for the first American colony. He died before his plans were realized, but his son, Stephen Austin, carried them out.

The trail is marked with 2 by 6 inch white rectangular blazes; a double blaze indicates an intersection or change in direction.

Elevation along the route varies from 920 feet in the valley of Scott Branch to 1,412 feet on the summit of Little Pilot Knob. Open meadows along the banks of Scott Branch offer good trail campsites.

Water from the creek or from a spring at trailside should be boiled before drinking. Scattered wildlife ponds indicated on the map may be full of cattails. Don't depend on them for a water source or cleared campsite.

If you begin the loop by heading north from the trail head, you will reach the spring after 3 miles and the side trail heading right to Little Pilot Knob and Floyd Fire Tower after 6½ miles.

You can also begin a hike at the fire tower—on Forest Road 2265, 5 miles west from its junction with County Highway AA.

Other roads on Forest Service or topographic maps may appear to provide access to the trail, but according to a brochure available from the sponsoring Boy Scouts, "none of these is usable except as an emergency exit to a main road. All are either impassable to passenger cars or cross private land."

Moses Austin Trail

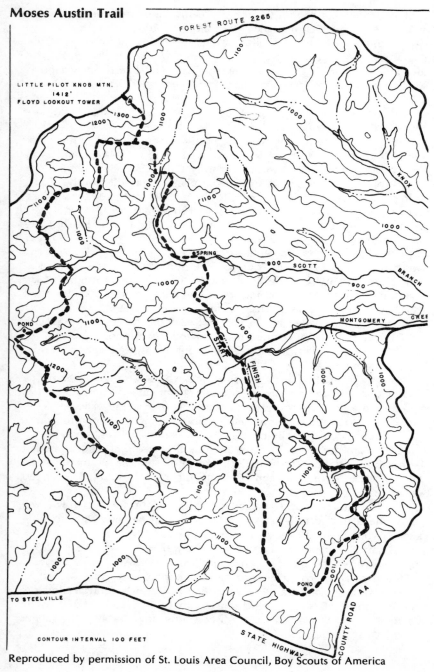

Reproduced by permission of St. Louis Area Council, Boy Scouts of America

For more information about Scout trails, write St. Louis Area Council, Boy Scouts of America.

VICTORY TRAIL

Location: In the Poplar Bluff Ranger District of Mark Twain National Forest. To reach the eastern trail terminus, drive north from Poplar Bluff 6 miles on U.S. Highway 67, then west 2.5 miles on U.S. 60 to a gravel road just west of Goose Creek. Turn right (north) on the gravel road a mile. The trail head is on the right where the road bends left. It is marked by a wooden Forest Service sign.

Length: Approximately 25 miles.

U.S.G.S. Quads: Williamsville, 15 minutes; Mill Spring, 7.5 minutes.

Description: This area of the forest is in the foothills of the Ozark Plateau. That means that the terrain is gentler and the elevation lower (400 to 700 feet) than in districts farther north and west. It also means there are plant species here that are more typical of more southern terrain. Baldcypresses, for instance, may show up on a creek bottom. Sweetgum and yellow poplar are more common than in other areas of the Ozarks.

The Victory Trail was designed for use by horseback riders, but the equestrians have apparently ignored it and it has been taken over by backpackers. The white rectangular blazes on trees are re-marked once a year.

Much of the trail is through deep woods; there are views from the ridge tops mainly in winter. The path crosses several perennial creeks, notably Cane and Brushy creeks, and numerous intermittent ones.

It heads north and west from the trail head near the Victory School, crossing Wiley King Hollow and Forest Road 3526 after 4 miles, and Forest Road 3111 (where there's a hitching rack) after 8 miles. Part of the route is along old logging roads. The rest is on a standard one-lane Forest Service trail.

At the 12-mile point, the trail reaches a parking area and alternate access point on County Highway A about 6 miles northeast of the town of Ellsinore. West of this point, the path follows a logging road for several miles to its end, then cuts cross-country again through Kelley Valley and across Forest Road 3129 before angling north to end at a hitching rack on County Highway KK.

TRACE CREEK TRAIL

Location: Potosi District of the Mark Twain National Forest. To reach Keith Spring, the forest recreation area that is the starting point for this trail, take State Highway 21 north to the junction with Missouri Highway 32 north of Belleview. Take 32 west about 11 miles to Keith Spring.

Length: 8 miles.

U.S.G.S. Quad: Johnson Mountain, 7.5 minutes.

Victory Trail

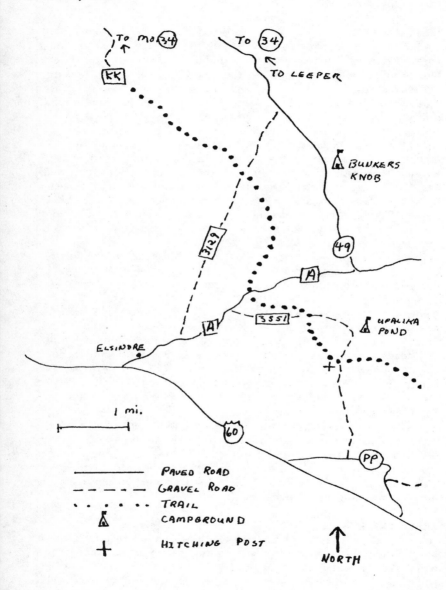

To mo 34

To 34

↑
TO LEEPER

KK

Bunkers Knob

JT29

49

A

A

3551

Upalika Pond

Elsinore

+

1 mi.

60

PP

————— PAVED ROAD

— — — — GRAVEL ROAD

· · · · · · TRAIL

Campground

+ HITCHING POST

↑
NORTH

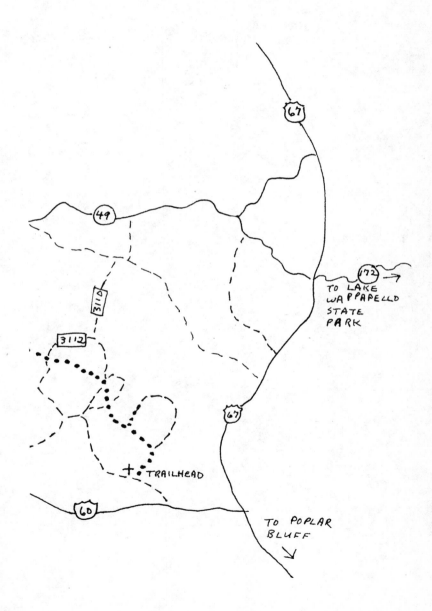

Trace Creek Trail

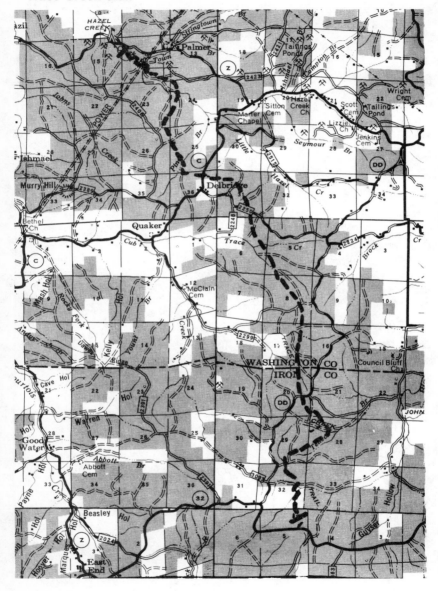

Description: This little trail runs entirely through deciduous forests and involves little climbing. There are three creeks to cross within the 8 miles, all of them ideal sites for a picnic. There are no campground facilities at Keith Spring, nor are there any along the trail, with the exception of a primitive hunter's cabin just before the junction of the trail with County Road DD.

The footpath comes to an end at a secondary road about half a mile west of another intersection with Highway DD. If you want to avoid retracing your steps back to Keith Spring, you can walk west and south along the road instead. When the county road intersects Forest Road 2391, take the forest road south to State Highway 32 and the state highway east for a mile to Keith Spring.

The Forest Service and the Sierra Club are working to lay out an extension for the Trace Creek Trail that will connect it to the Moses Austin and Berryman trails for a 120-mile loop.

BIG PINEY TRAIL
Location: Houston District of the Mark Twain National Forest. To reach the trail head at Paddy Creek Campground, travel east on Missouri Highway 32, 15 miles from its junction with U.S. 63, then north 10 miles on Forest Road 220. You may also begin your hike from the westernmost point at the Roby Lookout Tower, 6 miles south of Fort Leonard Wood on Missouri Highway 17.
Length: 17-mile loop.
U.S.G.S. Quad: Slabtown Spring, 7.5 minutes.
Description: Nearly 7,000 acres of the area this trail traverses have been nominated for designation as Paddy Creek Wilderness. Its strongest claims for such designation are the fine stands of mature pine and two clear and fast-moving streams—Little Paddy and Big Paddy creeks. Both are offshoots of the Big Piney River.

Paddy Creek Campground is the only designated campsite on the trail, but backcountry camping is allowed.

Special attractions along the route include a small cave, a box canyon that formed when fallen sandstone choked off the upper valley, a spring at the base of the box canyon and another 4 miles west, and a spectacular bluff-top view of the Little Piney River.

WHITES CREEK TRAIL
Location: Van Buren Ranger District of the Mark Twain National Forest. To reach the trail's easternmost end at Camp Five Pond, take State Highway 160 west of Doniphan to County Highway J. Take J north about 6 miles to the camp. There is ample space for car parking there and picnic tables with fireplaces, but no overnight camping is permitted.
Length: 20 miles.
U.S.G.S. Quads: Wilderness, Riverton, both 7.5 minutes.

Big Piney Trail—west section

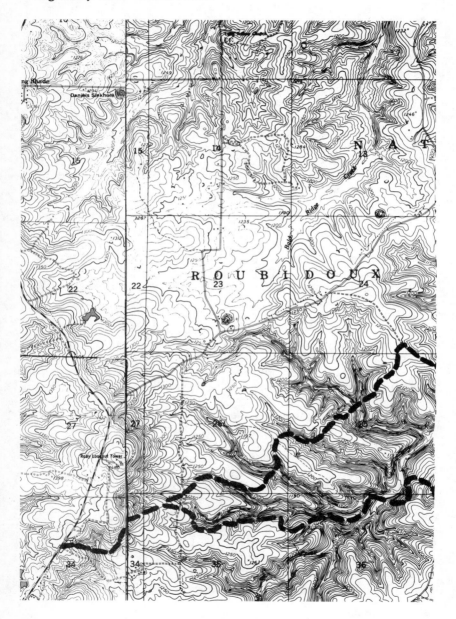

Big Piney Trail—east section

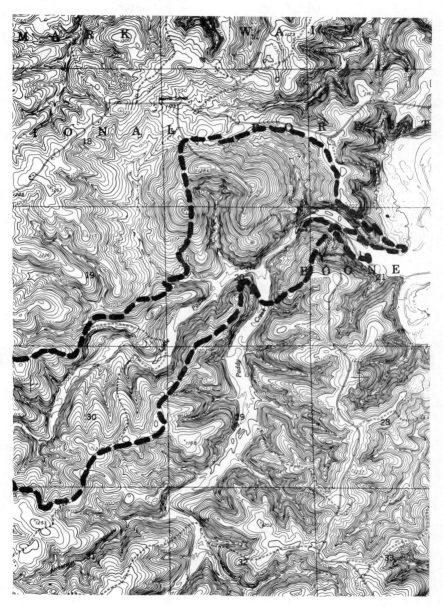

Description: The steep hills and deep hollows in this region were formed by tributaries of the Eleven Point River cutting into the impressionable limestone.

The trail lies entirely within the boundaries of the 17,562-acre proposed Irish Wilderness. It is undoubtedly revered more by environmentalists for its wilderness qualities than any of the other proposals, but it was tabled by the Carter Administration in 1979 for "further study," mainly because of the local congressman's opposition.

The name "Irish Wilderness" derives from a former pioneer religious settlement of Irish immigrants led by Father John Hogan.

The mature forests of the region, approaching "virgin" status, contain an astounding variety of oak species: white, chinquapin, red, scarlet, pine, shumard, Spanish, blackjack, and post oak, to name some.

The Whites Creek Trail makes a good 2-day hike if you get an early start. Bliss Spring Campground is located about halfway along the loop trail.

West of Camp Five Pond the trail winds along on more or less level ground through heavy hardwood forest for a couple of miles before beginning a gentle ascent to Whites Creek.

At the creek about 3½ miles from the trail's beginning, the trail branches to begin the loop. If you take the northern route you will begin climbing almost immediately, ascending 300 feet to the top of a mountain in less than 2 miles. From this peak you will have a good view of Bliss Hollow to the south and the impressive Eleven Point River itself. The Corps of Engineers waged a campaign several years ago to dam the Eleven Point, but conservationists prevailed and it was made a National Scenic River.

The west slope of the mountain is gentle, and the trail follows a ridge line for about 2 miles between Bliss and Brawley Hollows.

It begins a sharp descent and a gentle curve to the south around mile 7. The Eleven Point River is almost immediately below you now at its spectacular Horseshoe Bend. The trail continues along a ridge, but at a lower elevation than before, between the river on the west and Barn Hollow on the east.

Bliss Creek Campground, about 8½ miles by trail from Camp Five Pond, is situated on the riverbank at the southern end of Bliss Hollow. Because this camp is so far from main roads, it is used almost exclusively by hikers from the trail and by fishermen floating the Eleven Point. There are no picnic tables, but there is a well.

Heading back east from Bliss Spring, the trail stays between steep hillsides in Bliss Hollow for most of a mile, then climbs sharply to a ridge overlooking Orchard Hollow. It follows the brow of the ridge around to the south for a mile, then descends again to Whites Creek Cave.

The trail from this point heads north and then quickly south in

Whites Creek Trail

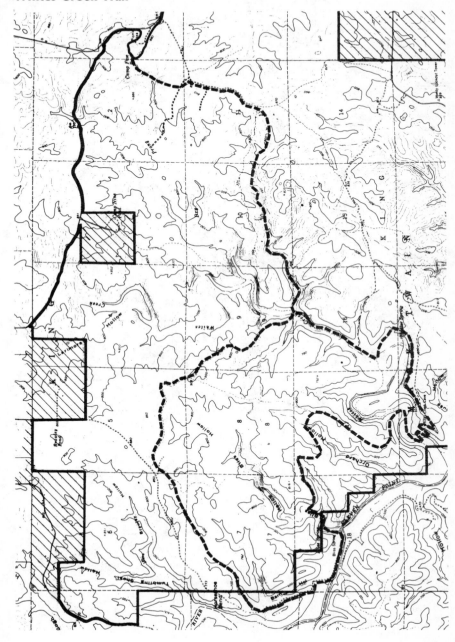

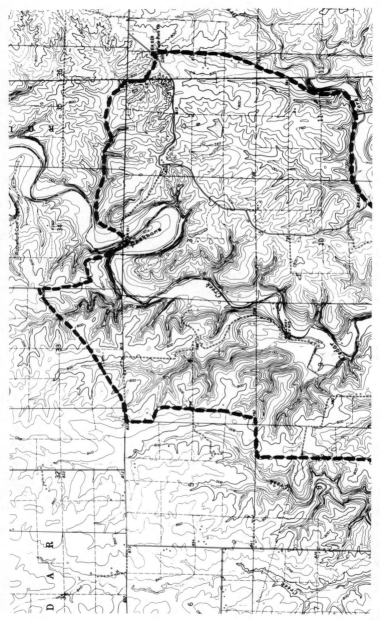

Devil's Backbone Trail—north section

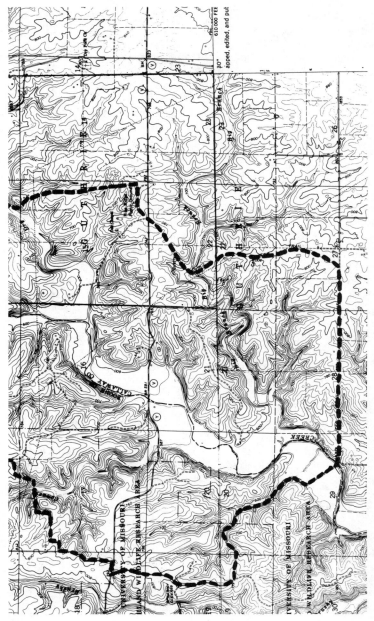

Devil's Backbone Trail— south section

another horseshoe bend for about 1½ miles along Whites Creek to Fiddler Spring.

It heads north then, still along the stream bed for about 1½ miles, to the point where the trail first branched. Retrace your steps of the previous day back east to Camp Five Pond.

DEVIL'S BACKBONE TRAIL

Location: In the Cedar Creek Purchase Unit of the Mark Twain National Forest. The land in this unit lies within a triangle bounded by the cities of Columbia on the northwest, Fulton on the east, and Jefferson City on the south. From the community of Ashland, 10 miles south of Columbia on U.S. 63, drive east on County Road Y about 5½ miles to the Pine Ridge Picnic Area and trail head.

Length: 20-mile loop.

U.S.G.S. Quads: Guthrie, Jefferson City Northwest, Millersburg; all 7.5 minutes.

Description: This newest unit of the forest, established in 1972, is the only one in the glaciated plain north of the Missouri River. It encompasses a 90,000-acre area, but only a little more than 13,000 acres are in public ownership at this point. For hikers that means that much of the trail will be crossing farm fields and other cleared areas. It also means that you can camp only when the metal signs on trees indicate that you are on Forest Service property.

The rock formation for which the trail was named is a horseshoe-shaped limestone bluff on a sharp bend in Cedar Creek.

Principal tree species in the area are white oak, black oak, red oak, hickory, and red cedar on high ground; basswood, walnut, maple, and ash on the slopes; sycamore and black ash in the bottomlands.

The return loop on the west edge of the purchase unit passes through the University of Missouri-owned Ashland Wildlife Research Area.

Fred A. Lafser Jr., author of a book called *Hiking and Backpacking in Missouri* (see our recommended reading list at the end of this chapter), says off-trail exploration through Brushy Creek Valley in this section is worthwhile. "The valley is in near wilderness state," he says, "and features tall limestone bluffs, waterfalls, and huge sycamore trees." Permission would need to be secured from the university.

AREAS TO EXPLORE CROSS-COUNTRY

ROCKPILE MOUNTAIN WILDERNESS (proposed)

Location: Fredericktown District of the Mark Twain National Forest. To reach the trail head at Faro Lookout Tower follow County Highway E

Rockpile Mountain Wilderness (proposed)

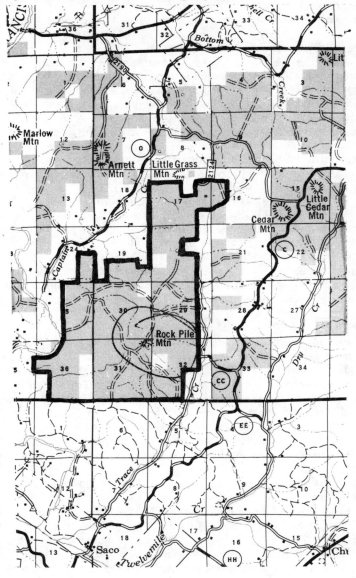

southwest from Fredericktown for 12 miles, then turn left (south) on Highway O for 2 miles.

Length: No formal trails, but about 6 miles of hiking on old logging roads.

U.S.G.S. Quad: Coldwater, 15 minutes.

Description: The 4,170-acre Rockpile Mountain area has been recommended by the Carter Administration for inclusion in the United States Wilderness system. It's a relatively small wilderness consisting mainly of Rockpile Mountain itself (elevation 1,305 feet) and the connecting ridge to Grass Mountain, where the Faro Tower is located. A circular pile of igneous rocks near the summit of Rockpile is thought to designate an Indian burial site.

A virgin cove hardwood forest in a ravine near the St. Francis River is also contained within the proposed wilderness boundaries. Tree species there include walnut, sugar maple, basswood, butternut, bitternut hickory, red oak, white oak, and Kentucky coffee tree.

The main trail route leads along the ridge from Faro Tower on Grass Mountain southwest to Rockpile Mountain. The first side trail on the left south of Faro Tower leads along a ridge to a bluff-top view of the St. Francois River Valley. The second trail to the left also follows a ridge and ends 300 feet above the river. A trail north from Rockpile Mountain leads three quarters of a mile to an intermittent stream carved in black granite; there are rapids in rainy seasons.

BELL MOUNTAIN WILDERNESS (proposed)

Location: South of Missouri Highway 32 and west of Missouri 21 near the town of Belleview in the Potosi District of the Mark Twain National Forest. To reach the main access point, head southwest from Belleview on County Highway O, 4 miles, then west (right) on Forest Road 2228, then south (left) on Forest Road 2359 to a parking area at the end of the road. An alternate access (with no formal parking area) is at the Joe's Creek Bridge on County Highway A southwest of Banner.

Length: No formal trails exist, but there are many old jeep roads and fire lanes. Hikers may also navigate cross-country with map and compass.

U.S.G.S. Quads: Banner, Johnson Mountain, Edgehill, Johnson Shut-Ins; all 7.5 minutes.

Description: This proposed wilderness of 8,530 acres lies in the heart of the St. Francois Mountains, highest in elevation and oldest among those on the Ozark Plateau. The bedrock is a combination of granite and cherty limestone, which makes for a particular kind of bare knobs and craggy, cliff formations unusual in the Ozarks. There are numerous outcroppings of felsite (a very dense igneous rock composed mainly of feldspar and quartz) and rhyolite (a rock that is the lava form of granite).

Bell Mountain itself, for which the wilderness is named, is a long,

Bell Mountain Wilderness (proposed)

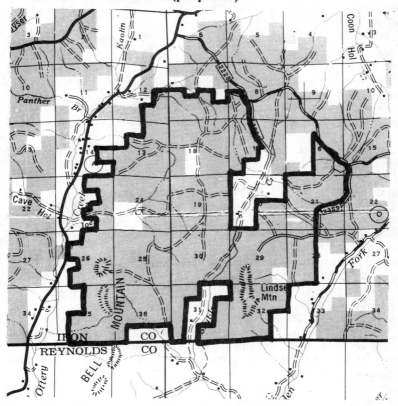

loaf-shaped knob running from north to south. At 1,702 feet, it is one of the highest in the state. (Nearby Taum Sauk Mountain holds the record at 1,772 feet.)

Shut-Ins Creek runs from north to south, bisecting the eastern third of the wilderness and separating Bell Mountain from Lindsey Mountain, the other major local landmark. Joe's Creek has its headwaters on the west side of Bell Mountain and empties into Ottery Creek on the western boundary of the tract.

Most of the forest is covered with oak-hickory and oak-pine forests with a few shortleaf pine plantations; but the crests and upper slopes of both Bell Mountain at its northern end and Lindsey Mountain are "barrens," or granite glades supporting only grasses and a few stunted oaks and shrubs. The Forest Service says 64 percent of the timber in the area is old growth.

Shut-Ins Creek contains a series of scenic waterfalls and "shut-ins," the latter an Ozark term for a place where a stream enters a narrow passage through unyielding igneous rock, forming a high narrow gorge and rapids.

Hikers who enter the wilderness at Joe's Creek often hike east up the creek, camping in meadows along the way, to the headwaters on the west slope of Bell Mountain. Continuing to the ridge top, one is offered a spectacular view of surrounding countryside and the steep 700-foot drop to Shut-Ins Creek east of the mountain.

Those who enter the wilderness from County Highway O on the east climb Lindsey Mountain first and descend to the east bank of Shut-Ins Creek.

Elevation varies from 1,702 feet on Bell Mountain to 970 feet in the Joe's Creek drainage.

DEVIL'S BACKBONE WILDERNESS (proposed)

Location: South of County Road CC and east of the North Fork River in the Willow Springs Ranger District of the Mark Twain National Forest. The main access point is at the North Fork Recreation Area Campground, about 20 miles west of West Plains on CC.

Length: Formal trails are planned but not yet built; logging roads, however, crisscross the area. Hikers are also free to navigate cross-country with map and compass.

U.S.G.S. Quads: Dora, Cureall Northwest, both 7.5 minutes.

Description: This 6,830-acre area was recommended by President Carter in 1979 for designation as Wilderness. A major Ozark stream, the North Fork River, passes through the area, and views are spectacular from the tops of McGarr Ridge, Turkey Point, and Devil's Backbone (the latter two both spurs of Collins Ridge).

Ciffs above the North Fork are formed from limestone and Gasconade dolomite; those above Crooked Branch, major watershed in this wilderness, are of Roubidoux sandstone.

The Devil's Backbone, for which the trail was named, is a horseshoe-shaped bend in a steep narrow ridge, which rises to 1,020 feet above Crooked Branch.

Blue Spring on the North Fork and McGarr Spring and Amber Spring on Crooked Branch provide high-quality sources of drinking water. Blue Spring is accessible by a quarter-mile nature trail from the North Fork Recreation Area Campground. It flows from a deep pool in a large cave opening.

Most of the forest consists of oaks of various species, and hickory. Shortleaf pine grows on the sandstone ridges. Sycamore, elm, witch hazel, cane, and willows thrive on the riverbanks.

The area is so remote that black bear, now absent from most parts of the Ozarks, have resisted extinction there. Bald eagles are seen occasionally along the North Fork River. Ruffed grouse were introduced in

1963 and are prospering. Locals claim to see mountain lion tracks now and then, but there is no official confirmation.

Large and smallmouth bass, rainbow and German brown trout are caught on the river. Professional river guide services (for both canoes and flat-bottomed motorized johnboats) operate out of West Plains and Willow Springs.

Address for the Willow Springs Ranger District of Mark Twain National Forest is P. O. Box 99, Willow Springs, Missouri 65793.

Devil's Backbone Wilderness (proposed)

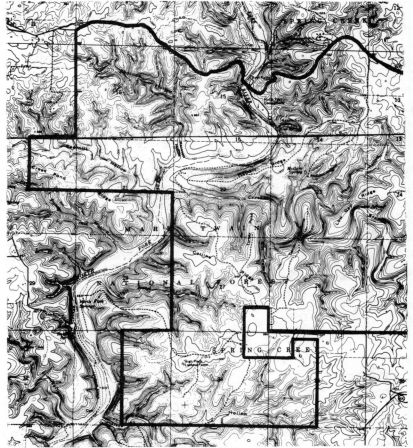

PINEY CREEK WILDERNESS (proposed)

Location: Cassville District of the Mark Twain National Forest. Travel west on Missouri Highway 76, 10 miles from its junction with Missouri

Piney Creek Wilderness (proposed)

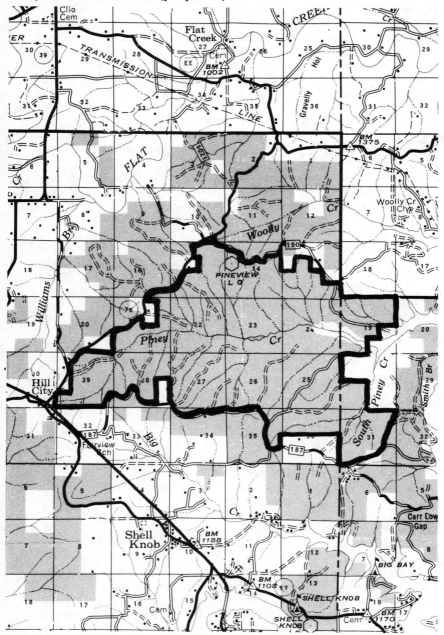

173. Turn southeast on a gravel road about 2 miles past County Highway EE to the Pineview Lookout Tower.

Length: No formal trails exist, but logging roads are plentiful, and cross-country hiking with map and compass is permitted.

U.S.G.S. Quad: Shell Knob, 7.5 minutes.

Description: President Carter recommended designation of this 8,430-acre area in 1979 for inclusion in the United States Wilderness system. Piney Creek, one of few streams in the state left undammed, flows through the area, and most of its watershed is contained within the proposed wilderness boundaries. It empties into the James River arm of Tablerock Lake.

The area has narrower ridges than in many areas of the Ozarks, and it has equally narrow valleys, making for strenuous hiking but also more frequent vistas than are common in other parts of the region.

The plant and animal species common to most of the Ozarks are common here as are a few wanderers from the adjacent prairie country in western Missouri, Oklahoma, and Kansas.

Bald eagles roost in protected areas along the creek; there is also a heron rookery. Hikers should stay away from these if they come on them by accident! Herons will not return to a nesting area that has been disturbed. Hikers may also be barred from future access if the environment is damaged.

Old fields along the banks of Piney Creek near the northern boundary make good campsites. They are also easily accessible for people hiking with children.

NATIONAL PARK SERVICE

BIG SPRING OZARK TRAIL

Location: In Big Spring National Park, administered as part of the Ozark National Scenic Riverways park along the Current River and its tributaries. Four miles south of Van Buren on Missouri Highway 103.

Length: 12.7-mile loop. Two cutoff trails provide shorter loops of 3.9 miles and 5.2 miles respectively.

U.S.G.S. Quads: Big Spring, Van Buren South; both 7.5 minutes.

Description: No other spring in the Ozarks matches Big Spring's flow of nearly a billion liters (277 million gallons) a day. The spring, about half a mile from the Current River it feeds, flows out of a cave in a high bluff and is the single surface outlet for a vast network of underground streams. The former Big Spring State Park and adjacent wildlife refuge were made part of the Ozark National Scenic Riverways in 1970, and the National Park Service now maintains the 5,000-acre property.

The trail begins at a boat landing next to the dining lodge in the park. Look for the standard National Park Service trail sign, a silhouette of a hiker with walking stick. These signs are missing on long stretches of the trail, so care will have to be taken to avoid getting lost.

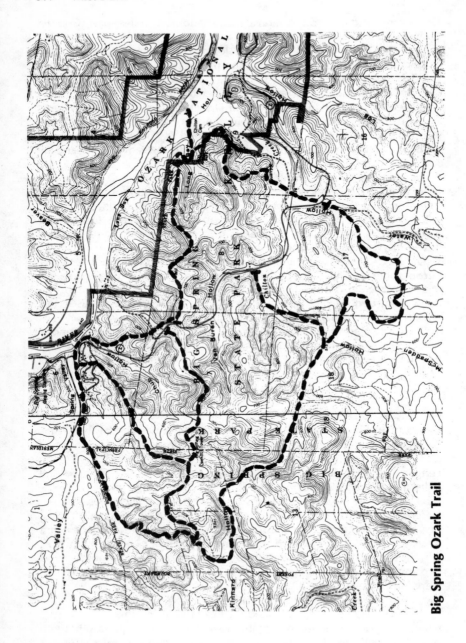

Big Spring Ozark Trail

Topographic maps and a compass are strongly recommended. Elevation ranges from 440 feet to 885 feet.

From the dining lodge the trail crosses an intermittent stream in Chub Hollow, a narrow ravine, then climbs steeply uphill through a rich woods of sugar. maple, walnut, and basswood, with sassafras, dogwood, and pawpaw trees in the understory.

It parallels County Road Z briefly, then cuts east on a ridge top along an old fire trail to a bluff overlooking the river just north of Long Bay.

Leaving the fire trail, it follows a single-lane path south along an east-facing slope above the river, then up a ridge line to join another old logging or fire road. It crosses Chilton Creek and County Road Z at a parking area that serves as an access point for the trail.

It follows an old road uphill to a knob 820 feet in elevation that offers a view of the surrounding area in winter when trees are bare.

As the path descends into McSpadden Hollow you will notice a change in vegetation. The oaks and hickories give way to maples, flowering dogwood and tulip trees, walnut and sassafras.

Wildlife that you are likeliest to see include wild turkeys, whitetail deer, fox squirrels, and gray squirrels. Fox and bobcat are present but more reclusive.

West of McSpadden Hollow the trail stays in a broad bottomland and passes through a series of old fields.

Markers on trees will indicate the point at which you pass into Mark Twain National Forest land. No backcountry camping is allowed in Big Spring National Park, but you can camp anywhere you like on the national forest property. There is a developed campground at Big Spring.

An interpretive post describes plant succession in a section logged over during the early 1970s.

The trail turns north on the Forest Service property. The Spring Valley Cutoff exits left and heads 2.9 miles down to the ranger station at the park entrance.

The main trail curves right (east) to junction with the Chub Hollow Cutoff Trail. The Chub Hollow Cutoff continues east (right) for 1.7 miles, passing a lookout tower (closed) on the way to intersect County Highway Z on the hill above the dining lodge.

The main trail heads north (left from the Chub Hollow junction) and sharply downhill on an old road back to the dining lodge.

More information about the park is available from Ozark National Scenic Riverways headquarters, Van Buren, Missouri 63965.

TRAILS IN STATE PARKS

LAKE WAPPAPELLO BACKPACK TRAIL
Location: Lake Wappapello State Park, about 20 miles north of Poplar Bluff, adjacent to the east boundary of the Poplar Bluff unit of the

Lake Wappapello Backpack Trail

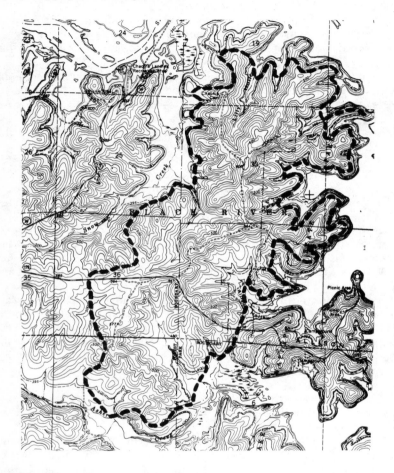

Mark Twain National Forest. To reach the park and trail head, drive north on U.S. Highway 67 from Poplar Bluff to Missouri Highway 172. Head east on 172 to its end at the park entrance.

Length: 10 miles.

U.S.G.S. Quad: Lake Wappapello, 7.5 minutes.

Description: The trail begins at a service area and parking lot on Highway 172 in Allison Hollow and for most of its route circles the edge of a peninsula that juts out into Lake Wappapello, a Corps of Engineers reservoir.

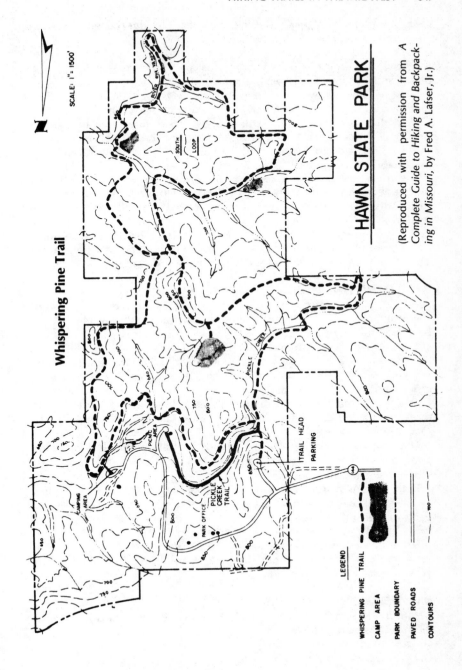

HAWN STATE PARK

(Reproduced with permission from A Complete Guide to Hiking and Backpacking in Missouri, by Fred A. Lafser, Jr.)

Whispering Pine Trail

SCALE: 1" = 1500'

SOUTH LOOP

PICKLE CREEK

TRAIL HEAD PARKING

PICKLE CREEK TRAIL

PARK OFFICE

PICNIC AREA

CAMPING AREA

LEGEND

WHISPERING PINE TRAIL

CAMP AREA

PARK BOUNDARY

PAVED ROADS

CONTOURS

The trail is marked with white paint blazes. Two designated campsites along the trail consist of cleared areas with fire rings.

From Allison Hollow, the path heads north along the lakeshore, following the sides of ridges for the most part but occasionally dipping down to the wooded rocky shoreline.

West of Lilly Hollow it moves inland to pass through several stands of mature oak, hickory, sugar maple, and yellow poplar (tulip tree).

Near the head of a ravine, where Snow Creek flows into the lake, a side trail heads north to a Corps of Engineers boat dock at Chaonia Landing. This side trail is not well marked and is difficult to locate from the Chaonia Landing end.

The main trail continues south across property owned by the Corps of Engineers, the University of Missouri, and private individuals. Trail easements have been secured, but no camping is allowed on these sections.

The path crosses Missouri Highway 172 again and continues south to a fire lane, which it follows briefly before turning east and then north again to the parking area and trail's end at Allison Hollow.

WHISPERING PINE TRAIL

Location: Hawn State Park, 11 miles east of Farmington on Missouri Highway 32, then south (right) 3 miles on Missouri Highway 144.
Length: 5-mile loop.
U.S.G.S. Quad: Weingarten, 15 minutes.
Description: The trail begins at a parking area just off Highway 144 near the park office. There are also short connecting trails from the campground and the picnic area.

The trail is marked with orange arrows. Yellow arrows direct you to three designated campsites along the route. The campsites are cleared spaces with fire rings.

The trail passes through several stands of mature shortleaf pine and also follows two very scenic streams—Pickle Creek and River Aux Vasse—for long stretches.

Both streams feature bluffs with outcroppings of LaMotte sandstone. Pickle Creek has occasional granite outcroppings as well. According to park ranger Bill Bonnell, there are nine beaver dams along Pickle Creek. Wild turkey and deer are abundant.

Elevation ranges between 650 feet and 900 feet.

For more information about the park, write Hawn State Park, Route 1, Weingarten, Missouri 63676.

MUDLICK MOUNTAIN TRAIL

Location: In Sam A. Baker State Park, about 45 miles north of Poplar Bluff on Missouri Highway 143.
Length: 12-mile loop.
U.S.G.S. Quad: Brunot, 7.5 minutes.

Mudlick Mountain Trail

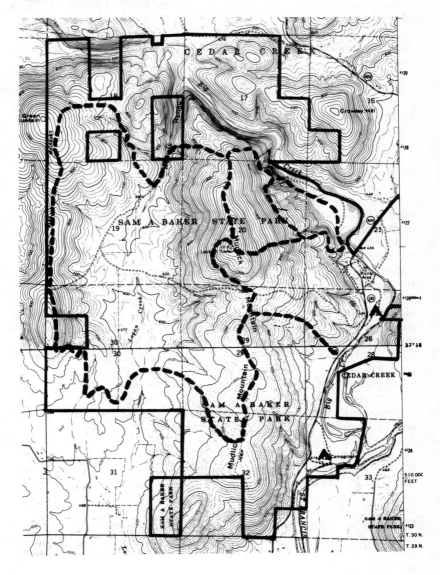

Description: Extremely rugged country in the St. Francois Mountains. These mountains are geologically unique in the state—the only area where a mixture of granite and cherty limestone forms the parent materials. The differences in weathering and erosion resistance between the two rock textures result in high local relief and a spacious, sweeping landscape.

Elevation on the trail varies 773 feet, from 540 feet in the bottomlands around Logan Creek to 1,313 feet on top of Mudlick Mountain.

The trail begins at an equestrian campsite north of the assistant superintendent's office and follows a horse trail, then a service road to the fire tower on Mudlick Mountain.

A grove of stunted oaks near the tower has been determined to be virgin timber. Winds and ice storms in winter on Ozark mountains can be severe, and this kind of gnarled oak forest is fairly typical.

A side trail heads right (east) from the fire tower back down to the park dining lodge. The main trail continues north along a ridge and gently downslope to intersect another trail that leads east to a series of three stone, three-sided camping shelters near a "shut-ins" area on Big Creek. You may camp wherever you like on the trail, but use of the shelters is encouraged.

The main trail begins heading west, with several meanderings along the way, to the park boundary where it turns south.

It joins an old dirt road for the climb to Green Mountain at an elevation of 1,200 feet, then descends by a series of switchbacks to a mixed pine and hardwood forest in the valley of Logan Creek (an intermittent stream). Remember to boil all water before drinking.

The trail climbs again to an elevation of about 900 feet and rejoins a service road for the last leg of the journey back north, and then east along the horse trail again, to where the trail began.

A dining lodge, which also sells a few groceries; cabins; a campground; and a canoe rental concession are located in the park. Mailing address is Sam A. Baker State Park, Patterson, Missouri 63956.

PEEWAH TRAIL

Location: In Trail of Tears State Park, 10 miles north of Cape Girardeau on Missouri Highway 177.
Length: 10-mile series of multiple loops.
U.S.G.S. Quad: Ware, 7.5 minutes.
Description: The trail head is on the left side of a road leading from the developed campground to a scenic overlook above the Mississippi River. It is about halfway between the park headquarters and the overlook.

The path winds through a rich mesic woodland of yellow poplar and sassafras, beech and cucumber magnolia. One stretch of about 3 miles follows bluffs above the Mississippi, but the rest is inland. Deep ravines cut into the landscape provide plenty of up-and-down walking, although the elevation ranges only from 400 to about 600 feet.

Designated campsites along the way are indicated by signs on trees that say "wigwa," which a park spokesman said means dwelling place. The same spokesman said that "Peewah," the trail's name, means "Come, follow me."

The 3,000-acre park was named as a memorial to the Cherokee Indians who passed nearby on their forced march west to Oklahoma in the 1830s.

The mailing address is Trail of Tears State Park, Route 4, Jackson, Missouri 63755.

Peewah Trail

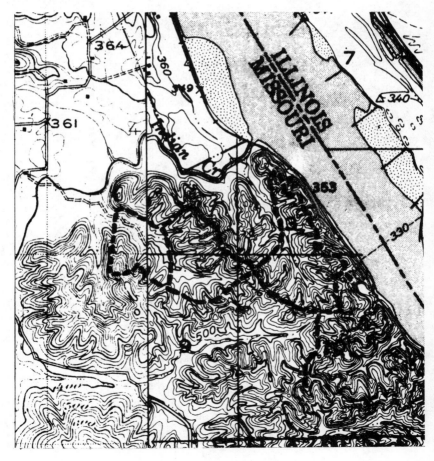

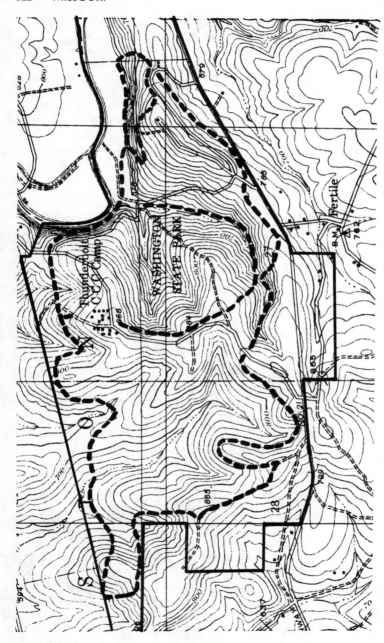

Rocky Wood Trail

ROCKY WOOD TRAIL
Location: Washington State Park, 45 miles southwest of St. Louis near the town of DeSoto on Missouri Highway 21.
Length: 10-mile loop.
U.S.G.S. Quad: Tiff, 7.5 minutes.
Description: Brown wooden signs with yellow lettering or orange arrows mark the trail's junction with roads. The trail itself is re-marked periodically with blue plastic tapes and occasionally with orange arrows.

Most of the path follows slopes or ridge tops through oak-hickory forest. There are some cedar glades on south and southwest slopes. There are open meadows where the trail follows Big River. The only designated backcountry campsite is marked with a stone fire ring.

There are scenic views from an old shelter that overlooks the bottomland along the river and also from a picnic area with a gazebo, which also overlooks the river.

Although this trail is 10 miles long, only the western half of the loop offers a real backcountry experience. The eastern half parallels park roads for much of its length and winds past various civilized trappings of the park—campground, dining lodge, nature center, swimming pool, etc. It obviously gets heavy use from day hikers.

The address of Washington State Park is Route 2, DeSoto, Missouri 63020.

TAUM SAUK TRAIL

Location: This trail lies between the Salem-Potosi and Fredericktown ranger districts of the Mark Twain National Forest. It runs south and west from the towns of Pilot Knob and Ironton on Missouri Highway 21 in Iron County to Johnson Shut-Ins State Park on Missouri Highway 178. Access at the trail's midpoint is on Iron County Road CC at the Taum Sauk Mountain Fire Tower.
Length: 20 miles.
U.S.G.S. Quads: Ironton, Johnson Shut-Ins; both 7.5 minutes.
Description: This path was developed and is maintained by the St. Louis Area Council of the Boy Scouts of America. Most of it crosses private land, so although trail easements have been secured, camping is allowed only at a designated campground just west of the fire tower and at Johnson Shut-Ins State Park.

The trail is marked with yellow and black St. Louis Boy Scout Council Historic Trail signs.

The portion of the trail between Pilot Knob and Ironton follows a jeep road up and then down Shepherd Mountain. (Elevation at the trail head is 1,050 feet; on top of Shepherd Mountain it is 1,608 feet.) If you're interested in hiking this part, drive west on West Maple Road from Missouri Highway 21 in Pilot Knob 0.1 mile to Shepherd Mountain Road. Follow it for a mile to the intersection with the jeep road. The

Taum Sauk Trail—west section

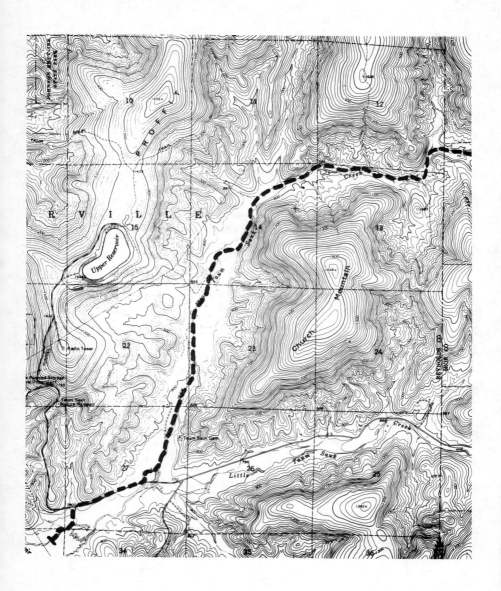

Taum Sauk Trail—central section

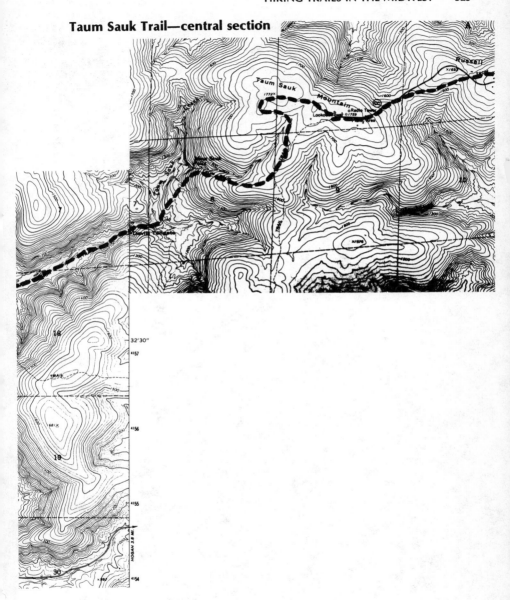

Taum Sauk Trail—east section

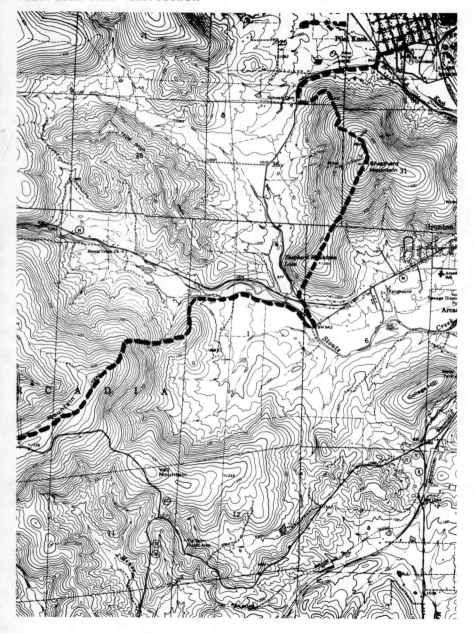

jeep road/trail rejoins Shepherd Mountain Road near County Road M in Ironton.

If you prefer to begin your hike in Ironton, take County Road M to the Ironton Municipal Water Works. Turn left (south) on a gravel road across Stout's Creek. Turn west again south of the bridge for a mile to the trail head.

The path heads southwest and uphill to the top of Russell Mountain, which, at 1,726 feet, is the second highest peak in the state.

The trail reaches and follows County Road CC west for just over a mile to the lookout tower on Taum Sauk Mountain, the state's highest point (1,772 feet).

Camping is available on a first come, first served basis at a primitive Scout campsite just west of the tower. There is no water available.

The path west of the tower follows a jeep trail briefly, then heads cross-country again to Mina-Sauk Falls, a cataract that falls 132 feet in three cascades. The trail leaves the falls by a path that descends the left side of the canyon and heads south for half a mile before turning right to join what was once a military road to Arkansas. This was part of the Trail of Tears over which 16,000 Cherokees from east of the Mississippi were driven by Presidential orders to a new reservation in Oklahoma in the winter of 1838–39. About a fourth of the Indians died in the march.

Between this point and the Johnson Shut-Ins Park, the trail crosses Taum Sauk Creek 20 times.

Points of special interest on this western half of the trail include the Devil's Toll Gate, a hole or split in the solid rock, so named, according to a brochure prepared by the Boy Scouts, "by the pioneers who were compelled to unload their long wagon trains and swing them around by hand in order to get through the sharp turn of the passage."

Sugar Camp Hollow west of Proffit Mountain along the trail route was named, also according to the Scouts, "because in pioneer days entire families would camp for ten days to two weeks in the hollow to tap maples for sap that would be made into maple sugar.

The trail ends at the mouth of Sugar Camp Hollow at Slick Rock Ford, where County Road N crosses the east fork of Black River. Turn left and cross the low water bridge. Continue west on N to Missouri Highway 178, which leads right (south) into Johnson Shut-Ins State Park. Fast water boiling around rocks that jut from the center of Black River and erosion-formed bathtubs and slides are the park's principal attractions.

MONITEAU WILDERNESS TRAIL

Location: Rudolph-Bennett State Wildlife Area about 25 miles north of Columbia. Take U.S. Highway 63 to County Highway F. Turn west (left) on F and then north (right) on County Highway for 3 miles to Fairview

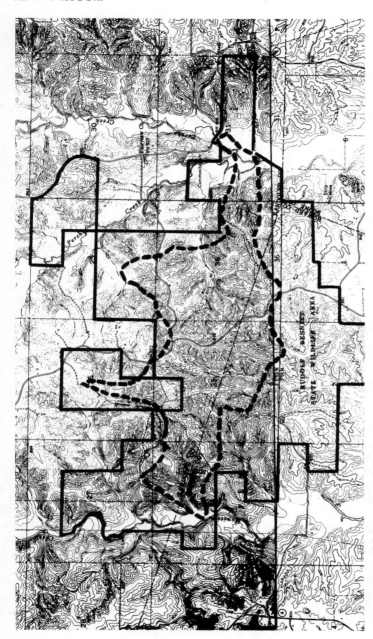

Moniteau Wilderness Trail

Church. A sign will direct you west (left) a mile to a parking area at the trail head.

Length: 18-mile loop.

U.S.G.S. Quad: Renick, 7.5 minutes.

Description: The hills in this part of the state are gentler and more rolling than those typical of the Ozarks farther south. There are, however, steep drainage channels which make for some rugged hiking. Elevation varies from about 750 feet to 880 feet.

Pine is also unusual here. The common trees are white oak, black oak, red oak, hickory, basswood, walnut, maple, elm, sycamore, hackberry, ash, and red cedar.

The Moniteau Wilderness Trail, in spite of its name, passes through several old fields in fairly civilized countryside, expecially along the northern half of the loop. The trail is maintained by the Boy Scouts of Moberly.

Featured attractions include the site of a boyhood home of General Omar Bradley; the gravesite of Lieutenant Leonard Bradley, a Revolutionary War soldier and presumably a relative of the later military figure; two swinging rope bridges (across Perch Creek and Moniteau Creek); the site of an Indian village and burial mounds of the Missouri tribe (the site long since combed clean by archeologists and curiosity seekers, needless to say).

Inquiries may be addressed to the Boy Scouts of Moberly, P. O. Box 463, Moberly, Missouri 65270.

OZARK TRAIL

Location: From Bunker, Missouri, take Missouri Highway 72 southeast 3 miles to County Road P. Take P south 2.4 miles to Forest Road 2220. Take this road south .4 mile and then southwest 2.8 miles to the trail head. Nearest road access to the south end of the completed section is on County NN about 3 miles east of County Road H. County Road H runs northeast from Winona, Missouri. In between, there is access from Missouri Highway 106 at Owl's Bend.

Length: 32 miles currently, with more planned.

U.S.G.S. Quads (north to south): Midridge, Missouri; Powder Mill Ferry, Missouri; Stegall Mountain, Missouri; all 7.5 minutes.

Description: The Ozark Trail is eventually supposed to run from St. Louis all the way to the Arkansas border. From there the dream is to tie it in with the Ozark Highlands Trail now being built in the Ozark National Forest. If all this becomes a reality, it will be possible to hike all the way from St. Louis to Oklahoma.

That goal is still a long way off, but in the meantime, this completed section provides some of the best hiking we have found in the Ozarks. Al Schneider, Ozark Trail Coordinator for the Missouri Department of Natural Resources, has laid out the trail on a route that takes hikers

Ozark Trail

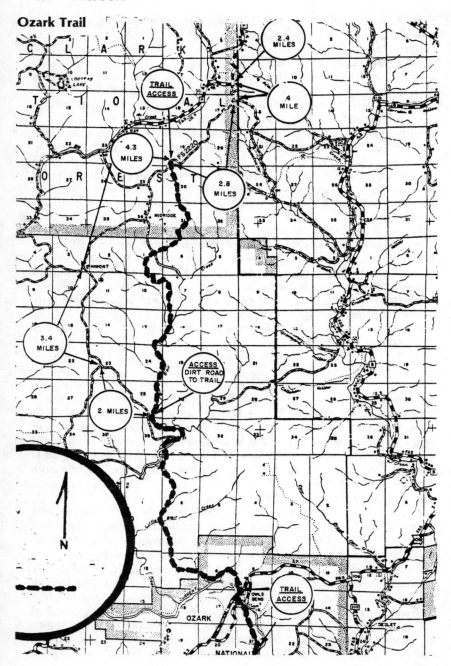

through all kinds of beautiful Ozark scenery—from ridge tops to creek bottoms, through thick woods and open glades, on steep bluffs overlooking the Current River and through narrow shut-ins where white water boils over hard igneous rocks. The trail runs across private land, as well as through state and national forest tracts and the Ozark National Scenic Riverway which is run by the National Park Service. Since the trail sections were built separately by each of these organizations, trail standards change dramatically from place to place.

On the private land, most of the work was done by volunteer crews under Schneider's direction. The trail here is quite narrow, deliberately left as natural as possible. You will occasionally have to step over small logs on the trail or duck slightly to avoid low branches. On Missouri State Forest land, the trail is wider, and the grades tend to be gentler. The Missouri Department of Conservation marks its sections with a sign showing the silhouette of a hiker and the words "Ozark Trail." Otherwise the trail is marked with white squares bearing the trail symbol, a "T" superimposed on an "O." The squares are usually nailed to trees. Marking is kept to a minimum in order to cause the least possible disturbance to the scenery.

From the north, the trail follows several creeks, eventually reaching the Current River just north of Owls Bend. The section along the river follows high bluffs that provide some spectacular views. South of Owls Bend the trail moves away from the river, crossing Indian Creek and Rocky Creek. Rocky Creek has some beautiful rapids created when the stream cut down to highly resistant igneous rocks.

South of County Road NN, the trail passes the spectacular Rocky Falls before climbing through mountaintop glades to the Stegall Fire Tower. The views from the glades are marvelous.

Work on extending the Ozark Trail is going on now, so by the time you read this, additional sections will probably be complete. To find out how far things have gone, write Ozark Trail Coordinator, Missouri Department of Natural Resources, P. O. Box 176, Jefferson City, Missouri 65102.

URBAN WILDS

Parks in St. Louis County don't offer a real wilderness experience, but many good day hikes and a few overnight trips are available within an easy hour's drive from downtown.

Camping is allowed in a designated off-road area along the 10-mile Green-Rock Nature and Conservation Trail in the western part of the county. The trail name reflects not the color of a stone but the fact that it passes through the A. P. Greensfelder County Park, the Rockwoods Range Tract, and Rockwoods Reservation (all administered by the St. Louis County Parks and Recreation Department). The path is maintained by the St. Louis Area Council of the Boy Scouts. Self-guiding interpretive trails branch frequently from the main trail. The path crosses roads five times in the 10-mile stretch and follows roads for short stretches. Maps are available from the Boy Scout Council, 4568 West Pine Boulevard, St. Louis, Missouri 63108.

A 5-mile trail encircles a campground and day-use recreation areas in Sioux Passage Park along the Missouri River off Old Jamestown Road in the northern part of the county.

There is a 13-mile trail network but no backcountry camping at Babler State Park, Missouri Highway 109 and Rieger Road.

There are 5 miles of trails but group camping only at Jefferson Barracks County Park, Kingston Avenue and South Broadway.

The Missouri Botanical Garden's Arboretum is along the Meramec River in nearby Franklin County on Missouri Highway 100 south of I-44 at Gray Summit. Maps and information about the arboretum are available from Missouri Botanical Garden, Box 93, Gray Summit, Missouri 63039.

Lake City Park and the Blue and Gray Park, both in the suburbs of Kansas City in Jackson County, each have 5 miles of trails. Swope Park, also in Jackson County, has a 4-mile trail. All three parks provide car camping facilities only. Siloam Mountain Park and Riverview Greenway Park in Clay County provide hiking trails of 4 and 5 miles respectively.

SOURCES

Missouri Department of Natural
  Resources
P. O. Box 176
Jefferson City, Missouri 65102
(coordinates information on trails
  in state parks and wildlife areas)

Missouri Department of
  Conservation
P. O. Box 180
Jefferson City, Missouri 65102

Mark Twain National Forest
P. O. Box 937
Rolla, Missouri 65401

St. Louis Area Council
Boy Scouts of America
4568 East Pine Boulevard
St. Louis, Missouri 63108

The Ozark Society
Henry Rowe Schoolcraft Chapter
P. O. Box 4761 GS
Springfield, Missouri 65804

Sierra Club
Ozark Chapter
Dorothy K. Stade, Chairperson
210 Wooster Drive
Ferguson, Missouri 63135

RECOMMENDED READING

Fred A. Lafser, Jr. *Hiking and Backpacking in Missouri,* 9506 Port Drive, Affton, Missouri 63123

Julian Steyermark. *Flora of Missouri,* University of Missouri Press, 1963, and *A Vegetational History of the Ozark Forest,* University of Missouri Press, 1959

T. R. Beveridge. *An Introduction to Geologic History of Missouri,* Department of Natural Resources, Rolla, Missouri 65401

Ramon D. Gass. *Missouri Hiking Trails,* Department of Conservation, Rolla, Missouri 65401